SKUAS AND JAEGERS

A GUIDE TO THE SKUAS AND JAEGERS

OF THE WORLD

SKUAS AND JAEGERS

A GUIDE TO THE SKUAS AND JAEGERS

OF THE WORLD

KLAUS MALLING OLSEN

AND

HANS LARSSON

YALE UNIVERSITY PRESS

NEW HAVEN AND LONDON

Published in the United States of America by Yale University Press.

Library of Congress Catalog Card Number 97-60338

ISBN 0-300-07269-4

First published in the United Kingdom by Pica Press.

A catalogue record for this book is available from the British Library.

The paper in this book meets the guidelines for permanence and durability of the Committee on Production Guidelines for Book Longevity of the Council on Library Resources.

10 9 8 7 6 5 4 3 2 1

CONTENTS

INTRODUCTION

The identification and distribution of one of the most challenging groups of seabirds, the skuas, is the purpose of this book. Some skuas are long-distance migrants (*Stercorarius* species and South Polar Skua *Catharacta maccormicki*) which are likely to turn up anywhere in the world. This is especially true of immatures, which may be present in any suitable habitat between their natal grounds and their winter quarters. The individual plumage variation in the *Stercorarius* skuas (jaegers) is enormous, creating one of the most puzzling yet fascinating challenges in modern field identification. This book presents the most up-to-date information on all the skuas, based on years of study in the field, and detailed examination of photographs and museum skins, as well as extensive research of the relevant literature.

The idea to produce a guide to the skuas stems from a 'Great Skua' which turned up at Falsterbo, Sweden in September 1981. This bird was subsequently reidentified as a Pomarine Skua, before photographs and minor (and at that time poorly understood) plumage details proved it to be an unusually large and fat juvenile Arctic Skua with unexpectedly large wing-flashes!

This book is the first complete identification guide to the skuas of the world, especially designed to enable species identification and correct ageing. Important supplementary knowledge such as moult, geographical variation, notes on aberrant plumages and hybrids, as well as biometrics, is included in each species account. Other sections deal with voice, food and migration, while shorter summaries are given of populations and breeding biology; the latter are treated in depth in O'Donald (1983) and Furness (1987).

Skuas make up a subfamily comprising seven species. They are divided into two main groups. The first of these, the large skuas *Catharacta*, consists of four species, of which three breed in the southern hemisphere. Great Skua *C. skua* breeds in the North Atlantic, while Brown Skua *C. antarctica* (with subspecies Subantarctic Skua *C. a. lonnbergi*, Tristan Skua *C. a. hamiltoni* and Falkland Skua *C. a. antarctica*), Chilean Skua *C. chilensis* and South Polar Skua *C. maccormicki* all breed in the southern oceans.

The treatment of the subspecies of Brown Skua, and their relationship with Great Skua, has caused much debate. We follow the latest taxonomic trends by treating Brown Skua as a different species from the monotypic Great Skua (Beaman 1994, del Hoyo *et al.* 1996), although other authorities (Devillers 1977, 1978; Cramp & Simmons 1983; Furness 1987; Higgins & Davies 1996) regard it as conspecific with Great Skua and thus treat the latter as polytypic. Sibley & Monroe (1990) recommend further splitting of Brown Skua into two species, with Tristan and Falkland Skuas forming one species and Subantarctic Skua another.

This may not be the ultimate solution to the problem. By treating Great Skua and Brown Skua in separate chapters, however, the information presented becomes more 'user-friendly'. Furthermore, distinguishing Great from Brown Skua is not really an immediate problem, as the two probably never meet, both being short- to medium-distance migrants which generally stay close to their breeding sites.

The three small species, Pomarine Skua *Stercorarius pomarinus*, Arctic Skua *S. parasiticus* and Long-tailed Skua *S. longicaudus*, fortunately create no such problems: they are clearly taxonomically separated from each other. All three breed in the northern hemisphere and winter in the tropics and south to the southern oceans. Notwithstanding the clear taxonomic differences among these smaller species, however, their enormous plumage variation, coupled with the fact that most observers see skuas flying past offshore, giving brief views and often under unfavourable weather conditions, creates an identification problem which is as difficult and time-consuming to unravel as the identification of the medium-sized *Aquila* eagles.

With the constant changes in taxonomic opinion and the enormous plumage variation involved within this group of birds, new information and points of view will surely develop in years to come. Any comments and new data will be welcomed by the authors, and should be sent to: Pica Press, The Banks, Mountfield, Near Robertsbridge, East Sussex TN32 5JY, U.K.

ACKNOWLEDGEMENTS

Producing detailed identification guides relies much on the help and willingness of the many people who are kind enough to supply photographs and share their knowledge with us. Our deepest thanks go to all.

Firstly, we thank the staff at the various museums visited: Peter Colston & Robert Prys-Jones, Natural History Museum, Tring (BMNH), Jon Fjeldså, Niels-Otto Preuss & Carsten Rahbek, Universitetes Zoologiske Museum, Copenhagen (UZM), Carl Edelstam, Göran Frisk & Per Eriksson, Naturhistoriska Riksmuseet, Stockholm (NRK), Christian Aas, Per-Göran Bentz, Jan Lifjeld & Tore Slagsvold, Zoologisk Museum, Universitetet i Oslo (ZMO), Sverker Wadén, Malmö Naturmuseum, Malmö (MN), Lennart Zederholm, Zoologisk Museum, Lund (ZML), Zoologisk Museum, Uppsala (ZMU), Pekka J. Nikander & Hannu Jännes, Zoological Museum, Helsinki (ZMH), M. Kreptowski & Edward Tranda, Museum of the Lodz University Institute of Evolution Biology, Poland (MLU), René Dekker & Peter van Dam, Nationaal Natuurhistorisch Museum, Leiden (NNH), C.J. (Kees) Roselaar, J.J. Wattel & T.G.Prins, Zoölogisch Museum (Instituut voor Taxonomische Zoölogie), Amsterdam (ZMA), Phil Angle, National Museum of Natural History, Smithsonian Institution, Washington (USNM), and Mary Le Croy, American Museum of Natural History, New York (AMNH).

Numerous individuals each contributed in their own way, many in the initial stages which led to earlier publications in Swedish, Dutch, English and German, or responded to our request in the monthly magazine *Birding World*. Our thanks to: Bob Abrams, Per Alström, Geir Andersen, Anders Andersson, Thomas Andersson, Olof Armani, Peter H. Barthel, Phil Battley, Michael Bayldon, D.G. Bell, Bengt Bengtsson, Per-Göran Bentz, Anders Blomdahl, Pieter Boesman, Leo J.R. Boon, Alan Brady, Bertil Breife, Michael Brown, Jens B. Bruun, Mads Jensen Bunch, C.J. (Kees) Camphuizen, Thomas Carlén, Rolf Christensen, Erik Christophersen, Hans Christophersen, David Cooper, John Cooper, Richard Crossley, Mark Curley, Kai Dallman, D.L. Davenport, Tom Davis, Don Desjardin, R.F. Dickens, Paul Doherty, Jon L. Dunn, Svend Dybkjær, Jan Elmelid, O. Endelweber, Hanne & Jens Eriksen, Rudolfo Escalante, Nils Fabæk, Knud Falk, Kim Fischer, G.T. Foggitt, Magnus Forsberg, Dick Forsman, Rosier de Fraine, P. Gasson, Hans Gebius, the late Peter J. Grant, B.J. Gregory, Alex Halley, Martti Hario, Peter Harrison, Erik Hirschfeld, Jan Hjort-Christensen, Norbert Hoffman, Claus Hornemann, Julian R. Hough, Bent Jacobsen, Jens-Kjeld Jensen, Stig Jensen, Ingemar Johansson, I.G. Johnston, Mikael Jonahsson, Rolland Kern, Jens Kirkeby, Henrik Kisbye, Nils Kjellén, Michael Knoll, Paul Knolle, Peter Koch, Folke Köhler, Bernd Koop, Niels Krabbe, Ed Kurater, Lasse J. Laine, Mike Langman, Gordon Langsbury, Knud Larsen, Anthony J. Lauro, David A. Leatherman, Alan McBride, Anthony McGeehan, R. McIntyre, Ed J. Mackrill, Stig Toft Madsen, Ingvar Martinsson, David Massie, Hans Meltofte, D.S. Melville, Åse Mielow, Karno Mikkola, Nigel Milius, Barry Mitchell, J. Moss, Jan Mulder, Killian Mullarney, Tomi Muukkonen, Ron Naveen, Howard Nicholls, John Damgaard Nielsen, Thorsten Nilsson, Andreas Noeske, Iwo Nörenberg, Pieter Nuyten, Daniele Occhiato, Urban Olsson, Phil Palmer, Jan Pedersen, Jens Skovgaard Petersen, Kim Petersen, Alf Pettersson, Göran Pettersson, Ove Pettersson, Stefan Pfützke, René Pop, Richard Porter, Michael Køie Poulsen, Carsten Rahbek, Christopher Randler, Lars Rask, Brian Rasmussen, Nigel Redman, The Royal Naval Birdwatching Society, Jürgen Ruddeck, Markku Saarinen, Hadoram Shirihai, Per Smitterberg, Uffe Gjøl Sørensen, Øystein Størkersen, Briand Strack, Rasmus Strack, M. Sundström, Lars Svensson, Ola Svensson, Alan Tate, Edward Thieme, Roderick Thorne, Antero Topp, Bjørn Olav Tveit, Magnus Ullman, Hans van Brandwijk, Arnoud B. van den Berg, M.C.M. van Lorven, Markus Varesvuo, R.R. Veit, Allan Kjær Villesen, P.J. Vines, P.M. Vizard, Michel Watelet-Cornet, Tony Whilde and Claudia Wilds.

KMO is especially grateful to Steen Christensen, Lars Jonsson and Knud Pedersen for long and most stimulating discussions, and for supplying numerous photographs. Ger Meesters provided the best of help in many ways, and gave us many useful contacts, as well as accommodating us during several visits to the Netherlands. In addition, KMO is most grateful to Claudia Wilds for her hospitality, great assistance and exciting field trips during several visits to the USA.

TAXONOMY, RELATATIONSHIPS
AND CHARACTERISTICS

Skuas constitute the subfamily Stercorariinae, forming a part of the family Laridae. Within this family, they are probably most closely related to gulls (Larinae), although studies of behaviour and DNA-DNA hybridisation suggest that they are equally related (as a sister-group) to all other Laridae. They probably diverged from gulls about 10 million years ago, towards the end of the Miocene. Among the few fossil skuas are finds from the northern hemisphere, indicating that skuas, like gulls, originated in that half of the world. Eventually, the skuas evolved into seven species divided almost equally between the two hemispheres. There appears to have been an early split into *Stercorarius*, which evolved in the northern hemisphere, and the *Catharacta* group, which colonised the south, where it more recently radiated into three species.

Skuas differ obviously from gulls in being darker, or showing distinct pale and dark morphs, but they also show a series of further differences. Their flight muscles and flight feathers are stronger, and they possess a unique combination of strongly hooked claws and webbing between the toes – amalgamating characters from both raptors and gulls. The tarsus has hard scutes similar to raptors, but differing from gulls, which have softer fleshy skin on their legs. The bill is rather short and heavy, with a hooked tip, and the rhamphotheca (horny covering of upper mandible) is complex, with four sections or plates: (1) sheath of lateral edge; (2) strongly curved distal sheath, smoother and more rounded than bill-tip of gulls and creating a strongly hooked tip of bill; (3) pair of separate, soft, thin dorsal plates covering the nostrils, forming a distinct cere that is lacking in all other Laridae. Unlike gulls, skuas have supraorbital salt glands, allowing them to drink salt water, although they prefer fresh water when available. The central pair of tail feathers protrudes to a greater or lesser extent, being shortest and least conspicuous on *Catharacta* skuas and longest on Long-tailed Skua. This tail projection is longest in breeding plumage, shortest in juvenile plumage, and between juvenile and adult length in immature plumages; from their second summer, birds may have a projection as long as that of adults.

Molecular data provide some indications of the skuas' evolutionary relationships with gulls. In the mitochondrial cytochrome b gene of gulls and skuas there are about 70 differences in 1,000 base pairs between present-day gulls and skuas and the most likely reconstructed sequence of their common ancestor. Arctic and Long-tailed Skuas and the *Catharacta* taxa differ from their most likely common ancestral sequence by about 50 in 1,000 base pairs (del Hoyo *et al.* 1996).

TAXONOMY

The current general consensus is that the skuas are divided into two groups, being classified as follows:

Family Laridae

  Subfamily Stercorariinae

    Genus *Catharacta* (large skuas) – four species

      1. Great Skua *Catharacta skua*
      2. Brown Skua *Catharacta antarctica* (with three subspecies: *antarctica, lonnbergi* and *hamiltoni*)
      3. Chilean Skua *Catharacta chilensis*
      4. South Polar Skua *Catharacta maccormicki*

    Genus *Stercorarius* (small skuas) – three species

      1. Pomarine Skua *Stercorarius pomarinus*
      2. Arctic Skua *Stercorarius parasiticus*
      3. Long-tailed Skua *Stercorarius longicaudus* (with two subspecies: *longicaudus* and *pallescens*)

Alternative names are used for the *Stercorarius* species in America: Pomarine Jaeger *S. pomarinus*, Parasitic Jaeger *S. parasiticus* and Long-tailed Jaeger *S. longicaudus*.

The molecular data would suggest that the small and the large skuas diverged into two genera relatively soon after the separation of the skuas from the gulls, rather than more recently (del Hoyo *et al.* 1996). The taxonomy of the genus *Stercorarius* is rather simple, although the division of *S. longicaudus* into two subspecies, nominate *longicaudus* (Western Palearctic to about Taimyr in Siberia) and *pallescens* (eastern Siberia and North America to Greenland), is debatable. No series of measurements has shown any mean differences in any parameter (remarkable among subspecies with rather similar plumage), and the only reason for treating *pallescens* as a separate subspecies is that adults on average have paler underparts than *longicaudus*; but, while birds from North America and Greenland do average paler below compared with West Palearctic series, overlap is considerable and in areas of possible sympatry there is virtually no detectable difference between the two in underpart coloration. In the present work we retain the two subspecies, but further investigation in the eastern Siberian areas of overlap is surely needed – a problem that has received little attention in recent years. Arctic and Long-tailed Skuas are more closely related to each other than to Pomarine Skua (Kranendonk 1981). Phylogenetic trees reveal that Pomarine Skua is closer to Great Skua, DNA sequences hardly differing between the two (only 8 base pairs in 1,000), making Pomarine Skua 'the missing link' between *Stercorarius* and *Catharacta*. Similarity of mitochondrial DNA (mtDNA) probably reflects hybridisation of a female Great Skua and a male Arctic/Long-tailed Skua, resulting in a new form (Pomarine Skua) carrying the mitochondrial sequence from Great Skua but nuclear genes from both Great Skua and *Stercorarius*. Another possibility is hybridisation between Pomarine and female Great Skua, leading to the replacement of the Pomarine mtDNA by Great Skua mtDNA. Differences in mtDNA sequences suggest that this occurred about 400,000 years ago. Divergence of *Catharacta* and Arctic/Long-tailed Skua is one order of magnitude older (Peter *et al.* 1994; del Hoyo *et al.* 1996; de Korte *et al.* in press). Pomarine Skua shows many similarities with Arctic and Long-tailed Skuas, but some aspects of its biology suggest strong affinities with Great Skua: for example, the wing-raising display with the 'long-call', typical of *Catharacta* skuas, is seen also in Pomarine Skua but not in Arctic or Long-tailed. In addition, multivariate analysis of skeletal measurements shows Pomarine Skua to be more closely associated with Great Skua than with Arctic and Long-tailed Skuas.

Although the *Catharacta* group is sometimes treated under *Stercorarius*, arguments for separating the two groups are strong. The *Stercorarius* skuas are smaller, have clearly different breeding plumages (with distinct patterning and plumage contrasts) and non-breeding plumages, and the juveniles show neat scaling on the upperparts and clear barring below (Brooke 1978; Furness 1987); all three *Stercorarius* species breed in the northern hemisphere, performing long-distance migrations to tropical wintering grounds. *Catharacta* skuas have much less varying plumage, the juveniles lack clear scaling and neat patterning in their much more uniform plumage, and most species stay close to the breeding grounds; apart from Great Skua (which breeds in the North Atlantic), all are southern-hemisphere breeders, larger and heavier than any *Stercorarius* and with striking white flashes on both surfaces of the wing. It should be noted that South Polar Skua exhibits different plumage morphs and is also a long-distance migrant, and thus may be the species most closely associated with the *Stercorarius* group; and that Pomarine Skua is between Arctic and Great Skuas in build, as well as being the most closely associated with the *Catharacta* group (Andersson 1973; Furness 1987), with which it has in common regular colonial breeding, often defending its small territory with aerial displays similar to those of *Catharacta* skuas.

The taxonomy of the *Catharacta* skuas is, on the other hand, widely disputed. Devillers (1977), Cramp & Simmons (1983) and Furness (1987) treat Great and Brown Skuas as conspecific within one polytypic species comprising four subspecies: Great Skua *C. skua skua*, Brown Skua *C. s. lonnbergi*, Tristan Skua *C. s. hamiltoni* and Falkland Skua *C. s. antarctica*. The last three forms are now generally accepted as representing a separate species (Brown Skua) from Great Skua, a treatment preferred by e.g. Harrison (1983, 1987) and del Hoyo *et al.* (1996); and Sibley & Monroe (1990) further split Brown Skua, regarding Tristan and Falkland Skuas as forming one species *C. antarctica* ('Southern Skua'), separate from *C. lonnbergi* ('Brown Skua'). The two other species of *Catharacta* are the South Polar Skua *C. maccormicki* and the Chilean Skua *C. chilensis*, which were formerly regarded as subspecies of Brown/Great Skua (*sensu lato*) but are now widely recognised as specifically distinct. Although interbreeding between Brown Skua and South Polar/Chilean Skuas is frequent, this also occurs among other avian forms regarded as closely related species showing distinct characters from each other (e.g. Red Kite/Black Kite *Milvus milvus/ M. migrans*, Herring Gull/Lesser Black-backed Gull *Larus argentatus/ L. fuscus* and Herring Gull/Glaucous Gull *L. argentatus/ L. hyperboreus*, especially when one species spreads into areas dominated by the other).

In the present work, we separate Great Skua *C. skua* from the southern Brown Skua *C. antarctica* (the latter including Subantarctic Skua *C. a. lonnbergi*, Tristan Skua *C. a. hamiltoni* and Falkland Skua *C. a. antarctica*). Although certain Falkland Skuas, in particular, are more similar to Great Skua than other subspecies, the differences in general plumage and the converse timing of breeding and moult (caused by Great Skua breeding in the northern hemisphere, Falkland Skua in the southern) are sufficient to warrant giving the southern Brown Skua the status of a full species distinct from Great Skua. It seems probable, however, that Great Skua expanded its breeding range to the North Atlantic not too long ago, probably invading from the southern hemisphere.

In the mitochondrial cytochrome b gene of the southern *Catharacta* skuas and their putative ancestor there are about 3 to 10 differences in 1,000 base pairs, indicating that southern *Catharacta* forms have only very recently diverged; the southern hemisphere group and Great Skua, however, show about 6 to 12 differences in 1,000 base pairs, suggesting that Great Skua diverged from the southern hemisphere *Catharacta* before the separation of the latter into three species (del Hoyo *et al.* 1996).

Future studies may even prove Tristan and Falkland Skuas to be specifically different from Subantarctic Skua, while the eastern populations of the latter vary so much from the South Atlantic and Antarctic populations that they may eventually be given subspecific status, being the largest and darkest of the population (see Measurements). This has already been recommended by Mathews (1913), who named populations from South Orkney as *Catharacta lonnbergi clarkei* and populations from Kerguelen Islands as *C. l. intercedens*.

Within the *Catharacta* group, the greyest and coldest-tinged individuals are certain South Polar Skuas, and the warmest and most reddish are Chilean Skuas. Most populations of Brown Skuas are dark and cold brown, whereas Great Skua shows the most variegated upperparts with golden, yellow and pale brown feathers intermixed in a medium brown plumage.

The final word on skua taxonomy is a long way off. Further studies of nuclear DNA and of feather lice may help to resolve the discrepancy between mtDNA and morphological phylogeny, which is partly due to the clonal maternal inheritance of mtDNA (Peter *et al.* 1994).

CHARACTERISTICS

Female skuas are larger than males. This is the reverse of the situation found in other Laridae, but it matches the pattern found in frigatebirds, raptors and owls - all families which take large prey (raptors, owls) or use kleptoparasitism as a feeding method (frigatebirds). The differences in weight between male and female skuas lie between 11% and 17% (Furness 1987), being least in South Polar Skua and Long-tailed Skua. The reasons for this sexual size dimorphism are probably related to the breeding strategy: the lighter males are better adapted to feeding, and the larger females are better at defending the nest and young. Several studies have demonstrated that males undertake a larger share of hunting than do females, and sometimes considerably so, especially at the end of the incubation period (Burton 1968; Andersson 1971; Kampp 1982; de Korte 1986; Furness 1987). This is again a pattern similar to that found in several species of raptor, where females are likewise larger than males. Sexual size dimorphism is most conspicuous in raptor species feeding on birds, where the taking by male and female of different species of different size is profitable, but it is negligible in carrion-eating raptors (Newton 1979). Studies of skuas failed to reveal any clear trend in feeding in relation to sexual dimorphism, making the theory that males and females feed on different food sources less plausible for skuas.

In the breeding season, males on average take more fish than females, which feed mainly on ground invertebrates and berries (Furness 1987). South Polar Skua, which shows the smallest difference in size between male and female, is more prone to feed on fish and krill during the breeding season than are its congeners in the southern hemisphere.

As with gulls, breeding and non-breeding plumages differ, and the adult plumage takes several years to develop. Differences between age-classes are greatest in the smaller skuas *Stercorarius*, where individual variation among juveniles is matched only by the plumage variation in certain raptors such as Common Buzzard *Buteo buteo*.

Catharacta skuas are predominantly brown, with a dark, strongly hooked bill and conspicuous white flashes on both upperside and underside of the wings. The differences between breeding and non-breeding plumages are small: prior to the breeding season, most species develop a broad necklace of fine yellowish streaks covering head and neck sides, hindneck and sometimes sides of breast, lacking in non-breeding, juvenile and immature plumage stages, although adult South Polar Skuas are said to show yellow head streaking all year round (Higgins & Davies 1996). Juveniles are cleaner-patterned than adults, a difference that is striking following the breeding season, when pale adults (most obvious in South Polar Skuas) are extremely bleached and worn.

Stercorarius skuas are smaller, with a longer tail and more pointed wings. In all but a few juvenile Arctic Skuas, they show only a diffuse pale area at the base of the primaries, as only the primary shafts and the basal part of the inner webs (not the basal part of both webs) are pale, but show much more striking projection of the central pair of tail feathers. Arctic Skua occurs in pale, intermediate and dark morphs, of which intermediates are the rarest (see Geographical Variation in the Arctic Skua account); so, too, does Pomarine Skua, but dark and, especially, intermediate morphs are much rarer. Adult Long-tailed Skua is monomorphic. All juvenile *Stercorarius* skuas show enormous variation from very pale-headed to almost blackish individuals. They have the shortest and broadest central tail feathers and show distinct pale fringes to the feathers of the upperparts and body. Juveniles may generally be aged by their warm brown coloration, although juvenile Long-tailed Skuas are always cold greyish-brown. The full scale of variation and the large numbers of dark juvenile Long-tailed Skuas (30% in all studies and skin series: Malling Olsen 1989) make it impossible to relate pale juveniles to pale adults. In general, *Stercorarius* skuas take four years to reach full adult plumage (see species accounts).

Skuas are long-lived birds. The yearly survival rate of adults is about 90% for Long-tailed and Arctic Skuas, and even higher (90-94%) for *Catharacta* species (Furness 1987). Slightly lower survival (80%, and even as low as 70%) found in a Shetland population of Arctic Skuas was probably a result of shooting (O'Donald 1983). The survival rate of young birds is probably 70-80% (Furness 1987).

POLYMORPHISM

Adult Arctic and Pomarine Skuas show strong plumage polymorphism, adults occurring in pale and dark morphs, with a limited number of intermediates. Polymorphism has yet to be substantiated for Long-tailed Skua; most claims of 'dark adults' probably relate to immatures, and no genuine dark-morph breeding adults are known to us. In the *Catharacta* skuas, only South Polar Skua shows a similar polymorphism, although the nature of individual variation in the Falkland Skua somewhat approaches polymorphism.

There are several theories on the strong plumage polymorphism of the Arctic Skua. The dark morph predominates in the southern part of the range in coastal populations, whereas tundra breeders consist mainly of pale-morph individuals. It also predominates in populations nesting close to seabirds, which are heavily parasitised for food. Dark birds are probably better adapted for approaching seabirds without being detected, the dark plumage camouflaging the skuas against a dark background (e.g. a dark sea). Thus they have the advantage of being able to take their victims by surprise, which is essential when using kleptoparasitism as a foraging strategy; attacks normally start in low flight, where the skuas are hard to see against the water. Raptors which use surprise tactics when hunting also have dark or cryptically patterned plumages. Juvenile skuas, too, are mainly dark when leaving the breeding sites and on their coastal migration. The theory that dark birds have the advantage of plumage camouflage is, however, overshadowed by the fact that pale and dark morphs feeding in seabird colonies have equal hunting success. On average, dark morphs breed earlier than pale morphs. There has been an increase in the percentage and populations of dark-morph Arctic Skuas since the 1930s, corresponding with an increase in seabirds such as Black-headed Gull *Larus ridibundus*, Black-legged Kittiwake *Rissa tridactyla* and Northern Fulmar *Fulmarus glacialis*. In Arctic and South Polar Skua breeding populations in total, more males than females are dark (Furness 1987).

Pale morphs are probably better adapted for hunting for themselves, feeding on a wide range of invertebrates and smaller vertebrates (rodents, birds) and fish in the breeding season. The more variegated plumage makes the pale morph harder to detect against a pale sky than a wholly dark bird, and is thus an advantage when the bird hunts live prey for itself (predation) instead of using kleptoparasitism. Predation is the primary feeding strategy of tundra-breeding skuas during the breeding season. It is also in tundra populations that the largest percentage of pale-morph adults is found, ranging from more than 90% in Arctic and Pomarine Skuas to 100% in Long-tailed Skua. In certain areas, however, pale-morph Arctic Skuas feed mainly by kleptoparasitism (Furness 1987). Local differences in the ratio of dark and pale morphs in certain populations may stem from a balance between opposing selection pressures that differ with latitude and colonies (O'Donald 1983).

Other bird families which catch their own fish, such as gannets, terns and gulls, have a whitish underbody. This explanation could be applied to pale-morph skuas, as the paler underbody is harder for the prey to detect than if the body were dark. Certain low-hunting raptors such as harriers *Circus* also show an underbody (and sometimes underwing, too) paler than the rest of the plumage surface, and even dark-morph skuas become paler on the underbody in winter plumage. Of the *Catharacta* skuas only South Polar Skua may show a very pale underbody, and this is the species which most frequently feeds by direct fishing.

In gannets, gulls and terns, the white mass created by feeding flocks makes it easy for birds farther away to locate a rich food source ('signal-plumage'). This is an advantage when food supply is plentiful but localised, in that as many birds as possible can profit from the rich food sources. It has been demonstrated that gulls and terns feeding in flocks have a higher hunting success than those feeding alone (Furness 1987), as flocks of feeding seabirds panic fish shoals, thus making hunting easier. Species feeding mainly by kleptoparasitism, such as skuas and frigatebirds, have much darker upperparts, as a white signal-plumage would depress feeding success by attracting other food pirates: the nature of kleptoparasitism is such that success is lower for birds hunting together in large flocks than for loners. Arctic Skuas, however, often hunt in groups of two or three individuals, success being greater when two birds collaborate than when one hunts singly.

A combination of the above theories may ultimately explain why certain skuas occur in pale and dark (and intermediate) morphs.

KLEPTOPARASITISM

Kleptoparasitism or piracy - the stealing of food from other birds - is not unique to skuas. Gulls, terns and frigatebirds also regularly attack victims in order to make them hand over food (by dropping or regurgitating it), but it is among skuas that kleptoparasitism is developed to its extreme. Arctic Skua in particular is an expert pirate, taking almost all its food at sea by stealing it from other birds. Skuas are the raptors of the seas, the sight of an Arctic Skua pursuing a tern being reminiscent of the aerial combats of First World War pilots.

Kleptoparasitism among birds is generally associated with the availability of hosts feeding on large, visible food items such as fish, and periods of food shortage (Brockman & Barnard 1979). The outcome of a piratical attack depends not only on the skua's experience, but also on the speed of reaction of the intended victim. Juvenile skuas are generally less successful pirates than are adults (own observations), and are more prone to use alternative feeding methods.

In Pomarine Skua and the *Catharacta* skuas the borderline between kleptoparasitism and predation is less clear. In these species, the attack often begins as kleptoparasitism, but may develop into a genuine attack on the victim itself, forcing it down to the water, where it is eventually killed.

THE SKUA SPECIES: A BRIEF OVERVIEW

CATHARACTA SPECIES

Of the four species within the *Catharacta* genus of larger skuas, only Great Skua breeds in the northern hemisphere. The other three coexist in the southern oceans, with limited hybridisation where their ranges overlap (see species accounts). This minor degree of hybridisation is sometimes cited as a reason for treating them as conspecific, but recent research has shown the separation of *Catharacta* into four species to be justified.

The Great Skua breeds in loose colonies on North Atlantic islands, and is in fact one of very few seabirds to breed solely in European waters. The densest colonies are found close to colonies of Northern Gannets *Morus bassanus*, a species which these skuas normally accompany also on migration. The Great Skua population has shown a continuing increase up to the mid 1980s, mainly a result of protection following heavy persecution in the 19th century, and has also expanded northwards. In areas where it coexists with Arctic Skua it takes a number of young and adults of the latter species, causing local decreases in the Arctic Skua population (see below). It is, however, much of an opportunistic feeder (as Brown Skua and probably Chilean Skua), feeding on virtually all available food. It may very occasionally kill lambs (or more often scavenge stillborn lambs), which in certain parts of the range has led to some persecution. The most severe threat facing it, however, is the decrease in the sand-eel population noted in the late 1980s, while changes in methods of commercial fishing (with larger mesh sizes leading to fewer small whitefish being available) may cause local declines.

The other members of this genus all breed in the southern hemisphere. South Polar Skua is the southernmost breeding skua, nesting entirely in Antarctica. In the breeding season it feeds mainly on fish, and to a much lesser degree on penguins and seabirds than does its larger and fiercer congener, the Brown Skua. For nesting, it selects open ground with very little vegetation; it may breed in the vicinity of penguin colonies. In areas where it breeds alongside Brown Skuas (with some hybridisation), it forages almost entirely away from the colony, by fishing.

The Brown Skua breeds in the subantarctic region, as three different subspecies: at the tip of South America and in the Falklands (Falkland Skua), north to Tristan da Cunha and Gough Island (Tristan Skua), and on the Antarctic Peninsula and on subantarctic islands right across the southern oceans (Subantarctic Skua). It is loosely colonial, breeding near petrel and prion colonies, which it plunders, or penguins, whose eggs and chicks form the main prey of some populations. Brown Skua, however, takes all available prey, not only being a pest to seabird colonies but also feeding on birds at sea, on weakened seals and on mammal carcases.

Chilean Skua is restricted to the southernmost coasts of South America, where it probably remains for most of the year, although with some dispersal along the coasts northwards to Peru. Unlike the other skuas, it often breeds in large dense colonies and seems to be adapted to a gull-like way of life, in many areas feeding at refuse tips alongside Kelp Gulls *Larus dominicanus*.

The *Catharacta* skuas are mostly shorter-distance migrants, the sole exception being the South Polar Skua. Great Skuas perform moderately long migrations, large post-breeding flocks gathering in the North Sea before the main passage southwards between August and October. The principal wintering area for adults is between the Bay of Biscay and the northern part of West Africa. Younger birds move farther, with winter concentrations south of the adults' main wintering range. In their first and second years immature Great Skuas disperse over the entire North Atlantic, and extending into the Mediterranean. Stragglers (mainly immatures) have reached the coasts of Central America and northern South America, and also the Black Sea.

The South Polar Skua, however, is a real long-distance traveller, and parts of its population (probably immatures) may undertake movements as noticeably long as those of the Arctic Tern *Sterna paradisaea*. This migration takes the birds from Antarctica on a clockwise route to the northern Pacific, where they spend the summer before heading southwards again; from August, probably part of the population migrates halfway back towards the south to 'summer' off coasts slightly above the equator. This long-distance migration is now well understood in the Pacific, but it was not until the 1970s that the phenomenon was proven to occur also in the Atlantic. This was probably because much lower numbers occur in this ocean, with a larger percentage of the harder-to-identify dark morph, and because of the presence there of the similar-looking Great Skua, a problem not encountered in the northern Pacific, where South Polar Skua is the only species of *Catharacta*. There are still many questions raised about the South Polar Skua in the northern hemisphere, especially concerning proof of its occurrence in the Western Palearctic, the regularity of its appearance in the Indian Ocean (and which of the *Catharacta* skuas is most regular there), and to what degree Atlantic birds follow larger shearwaters to their non-breeding grounds (as has been proven for the Pacific birds). If South Polar Skuas do follow shearwaters in the Atlantic, they are likely to occur regularly off Greenland (from where there are four records) and then to migrate south to central parts of the Atlantic, with passage reaching western Britain and the Bay of Biscay. Amazingly, several hundreds were noted off Senegal in the autumns of 1995 and 1996 (R.F Porter *in litt.*), in an area with just one previous record of the species. Most older South Polar Skuas probably remain in the southern oceans in winter.

Brown Skuas of all three subspecies stay closer to their breeding range. This is especially true of populations breeding in the vicinity of colonies of petrels and prions; the latter may breed all year round, providing a continuous food source for the skuas. The Brown Skuas breeding in more southerly waters, which are deserted by most seabirds in winter, perform an east-west migration, remaining in the southern oceans. Most of the population occurs well south of the continents. The most widespread subspecies, the Subantarctic Skua, is the one which disperses most widely, but even the other two, geographically restricted subspecies (Tristan and Falkland Skuas) expand somewhat across the southern Atlantic. There have been several records of Subantarctic Skua in the Indian Ocean north to the coasts of the Indian subcontinent, indicating an immature dispersal similar to that found in South Polar Skua. It is thus now established that two of the southern *Catharacta* species regularly cross the equator. The occurrence of Brown Skua in the northern part of the Atlantic and the Pacific, areas which form part of the non-breeding range of South Polar Skua, remains to be proven. A record from well-watched countries such as those in northern Europe, or the United States, is not so unlikely as was recently thought. There have been claims of Brown Skua from several Central American countries, but all are considered to have been referable to South Polar Skua.

Effects of Great Skuas on other species

Since 1900, the British population of Great Skuas has increased, mainly because of extra food provided by a growing population of sand-eels *Ammodytes*. Great and Arctic Skuas compete for territories, the former establishing its territory 2-3 weeks before Arctic Skua and always dominating it. Isolated pairs of Arctic Skuas, in particular, are highly vulnerable to Great Skuas. On Foula, Shetland, Arctic Skuas have been driven to poorer areas or smaller territories, and have become gradually more exposed to predation from the larger species. The total Arctic Skua population has not dropped (and has even increased locally), but its breeding success has been reduced in areas also occupied by Great Skuas (Furness 1987). In some years a percentage of adult Arctic Skuas has been killed by Great Skuas, probably when other food sources have been poor. Furness (1977) showed that as many as 20% of adult breeding Arctic Skuas are killed by Great Skuas, and O'Donald (1983) found that, on Fair Isle, 4.4% of adults and 31% of fledglings were killed by Great Skuas.

The Great Skua also takes a small quantity of other bird species. Although its total population seems too low to have any serious effect on other avian species, it may have a noticeable influence on the numbers and/or breeding success of European Storm-petrel *Hydrobates pelagicus*, Black-legged Kittiwake *Rissa tridactyla*, Black Guillemot *Cepphus grylle*, Common Eider *Somateria mollissima* and Eurasian Oystercatcher *Haematopus ostralegus* (Furness 1987). The decline of the sand-eel population from the 1980s has probably forced Great Skuas to exploit breeding seabirds to a higher degree.

STERCORARIUS SPECIES

The three species of *Stercorarius* skuas, Pomarine, Arctic and Long-tailed, all breed in the northern hemisphere. Arctic Skua is the most widely distributed, and its breeding range is almost circumpolar. While its northernmost populations are mostly tundra breeders, most of the population in the southern part of its range breed in coastal habitats, where they are typically associated with large seabird colonies. Arctic Skuas feed opportunistically in the breeding season, taking invertebrates, birds, insects and plant berries; although they do not ignore rodents, they are less dependent on lemmings than are Pomarine and Long-tailed Skuas. North Atlantic populations, however, feed mostly on sand-eels *Ammodytes*, by kleptoparasitising other seabirds; as a result, they suffered in the late 1980s owing to a drastic decline in the sand-eel population, but have shown some recovery since then. Locally, a limiting factor on the Arctic Skua population is the presence of high numbers of Great Skuas in the same area.

Long-tailed and Pomarine Skuas breed on the same arctic tundra. Both have an almost circumpolar breeding range, but with a gap in lemming-free areas. While both species feed mainly on lemmings when these are present, Long-tailed Skua will also accept a range of smaller animals (similar to those taken by Arctic Skua) and berries, allowing it to breed even in years when lemmings are scarce or absent. Pomarine Skua, on the other hand, is extremely dependent on lemmings as a food source in the breeding season, and breeds only in areas where these rodents are present in some numbers. In the spring and the early part of the arctic summer, Pomarine Skuas wander around the Arctic, often in huge flocks, in search of lemmings; if unsuccessful in their search, they do not breed. By contrast, the density of Pomarine Skuas is locally very high when lemmings are present, and this is true also, though to a lesser degree, of the Long-tailed Skua. Following summers with a good lemming population, numbers of juvenile Pomarine and Long-tailed Skuas (and to some extent also Arctic Skuas) are very high. This is not only a result of good food availability, but also because Arctic Foxes *Alopex lagopus*, the main enemy of breeding skuas, also feed mainly on lemmings in such summers, ignoring the large number of birds around. In Western Europe, a large percentage of juvenile *Stercorarius* skuas has occurred at three-year intervals, with noticeable influxes in 1976, 1982, 1985, 1988, 1991 and, to a lesser degree, 1994. It is since the identification of the smaller skuas has been better understood that this phenomenon has been revealed. Local weather conditions, however, have a great influence on the numbers of skuas seen from shore each year: high pressure with little or no wind always produces far fewer skuas at seawatch points than do low-pressure systems (depressions) with strong winds, rain and fog.

Both Pomarine and Long-tailed Skuas occur mainly as pale morphs (a genuine dark-morph adult Long-tailed has still to be proven), whereas dark morphs predominate in the southern populations of Arctic Skua, which feed mainly by kleptoparasitism; such piratical behaviour is apparently aided by dark coloration. Interestingly, all three species feed at sea in winter, when they develop a much less conspicuous winter plumage, closer to the juvenile and immature plumages.

All three *Stercorarius* skuas make long migrations, bringing Long-tailed and Arctic Skuas to the southern oceans, with their main wintering ranges in the oceans south of the equator; Pomarine Skuas normally winter slightly north of the equator. Non-breeders as a rule remain in the winter quarters or migrate only halfway towards the breeding range. The three small skuas are therefore likely to be encountered in almost any area between the high Arctic and the southern oceans, and, although normally strongly associated with the sea, pirating food from seabirds or feeding on fish, the rather large number of inland records demonstrates that they migrate over large parts of the continental landmass. Not unexpectedly, few other bird species have occurred in a larger number of countries than have the three *Stercorarius* skuas.

BREEDING BEHAVIOUR

All skuas apart from Pomarine Skua exhibit mate and site fidelity from year to year. By using the same territory and mate for many years, they allow themselves to breed earlier and more successfully.

The Pomarine Skua is dependent on lemmings during the breeding season, and it is so specialised a predator that it is unable to breed unless lemming numbers are sufficient. It wanders around the arctic tundra until sites with an abundance of lemmings are found. Lemming populations are not stable, but show more or less cyclic fluctuations: an area with no lemmings in one year may have a plentiful supply of these rodents in the next year. It is therefore normally possible for Pomarine Skuas, following extensive searches, to locate areas with lemmings. This explains the large summer migration noted along the north coast of Siberia in certain summers. As soon as a site with lemmings is found, the male defends a territory, and soon attracts a female. Under such circumstances, mate fidelity could be a disadvantage. Pomarine Skuas are not able to build up sufficient body-fat reserves on berries and insects alone, but need a supply of lemmings.

Long-tailed Skua is also dependent on lemmings, but to a lesser degree, returning year after year to the same site and changing to other food sources in years when lemmings are scarce (Andersson 1981).

The territory is established almost immediately after arrival on the breeding grounds, at which time the skuas carry large fat reserves, enabling them to reoccupy the territory at a period when food is short. Great Skuas weighed up to 25% more and Arctic Skuas 10% more on their return than during the incubation and hatching period (Belopolskii 1961; Furness 1987). Conversely, Tristan Skuas did not show any significant difference in weight during the breeding season, probably owing at least partly to the constant availability of food at their breeding sites. Birds which establish territory the soonest generally have the best breeding success.

Apart from Pomarine Skua, skuas form lifelong pair-bonds, being monogamous. Males of Great and Brown Skuas sometimes mate with several females, forming trios, although such trios seemingly do not last for long (Burton 1968; Furness 1987).

In Subantarctic Skua (and to a lesser degree Tristan Skua), two males and one female often form a trio, locally an important breeding strategy among skuas feeding at petrel colonies. This is an unusual strategy among birds, and a remarkable one in this case, as the female skuas are highly aggressive towards other females invading the territory. Sometimes, aggressive behaviour by intruding females causes the established female to leave, giving way to the newcomer.

The territory is largely concerned with nesting, its size varying considerably. Generally, skuas feeding well away from the colony hold the smallest territories. Also, the more aggression encountered from neighbours (which varies considerably from bird to bird), the smaller the territory. The territory is aggressively defended against intruders by swooping and dive-bombing, this being especially fierce when both mates are present, and most enthusiastic in the middle of a colony, where the oldest, most experienced birds gather.

Breeding density varies from site to site. The smallest territories are found in skuas nesting close to seabird colonies. Here, kleptoparasitism or active fishing are the main feeding strategies, although a certain proportion of South Polar Skuas feeding on penguin eggs and chicks also established large territories (Trillmich 1978). Brown Skuas nesting among petrels (which then constitute the main food) defend smaller territories, but this is probably a result of an unusually high density of potential prey. Generally, however, the larger the territory defended, the greater the amount of food taken within the territory. This is particularly the case among Long-tailed Skuas.

Skuas breeding in colonies are often seen attacking 'clubs' of younger, non-breeding birds. This is especially true of large, successful colonies, whereas a constant decrease in colony size/success forces younger birds to move elsewhere.

BREEDING

During courtship, the elongated central tail feathers of *Stercorarius* skuas play an important role in their aerial displays. *Catharacta* skuas, all of which show minute tail projections varying little among the species, display on the ground, uttering a characteristic 'long-call' and spreading their wings to reveal the striking large white wing-flashes.

The eggs are laid 10-30 days after territory establishment. Laying takes place much more quickly at higher latitudes than at lower ones, as the time available for breeding is much shorter there. Before the eggs are laid, the male feeds the female in order to ensure that she is in adequate breeding condition. During the rest of the breeding period, too, males undertake a greater share of foraging, whereas females spend a larger part of the time within or close to the territory. As mentioned previously, this may explain why males are smaller than females: the smaller, more agile males are better hunters, whereas the larger females are more effective and aggressive defenders of the territory and offspring against intruders. Territory defence is especially fierce in older breeders. The *Stercorarius* skuas often feign injury in a manner similar to that of shorebirds in order to lead intruders away from the young.

The clutch normally contains two eggs, but clutch size varies slightly depending on food availability. O'Donald (1983) found 87% of Arctic Skua clutches to consist of two eggs. Skuas have two brood-patches and are able to take only two eggs onto their feet. Single-egg clutches are the rule if the first clutch is lost, but are also normal among late layers or younger adults. In Long-tailed Skua, clutch sizes were 1.9-2.0 in 'rodent years' and 1.4-1.7 in years of food shortage (Andersson 1981). Exceptionally, three or even four eggs are laid.

Hatching success varies between 60% and 73% for all skua species, but can naturally be affected by severe weather such as storms and snow. A particularly low hatching success was found among South Polar Skuas at Cape Bird, Antarctica, in 1977-78, caused by unusually heavy snowdrifts at a time when the snow normally would have melted (Ensor 1979). In tundra-breeding *Stercorarius* skuas, most eggs are lost to Arctic Foxes *Alopex lagopus*.

THE CHICK STAGE

There is an interval of several days between the hatching of the two eggs. Consequently, the first-hatched chick is larger than the second and thus better able to survive. Sibling aggression often reduces breeding success, as the older nestling regularly dominates and eventually eats its younger brother or sister. This is the normal case in years with short food supply, and enables one young to survive. In years when food is plentiful, both young normally fledge. Cannibalism among young is, however, the rule in South Polar Skua.

The coloration of young *Stercorarius* skuas is cryptic, averaging darkest in Arctic Skua and palest and greyest in Long-tailed Skua. Young of *Catharacta* species are much more conspicuous, being pale sandy to pinkish, but South Polar Skua is greyer, varying from pale bluish-grey to dark brownish-grey. That young Great Skuas have the 'wrong' coloration for their background is puzzling; Great Skuas probably colonised the North Atlantic from the south, and have not yet had time to evolve a more appropriate colour (Furness 1987).

The young skua begs for food by pecking at the breast of the parent bird or by moving up and down. The begging behaviour thus differs strongly from that of young gulls, which peck at the parent's bill in order to make it regurgitate food.

Chick development differs between the two genera of skuas. *Stercorarius* young sprout feathers early in their growth and do not put on much fat, probably because the weather in the arctic summer is rather stable, allowing chicks to expect good conditions during the period of their growth. Furthermore, their development is rapid, enabling them to leave the breeding site shortly after fledging. *Catharacta* young remain down-covered until almost reaching their peak weight, and put on much fat, this strategy having presumably evolved as a result of breeding in the severe antarctic summer, the growing young being protected by fat reserves and down for quite a long period. (The fact that this latter strategy is also adopted by the Great Skua may be further evidence that it colonised the North Atlantic rather recently.) Most *Catharacta* skuas are short-distance migrants, leaving the breeding site relatively later than *Stercorarius* young; this is the case even with the South Polar Skua, which migrates longer distances.

In all skuas, the tarsus and bill develop rapidly during the first half of the growth period, whereas wing development begins slowly and then accelerates.

BREEDING SUCCESS

The breeding success of *Stercorarius* skuas in the tundra is highest in peak years for lemmings. Pomarine Skuas breed only where lemmings are abundant, and Long-tailed Skuas prefer areas with lemmings, though Arctic Skuas are not especially lemming-dependent. In lemming years, several factors influence breeding success. First, the large numbers of these rodents enable skuas to breed in denser populations and to raise more young than in other years; secondly, skua predators such as Arctic Foxes feed almost solely on lemmings in peak lemming years, whereas in normal years young of seabirds (including skuas and birds up to the size of geese) form the main part of their diet. Thus, in lemming years, large numbers of young are raised by several tundra-breeding bird species: in north and west Europe, large autumn influxes of Pomarine and Long-tailed (and to a lesser degree Arctic) Skuas coincide with years when above-average percentages of juveniles of Brent Geese *Branta bernicla*, Little Stints *Calidris minuta* and Curlew Sandpipers *C. ferruginea* are seen (Breife 1989; own observations). The following year, with a shortage of lemmings and a large population of Arctic Foxes, is normally characterised by skuas breeding in only very small numbers. Note that annual fluctuations in lemming populations do not occur uniformly throughout the entire Palearctic, but vary in timing from one region to another.

Fledging success is very high in Great, Tristan and Subantarctic Skuas, as well as in Arctic Skuas breeding at lower latitudes, being 80-95%. It is most variable in tundra-breeding *Stercorarius* skuas and South Polar Skuas; in the latter it decreases with increasing latitude (Furness 1987), but at Signy Island (South Orkneys), one of their northernmost breeding sites, it is as high as that of Subantarctic Skua (Hemmings 1984).

AGE OF FIRST BREEDING

Stercorarius skuas normally start to breed at an age of three years, although Pomarine Skuas may first breed at two years and tundra-nesting Arctic Skuas are known to breed at one year of age (Belopolskii 1961; Maher 1974; Furness 1987). In Shetland, Arctic Skuas were found to breed first at an average age of 4.2 years (Davis 1976).

South Polar Skua breeds mostly when five or six years old; in one study, 0.8% bred at four years of age and 58% at eight years (Wood 1970). Brown Skua shows the same pattern, the youngest breeding bird being six years old (Parmelee & Pietz 1987). Great Skuas normally do not breed before they are five or six years old, but exceptionally may do so from four years of age (Furness 1987).

AGE DEVELOPMENT OF SKUAS

The *Stercorarius* skuas (known as jaegers in North America) take about four years to develop full adult plumage. The timing of this development is similar to that of the larger gulls, but with a frustrating intraspecific variation, making safe ageing of all but juveniles and adults in the field almost impossible. Nevertheless, by classifying immatures according to particular characters, most individuals can be linked to an 'age type'.

Juveniles are characterised by pale feather edges to all upperpart feathers, creating a neat scaly pattern, most pronounced on Long-tailed Skua. The juvenile plumage of Arctic and certain Pomarine Skuas shows warm brown colour tones, not present in other plumages. The underwing and rump are barred pale and dark. The central pair of tail feathers is shorter and less pointed than at other ages. Dark-plumaged skuas often look uniformly dark in the field. With such birds, look for projection and shape of the central tail feathers and the bare-part coloration. The bill is pale with a black tip, and the legs pale with black outer part to the feet, showing almost no intraspecific variation. Note that there is a sliding scale of variation between dark and pale individuals, generally not linked to eventual development of dark and pale morphs, although very pale-headed birds probably become pale adults.

Plumage wear causes fading, especially of the head, body and greater coverts, which may be unusually pale during the first winter. Most birds retain juvenile plumage (or most of it) into their first winter, the post-juvenile moult not being completed until summer of the second calendar-year, followed by a moult directly into second-winter plumage.

First-summer plumage is similar to juvenile, but colder greyish-brown above, lacking pale feather edges on upperwing-coverts. Some individuals become much worn and faded, appearing very different from the fresh juveniles of late summer and autumn. The juvenile underwing pattern is retained, but the tail projection is longer, and on Arctic and Long-tailed Skuas now sharply pointed. Pale birds develop paler areas on the head (especially hindneck) and belly. A few probably acquire a distinct dark cap at this age, but this has been proven only for Long-tailed Skua. Dark colour starts to appear on the cutting-edges of the bill and on the tibia, and the entire foot is black.

Second-summer retains juvenile underwing and barring on rump (often even more striking, as the bars are clearer white and very dark). Pale morphs acquire adult-like head and underbody, but the pattern is less clean. A few show head and body plumage less advanced, being virtually identical to first-summers, but generally the tail projection is longer (from this age overlapping with adult summers), the bill is less strikingly two-toned (often with pale only on upper mandible), and the legs are predominantly dark with scattered pale spots. From this stage, dark birds are impossible to age in the field if not seen very well.

Third-winter is similar to adult winter, but still with underwing predominantly barred pale and dark. Typically, the lesser underwing-coverts and the axillaries start to develop the uniform dark colour of adults, followed later in winter by the rest of the underwing-coverts, although some barred coverts (especially greaters) are normally present. Bill and legs are identical to those of adults.

Third-summer is similar to adult, and many are probably inseparable. Individuals showing a few barred underwing-coverts, a less clean pattern on the underparts and scattered pale-barred feathers on the rump can be referred to this age, although retarded adults may be identical. Pale markings on otherwise dark tarsi are a safer immature character.

The subsequent plumages are similar to adult. Note that individual variation is large, and it is always safest to assign immatures to e.g. 'first-summer type', 'first- or second-summer type', and so on.

Adult summer is the cleanest and neatest plumage. Pale morphs show a striking blackish cap, uniform blackish underwing-coverts, and the longest, most typical tail projection. There is a rather sharp division between pale and dark morphs, with intermediates common only among Arctic Skuas.

Adult winter is similar to immatures in showing a less clean pattern than adult summer, as well as developing a barred rump and having a shorter tail projection. The mantle shows pale feather edges, on some creating a paler saddle, which soon disappears with wear. Adult winter can be aged by the uniform dark underwing-coverts and the adult bare-part coloration.

Ageing of *Catharacta* skuas is much more complicated, and rarely possible in the field. Typically, **juveniles** have clean-patterned underparts and rather uniform upperparts, only with narrow pale edges to the mantle and scapulars. In species showing a dark cap in adult plumage, juveniles generally have a uniformly dark hood. Unlike in *Stercorarius* skuas, the underwing is identical at all ages. The bare-part coloration is in most species similar to adult (see species accounts), but juveniles and younger immatures often show pale spots on the tarsus. **Immatures** are similar to adults, often with more irregular mottling on mantle and underbody. They lack the pale streaks on the hindneck and sides of neck of adults, which are most pronounced during breeding. **Adults** have narrow pale streaks on the hindneck and sides of neck, accentuating the dark cap of those species (or subspecies) showing the latter feature. The mantle and underparts are typically blotched with feathers of different coloration, unlike the clean pattern of juveniles.

TERMINOLOGY

As winter and summer seasons of the northern hemisphere are reversed in the southern hemisphere, terms such as first-winter are not always appropriate. Alternative terminologies for naming age and plumage were introduced by Humphrey & Parkes (1959), and these are the most widely accepted terms in North America. Listed below are examples of alternative terminologies, with the Humphrey & Parkes terms given in parentheses:

> First-winter plumage (first basic plumage)
> First-summer plumage (first alternate plumage)
> Winter plumage (basic plumage)
> Summer plumage (alternate plumage)

These alternatives are also included in the species accounts, in the section 'Detailed Description'.

MOULT

Adults moult to summer plumage before reaching their breeding sites, long-distance migrants (*Stercorarius* species) typically moulting in the winter quarters. This moult is partial, involving head, body and central pair of tail feathers. Following breeding, a complete moult takes place, in *Stercorarius* mostly after arrival in the winter quarters, although minor parts of the plumage may be moulted close to the breeding grounds (especially in the case of Pomarine Skua). The flight feathers are moulted on the wintering grounds, rarely with a few feathers renewed close to the breeding grounds. The moult of immatures is similar. **Juveniles** have a complete moult on the wintering grounds, generally later than that of adults, and may retain parts of juvenile plumage in their first summer (especially those birds, probably weakened, which winter outside the normal winter range). Moult of flight feathers is later than in adults, and often not completed before late in the first summer. There is no moult to a first-summer plumage, but a direct moult into second-winter plumage. See species accounts.

BLEACHING AND WEAR

Apart from first-years with retarded moult, plumage wear is not pronounced in skuas. The exceptions are worn pale South Polar Skuas and (rarely) paler, retarded Great Skuas, which may become unexpectedly pale on the head (and to a lesser degree the body) with wear.

Note that, during moult of the greater coverts, the pale bases to all flight feathers (including secondaries) may produce a much larger pale area on the wing than is normal. This is evident from photographs of moulting *Stercorarius* skuas in the northern hemisphere winter, and has confused observers of Great Skuas in October-November (Norman & Tucker 1979).

Some first-summer *Stercorarius* skuas are more worn than any others, having forgone the normal moult cycles. Pale-headed birds may then look unusually pale-headed, this often combined with extremely worn coverts and unmoulted juvenile flight feathers. This effect, however, is rare, as such birds have probably suffered from sickness or disease, quickly weakening them to the point that they are unable to feed in the skuas' highly specialised way and therefore succumb.

DEFINITIONS

Adult: Term used to describe plumage worn by a bird capable of reproduction.

Immature: All plumage stages between juvenile and fully adult plumages.

Juvenile: The first plumage, worn at time of fledging.

t: Tail feather (rectrix); t1 is the elongated central pair of tail feathers, t6 the outermost pair.

Calendar-year: The period from when the bird hatches until 31st December of the same year is referred to as its **first calendar-year**. **Second calendar-year** is from 1st January to 31st December of the following year, and so on.

Summer plumage: The plumage worn in the breeding season. Acquired by the partial moult of head and body plumage (even t1 in *Stercorarius*); in long-distance migrants, this moult is undertaken before leaving the wintering grounds.

Winter plumage: The plumage worn in the non-breeding season. Acquired by a complete moult after the breeding season. In *Stercorarius*, this moult is typically undertaken on the wintering grounds.

SKUAS AND MAN

AGRICULTURAL CONFLICTS

Most skuas breed in remote areas not exploited for agriculture. Great Skuas, however, breed on islands also inhabited by farmers, and at several Scottish sites they are illegally shot in order to protect animals, although they only occasionally kill weak lambs. They are attracted by lambing, especially in areas with poor husbandry, but normally eat just the afterbirth and rarely harm the lamb itself or the ewe. Unfortunately, the time of lambing coincides with the period when other food items are in short supply (Furness 1987).

Brown Skuas on Rangatira, New Zealand, feed more exclusively on lambs; removal of sheep was followed by a drop in the numbers of skuas, which eventually learned to feed on petrels (Fleming 1939; Young 1978). Heavy persecution of the Tristan subspecies of the Brown Skua on Tristan da Cunha led to a decrease in the population to 5-10 pairs (Furness 1987).

The conflict between farmers and Great Skuas (and, in certain areas, Arctic Skuas) is as much a result of the skuas' fierce defence of their offspring in the breeding season, especially against sheep and sheepdogs. The aggressive behaviour of *Catharacta* skuas towards intruders was noted as being less marked among Great Skuas, which have probably learnt the disadvantages of aggression towards man, than among their southern hemisphere cousins (Furness 1987). Arctic Skuas attack more violently, using their voice as well as dive-bombing, but they are generally shown more tolerance by farmers, who regard this species as a victim of the growing population of Great Skuas in certain areas.

In only a few areas has habitat destruction reduced the numbers of breeding skuas, although agricultural changes may have a local effect on skua populations. One example is the destruction of moorland habitats in the Orkney Islands, where the Arctic Skuas decreased following agricultural improvement (Meek *et al.* 1985), but it seems improbable that loss of marginal land will be extensive enough to reduce the overall population (Furness 1987).

PERSECUTION BY MAN

Skuas are protected by law in the Western Palearctic. In the northern isles of Scotland, illegal shooting has held down the numbers of Great Skuas on Fair Isle, Hascosay, Mousa and Papa Westray, but the shooting of an estimated 30-500 Great Skuas annually on Foula does not appear to have had any severe effect on the population (Furness 1987).

Thousands of pairs of Great Skuas formerly bred in the Faeroe Islands, where, as well as being persecuted, they were heavily harvested for food. In 1792, 6,000 juveniles alone were taken for food (Glutz von Blotzheim & Bauer 1982). In 1741, it was decided that every man between the ages of 15 and 50 should pay a 'bill-tax', which involved handing over the bills of two Great Skuas (or Common Ravens *Corvus corax*) each year (if a bill of a White-tailed Eagle *Haliaeetus albicilla* was delivered, the hunter was free from bill-tax for the rest of his life!). Towards the end of the 19th century, an even heavier toll was taken by taxidermists and 'sportsmen'. Such heavy persecution, which occurred both in the Faeroes and in Scotland, almost wiped out the skua population, which by 1897 numbered just four pairs in the Faeroes (isolated pairs on four islands). This led to protection of the Great Skua, the Faeroese population of which eventually increased to 550 pairs in 1961 (Bayes *et al.* 1964; Joensen 1966).

EFFECTS OF POLLUTION

Skuas are one of the top predators in the marine ecosystem, and are obvious species to use for monitoring pollutant levels in the seas and oceans. This is especially true of *Catharacta* skuas, whereas *Stercorarius* species are less useful indicators in the breeding season, when they feed mainly on terrestrial prey or smaller food items (Furness 1987).

The organochlorines found in seabirds are DDT and its metabolites DDD and DDE, and the industrial compounds PCBs. The highest levels have been found in Great Skuas, especially from Iceland (Furness 1987), but high levels have also been found in Brown Skuas, which had greater concentrations of DDE than other antarctic seabirds, while a Tristan Skua showed levels equal to those of the most heavily affected Great Skuas. PCB levels are highest in Great Skua, much less in Brown Skua, indicating that PCBs have not yet been carried into southern-hemisphere marine ecosystems to any great extent.

DDT was developed as an insecticide in the 1940s, but, following research on its harmful effects on wildlife, it has been replaced in the northern hemisphere by less persistent pesticides; on a worldwide scale, however, its use has increased, especially in the so-called underdeveloped countries. The tendency of PCBs to accumulate in the fat reserves of wild animals was noted in the 1970s, but the total worldwide production of these substances has not diminished, and restrictions on their use have little or no effect on reducing PCB levels in animals, as they are even more resistant to biodegradation than is DDT.

The only skua species analysed over a longer period is Great Skua. During the 1970s, levels of DDT and dieldrin in tissues and eggs declined, but PCB levels in livers of Great Skuas showed a slight increase, reaching 99 ppm in wet weight (Furness 1987). PCB levels in eggs have fallen since reaching a peak in 1974. DDE and PCB levels tend to increase with age, but the sample is rather small. There is, however, no clear evidence that any skua population has been severely affected by pollutants, although the numbers of addled eggs and deformed or dying chicks are higher than in other seabirds (Furness 1987). The breeding success of Great Skuas investigated was rather stable, and eggshell-thinning minimal. A reduction of 15% or more in eggshell thickness may lead to increase in egg breakage and lower hatching success, but thinning has not been found to any significant degree in Great Skua eggs (Furness 1987). It is possibly a result of the opportunistic way in which Great Skuas feed that they show such low levels of pollutants, these probably being highest in individuals which kill seabirds.

OBSERVING SKUAS IN THE FIELD

Field identification, including the recognition of differences in shape and flight between the species, is learned only with experience, preferably acquired from prolonged hours of seawatching in different wind conditions. Once this has been achieved, however, the knowledge gained is extremely useful. In areas inhabited by only one species of skua, such as certain breeding sites, the observer can concentrate patiently on getting to know that species' jizz and flight without needing to worry about similar species. In northern Scotland, for example, Arctic Skua is the only breeding *Stercorarius*, often being seen together with Great Skua, whereas the Scandinavian tundra harbours only the Long-tailed Skua in summer. Once an observer is familiar with the way in which an Arctic Skua behaves and its manner of flight, a sudden and unexpected encounter with a Pomarine or Long-tailed Skua (especially adults) becomes something of a revelation!

Nevertheless, learning the clues to identification is certainly better achieved in situations where several species occur together. The best time for this is during migration periods, when a number of skua species may be observed on the same day (typically with one species dominating); this is particularly the case in autumn, when it is by no means unusual for all four northern skuas to be seen in a single day, especially in September. At this time, the possibilities for observing most plumages are good and, since immatures of the three *Stercorarius* skuas show considerable overlap in plumage characters, it becomes obvious that a thorough knowledge of differences in jizz and flight attitude is essential.

From land, skuas are observed mainly during seawatches, with most birds passing in conditions of strong oceanic winds. A careful check of weather forecasts on the days before a planned trip will add to the chances of success. Be ready if low-pressure systems are predicted - and, if 'advantageous' weather suddenly approaches, go! Always be prepared to be patient; take a whole day off, and bring plenty of warm clothes and coffee. You must accept that skuas sometimes have plans other than yours, although only rarely do days with the 'right' weather fail to produce skuas. Note that migration may cease in gale-force winds, as these make active migration difficult; days immediately preceding and following the passage of low-pressure systems are often better. Finally, remember that, if you really want to see skuas, ignore everything else that moves past. The chances are that the main skua migration will pass in one day but, if you miss the skuas, something else of interest will almost surely turn up. In the northern hemisphere, the best localities in autumn are headlands and promontories facing the ocean and along the North Sea coast (the Norfolk coast is magnificent). That is, of course, unless you are able to join a pelagic trip.

Skuas normally pass by merely as dark shadows which soon disappear in the distance, often as a dark W-shape suddenly rising up, only to vanish below the wave-tops. In most cases, however, patience pays: migrating skuas are rarely blown strongly off their flight path and are usually easily relocated, especially when many seawatchers are present. With high waves, the larger species are the most difficult to keep track of as their flight is low. Make sure to identify fixing-points such as ships, and do not forget to name them, e.g. 'white fishing-boat', 'blue coaster with red funnel' or 'large vessel', (but do not assume that your fellow birders know the difference between a tanker, a bulk-carrier and a ferry!). Naturally, this is much easier when characteristic landmarks are within view. Remember also that plumage details are easier to observe through a telescope than through binoculars, although the latter are often more helpful when judging size and jizz (and, if you are lucky enough to have birds at close range, examine them with the naked eye, which gives an even better impression of the bird in relation to its surroundings). Be sure that your tripod is stable: weather conditions when seawatching are notoriously rough.

Fortunately, many skuas will suddenly interrupt their migration in order to chase other seabirds, and identification can then be less problematic. In the northern hemisphere, *Stercorarius* skuas often pursue gulls and terns, and in such cases size and jizz are often of greater value than plumage characters. If the skua's size and flight approach those of a larger gull, it is a Pomarine

Skua (or a *Catharacta* skua); if its size is about that of a Common Gull *Larus canus* or Black-headed Gull *L. ridibundus*, then it is either Arctic or Long-tailed Skua. Note, however, that their dark plumage sometimes makes skuas appear larger than similar-sized pale gulls; comparison with terns and gulls is best made when skuas are chasing these. In moderate winds, high arcing flight up and down waves, with fast wingbeats alternating with passive gliding flight as in shearwaters, is performed only by Arctic and Long-tailed Skuas; 'shearwatering' is more frequent in tail-winds, when even *Catharacta* skuas perform it.

Light conditions affect the overall impression given by any bird. In direct light, plumage is more important than shape; in backlighting, the reverse is the case. Strong sunlight generally illuminates warm-coloured parts such as orange or reddish and, of course, pale areas, whereas overcast and poor light conditions tend to impart a 'brown tinge' to the general coloration. It is unlikely that the first opportunity a birder has to confirm this will be for skuas, but observers should test the effects of different lights on much commoner seabirds, such as gulls.

Against a pale background, dark birds show their shape very well. The pale parts of skuas are sufficiently restricted not to distort this, although the pale tinge to the forehead of Arctic Skua and (to a lesser degree) of *Catharacta* species may show a tendency to disappear against a pale sky. Against a dark background, pale areas (such as a pale belly and wing markings) may be the first things that attract attention.

A final point to bear in mind: not all people interpret descriptions of colours or tones in the same way and, moreover, for anybody suffering the disadvantage of being colour-blind, phrases such as 'warm tinge' or 'strongly orange neck-band' may seem rather meaningless.

SKUA TOPOGRAPHY

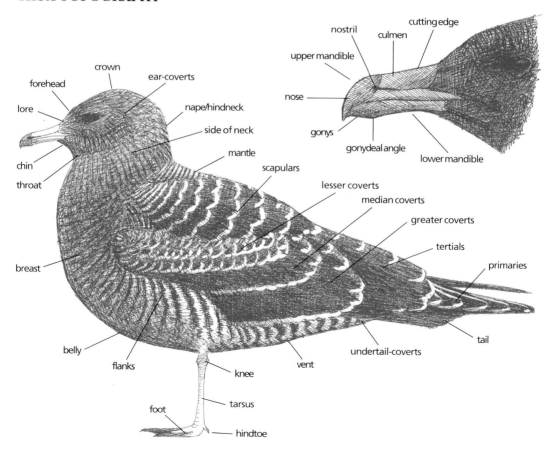

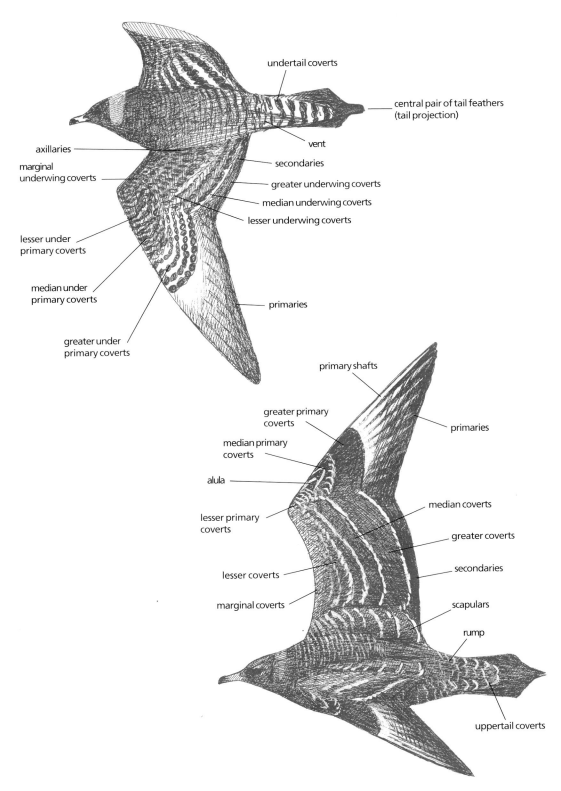

undertail coverts

central pair of tail feathers
(tail projection)

axillaries

marginal
underwing coverts

vent

secondaries

greater underwing coverts

median underwing coverts

lesser underwing coverts

lesser under
primary coverts

median under
primary coverts

primaries

greater under
primary coverts

primary shafts

greater primary
coverts

primaries

median primary
coverts

alula

median coverts

lesser primary
coverts

greater coverts

secondaries

lesser coverts

scapulars

marginal coverts

rump

uppertail coverts

EXPLANATION OF THE SPECIES ACCOUNTS

Each species is dealt with under the following subheadings.

FIELD IDENTIFICATION

Each species account opens with a presentation of the identification of the species in the field, concentrating on jizz, behaviour, short plumage descriptions and separation of age-classes, as well as notes on field separation from similar species. This section is intended to be immediately readable, the section in which to find the solution to most field problems, and is based mainly on personal field observations.

VOICE

Brief notes are given on calls.

MOULT

A description follows of moult in different age-classes. This is based mainly on museum skins, supplemented with field notes and photographs. Included both in this section and in the detailed descriptions are notes on bleaching and wear.

DETAILED DESCRIPTION

A detailed description is given of plumage and bare parts of the different age-classes. This section is based largely on studies of museum skins, supplemented with information from the relevant literature, especially Cramp & Simmons (1983), Glutz von Blotzheim & Bauer (1982) and Devillers (1977, 1978). The plumage topography follows in principle that given in Cramp & Simmons (1977): see illustrations on pages 26 and 27.

Detailed descriptions are given in the sequence of **Adult**, **Adult summer** (breeding), **Adult winter** (non-breeding), **Juvenile**, **first-winter**, **first-summer**, **second-winter**, and so on. Under **Adult**, characters applicable to adults of all morphs at all seasons are included. Descriptions generally follow the order used in other similar works, starting with head, upperparts, wings, tail and underparts, and ending with bare parts. Certain features which may be exceptional are included here, rather than being listed under a separate heading, although genuine aberrants (such as leucistic or albinistic individuals) are mentioned under 'Variants'.

Generally, all plumages are detailed in full, but in cases when age-classes are similar, the main description is found under 'Adult'. Furthermore, it should be noted that the immature (or some juvenile) plumages of the *Catharacta* skuas are still poorly understood.

This section is written mainly for the scientist, working with birds in the hand (e.g. when handling live birds or specimens), but it should be very useful also to field observers with regard to the enormous plumage variation found, especially in the *Stercorarius* skuas.

GEOGRAPHICAL VARIATION

If a species has several subspecies, detailed information on their plumage differences is given in this section, as well as comparisons between skin series from different areas within the species' range. In addition, details concerning regional plumage variation (e.g. occurrence of pale and dark morphs in different parts of the breeding range) are included.

VARIANTS

If any aberrant individuals are known, they are mentioned in this section.

HYBRIDISATION

Details of hybridisation between species are given where appropriate.

MEASUREMENTS

Details are given for the most important measurements, based on skin studies by KMO in the museums cited. Measurements are presented in three columns: range of measurements for all specimens measured, mean (in parentheses), and number measured. Included are: wing length, projection of central pair of tail feathers, bill length, depth of bill at gonys, depth of bill at base, gonys length and tarsus length. We believe that these measurements, of the most easily visible parts of the bird, may be helpful not only to ringers but also to experienced field birders, who may find comparison between several species informative.

Wing length (carpal joint to tip of longest primary) is maximum chord, with the wing flattened and straightened against the ruler. Bill length is from the feathering at the base of the upper mandible to the tip of the bill. Bill depth at gonys is from the culmen to the gonydeal angle. Tarsus length is from the intertarsal joint to the distal end or the last undivided scale before the toes diverge. Some measurements are followed by notes giving additional data from other measurement series (if these differ considerably from those made by KMO).

WEIGHT

Weights (in grams) are taken from notes on skin labels and from relevant literature.

FOOD

Short summaries of prey items and feeding techniques are given in this section.

BREEDING

Brief details of nesting sites are given, together with the latest published population estimates if available.

MIGRATION AND WINTERING

This section gives full details of migration routes, timing and numbers, based on personal experience and published references. This information should be used in conjunction with the maps.

REFERENCES

The most important sources of information are cited (author and year), but many more references have been extensively consulted during research for this book. All literature cited and checked is listed in the bibliography at the end of the book.

THE MAPS

Maps show the breeding distribution and wintering ranges of the different species of skua. Arrows indicate the best-known or most heavily used migration routes.

THE PLATES

Each species is comprehensively illustrated, concentrating on variation in breeding and juvenile plumages, but with all known immature plumages depicted as well. The plates have been specially prepared for this guide by Hans Larsson, and are designed to complement the text; they are painted from studies of live birds supplemented with information from skins and photographs. Each single image is based on a certain, known individual bird, in order not to 'mix' characters from several individuals (which could result in plumages which may be rare or exceptional).

THE PHOTOGRAPHS

Each species account is accompanied by a series of photographs showing the different age-classes and the range of variation of some ages, including birds both in flight and settled. Each photograph is captioned with brief notes on identification, followed by the place and month where taken, and the name of the photographer. Eight pages of colour photographs follow the species accounts. These have been chosen as a showcase to illustrate the beauty and diversity of skuas, but each photograph is also captioned with brief notes on identification.

PLATES
1-13

Great Skua *Catharacta skua*

The *Catharacta* of the northern hemisphere, breeding mainly on islands in the North Atlantic; outside breeding season spreads over entire North Atlantic.

Deep, barrel-shaped body with large, protruding head and very short tail lacking obvious projection. White patches on both upperwing and underwing conspicuous, even at great range. Note warm tinge to plumage and, on older birds, medium brown back and upperwing-coverts contrasting with blackish flight feathers and tail to create two-toned pattern on upperparts.

1 **Juvenile** Note warm brown overall coloration (head often darker than body), narrow rufous streaking along leading edge of inner wing, and warm brown pattern to upperparts. White wing-flashes generally reduced compared with adult, and sometimes lacking on upperwing.

2 **Juvenile, darkest variant** Almost blackish, but typically with a rusty tinge. Note restricted white wing-flash (sometimes similar to Pomarine Skua).

3 **Adult** Note well-defined dark cap against yellow-streaked sides of neck, two-toned upperparts and darker blotching on underbody.

4 **Adult** Note paler back and upperwing-coverts contrasting with blackish flight feathers and tail.

5 **Juvenile** Note bicoloured bill (not always so obvious as on this individual), complete dark head forming dark hood, strong reddish-brown tinge to underbody, and scaly pattern on upperparts.

6 **Juvenile** Certain very dark juveniles show reduced pale pattern and may look blackish at distance.

7 **Adult** Pale individuals often show dark mask against strongly pale-streaked head, irregular white blotches on mantle and pale streaking on coverts. With wear, may develop pale frontal blaze, although rarely so conspicuous as on South Polar Skua.

8 **Adult, dark type** Note dark brown overall appearance, and yellow streaks on hindneck, mantle, scapulars and upperwing-coverts.

9 **Adult, average type** Shows dark cap, small amount of pale crown spotting, and strong yellow streaks on hindneck and upperparts.

PLATE 2: CHILEAN AND BROWN SKUAS

Chilean Skua *Catharacta chilensis*

Breeds in southern part of South America. Short-distance migrant, normally wintering close to breeding grounds.

Brown Skua *Catharacta antarctica*

Circumpolar distribution in southern oceans, mainly on islands. Three subspecies: *hamiltoni* on Tristan da Cunha and Gough Island, *antarctica* on Falklands and Patagonia, and *lonnbergi* in rest of range.

1 **Chilean Skua, juvenile** Note dark cap (on juveniles often creating hood), orange-brown underparts, including tips to lesser and median underwing-coverts, and slightly two-toned upperwing. Bill bicoloured as on adults. Legs pale, with dark feet.

2 **Chilean Skua, adult** Note dark cap and breast band, strong rusty to reddish tinge to body and underwing-coverts, and bicoloured bill. With wear, underparts become greyer, but rusty tinge is retained on cheeks/throat and undertail-coverts, often striking against colder surrounding plumage.

3 **Brown Skua of ssp. Falkland Skua *antarctica*** Unlike other subspecies, often shows slight contrast in upperwing similar to Great Skua (although generally weaker). Slightly capped appearance similar to Great Skua. Head and underbody more variable than in other subspecies; some are paler on head with dark eye mask, others blackish-brown. Sometimes shows a few scattered rusty feather edges to underwing-coverts, as illustrated here.

4 **Brown Skua of ssp. Tristan Skua *hamiltoni*** Similar to Subantarctic Skua, but slightly smaller, generally with deeper yellowish streaks on neck sides (often also on mantle). With wear, flanks become white-patterned (shown also by other subspecies, though less prominent on all but certain Subantarctic Skuas).

5 **Brown Skua of ssp. Subantarctic Skua *lonnbergi*** Largest and fiercest skua. Dark brown, with narrow pale hindneck streaking and variable, irregular pale blotching on mantle, latter creating pale saddle on most strongly marked birds. The very heavy bill of this individual is typical of birds from the easternmost part of the range.

6 **Chilean Skua, adult** Note bicoloured bill, and reddish overall coloration (with wear, most conspicuous on cheeks and throat). Dark cap against pale neck sides more developed than on other *Catharacta* skuas.

7 **Brown Skua of ssp. Subantarctic Skua *lonnbergi*, adult** Note deep, black bill, and narrow white shaft-streaks on hindneck and neck sides. Worn birds often show traces of pale frontal blaze.

8 **Brown Skua of ssp. Falkland Skua *antarctica*, adult** Similar to Great Skua, thus showing stronger head contrast and less heavy bill than Subantarctic Skua. Yellow streaking on hindneck and neck sides much stronger than in other subspecies of Brown Skua. With wear, breast and flanks often show pale blotches.

South Polar Skua *Catharacta maccormicki*

Breeds Antarctica. Younger birds migrate to northern hemisphere in southern winter, performing clockwise migration; well known in the Pacific but less understood in Atlantic. Has reached north as far as Alaska and Greenland. Straggler to the Indian Ocean. Regular off West Africa in October.

Approaches Great Skua in size, but always lacks warm colour tones, typically appearing greyish or cold brown. Upperwing rather uniform, lacking contrast between coverts and flight feathers characteristic of most Great Skuas. Typically, shows striking paler hindneck contrasting with dark hood, and sometimes penetrating onto mantle to create pale saddle against dark wings. Bill and legs less heavy than on Great Skua and, especially, Brown Skua. Adult occurs in three colour morphs. All are coldish-tinged, with black bill and legs.

1 **Juvenile** Similar to intermediate adult, but cleaner grey, lacking any brown tinge to plumage. Mantle and coverts greyish-black with indistinct grey fringes, latter normally not visible at range. Bill bicoloured. Juvenile shows much less variation than adult: most are medium grey on head and underbody; a few are blackish-grey or with head paler than body.

2 **Adult, intermediate morph (dark type)** Note dark hood contrasting with paler neck sides and hindneck, traces of pale blaze, and cold greyish-brown underbody, often showing pale blotches or bars. Upperwing dark, often contrasting with pale-streaked mantle and scapulars. Axillaries and most underwing-coverts blackish, contrasting with underbody.

3 **Adult, intermediate morph (pale type)** Often strikingly cold creamy on head and underbody, but on pale intermediate types (or 'dark' pale types) often with even paler neck bar and some dark shading on flanks. Note conspicuous contrast between pale underbody and dark underwing; also pale bar on underwing created by exposed pale bases to secondaries (owing to moulting of greater coverts). This individual shows simultaneous moult of 3-4 inner primaries.

4 **Adult, pale morph** Head and underbody almost uniform creamy to pale greyish-brown; with wear, becomes almost white-headed. Pale adults sometimes show slightly paler leading edge to upperwing, created by pale fringes to lesser and median coverts; these areas always coldish-tinged, never warm brown or strongly yellow as on Great (and some Falkland) Skuas. Typically, head and body contrast well with dark wings and tail.

5 **Adult, dark morph** Almost blackish-brown, lacking any warm coloration apart from numerous golden streaks on neck sides. A certain percentage of dark adults still show pale forehead blaze.

6 **Adult, intermediate morph** Note pale blaze against dark hood, paler hindneck, and regular but narrow, pale mantle streaks.

7 **Adult, pale morph** Note creamy head and underparts, with wear appearing almost whitish, especially on hindneck, but sometimes penetrating onto mantle.

8 **Juvenile** Cleaner grey than adult, with bicoloured bill and more uniform upperparts, with only narrow pale fringes to mantle and scapulars.

9 **Adult** Note pale hindneck and mantle contrasting with uniform wings and dark rear end: a diagnostic difference from Great Skua.

PLATE 4: SOUTHERN *CATHARACTA* SKUAS

1 **Chilean Skua, adult** Note dark cap, bicoloured bill, strong rusty tinge to cheeks, throat, neck sides and undertail-coverts, and strong pale streaks on hindneck. Mantle sometimes with similar pattern to that of young gulls. Many show dark-spotted breast band. This individual shows rather coldish brown underbody, often due to wear. Extremely worn birds may lack any reddish or rufous apart from on cheeks and throat.

2 **Chilean Skua, adult** When fresh, entire underbody strongly rufous-tinged and pale streaks on hindneck conspicuous. Note more uniform bill than on figure 1; adults show variation in bill pattern.

3 **Chilean Skua, juvenile** Generally similar to adult, but underparts cleaner (and often even more strongly reddish), bill contrast stronger, and upperparts normally with weaker, more scaly pattern. Many show dark hood; individual with cap similar to adult illustrated.

4 **Chilean Skua x Falkland Skua hybrid** This individual is similar to Chilean Skua, showing latter's strong reddish tinge to body and strongly capped appearance, but with uniform dark bill, darkish chin and throat, and upperpart pattern similar to Falkland Skua. See text for details concerning hybrids.

5 **Brown Skua of ssp. Falkland Skua, adult** Similar to Great Skua, but wings and upperparts with narrower pale markings. Compared with Subantarctic Skua (figures 6 & 7), is less heavy, with more conspicuous yellow streaks to sides of neck contrasting somewhat with dark cap or hood, stronger rusty wash to pale upperpart coloration, and stronger yellow streaks on breast. Never so fierce and 'grotesque-looking' as certain large Subantarctic Skuas.

6 **Brown Skua of ssp. Subantarctic Skua, adult** The largest skua. Typically cold blackish-brown, with flat forehead, very heavy bill with bulbous tip and irregular pale blotches on upperparts; blotching especially conspicuous with wear, when it creates strong whitish saddle against dark wings. Pale patterning with wear also conspicuous on flanks and sometimes around dark bend of wing.

7 **Brown Skua of ssp. Subantarctic Skua, adult** Note blackish-brown overall coloration, hooded appearance, narrow yellow streaks on neck sides, and irregular pale patterning above. With wear often shows inconspicuous pale feathering around base of upper mandible (cf. figure 9). Bill heavy, with gonydeal angle located about halfway from bill-tip.

8 **Brown Skua, juvenile** Uniform blackish-brown apart from narrow pale fringes and shaft-streaks to mantle and scapulars, slightly bicoloured bill, and pale, dark-spotted tarsus. Pale wing patches smaller than on adult, often not visible on swimming or perched birds (cf. figures 6 & 7).

9 **South Polar Skua, intermediate adult** Note more conspicuous pale feathers around base of upper mandible than on Brown Skua, cleaner pale hindneck, regular but narrow pale streaks on mantle and scapulars, and tendency to show dark mask. Also, head is rounder, legs shorter, and bill less heavy than on Brown Skua; gonydeal angle situated 35-45% from bill-tip. Rounded head often striking compared with Brown Skua at breeding sites; migrants in northern hemisphere, however, often appear small-headed, probably an effect of moult.

Pomarine Skua *Stercorarius pomarinus*

Almost circumpolar breeding distribution in the Arctic. Winters generally north of the equator (but also as far south as southern oceans) and usually north of the wintering ranges of Arctic and Long-tailed Skuas.

Juveniles

Pomarine is the largest *Stercorarius* skua, with size and flight approaching those of a larger gull (Ring-billed Gull *Larus delawarensis* or even Herring Gull *L. argentatus*). Steady flight sometimes remarkably similar to *Catharacta* skuas. Heavy-looking, with full body, broad arm but narrow hand, and short tail. Bill looks bicoloured even at distance, sometimes recalling first-winter Glaucous Gull *L. hyperboreus*. Head rounded, with full neck; body well rounded, as centre of gravity between breast and belly. Tail looks triangular, with barely visible projection of central pair of feathers, tip appearing broadly rounded. All but extreme dark juveniles show pale-barred uppertail-coverts, and none shows pale neck bar against darker hood as on juveniles of Arctic and Long-tailed Skuas. Below, note pale 'double patch' on hand, created by pale bases to primaries and their coverts, and typically paler underwing than body. Shows much less individual variation than juvenile Arctic and Long-tailed Skuas: 90% or more of juvenile Pomarine Skuas are covered by figures 2-4.

1　**Juvenile, dark type** Rarely, almost lacks pale underwing barring, which can be reduced to isolated inconspicuous pale spots on axillaries and median coverts, as shown here.

2　**Juvenile, dark type** Note contrasting pale barring on uppertail-coverts; combination of pale barring and dark head never shown by dark juvenile Arctic Skuas. Tail projection short and rounded, inconspicuous in the field.

3　**Juvenile, dark intermediate type** Most frequent type shows rather uniform dark greyish-brown head and body against paler underwing, and distinct pale barring on undertail-coverts.

4　**Juvenile, intermediate type** Note dark face against uniform-looking greyish-brown head, darker-streaked breast band, and conspicuous flank streaks. This individual shows reduced pale 'double patch' on underwing and slightly paler crown and hindneck (lacking cap).

5　**Juvenile, pale type** Note creamy head; if hindneck is pale, crown is also pale, but face often darker, creating angry look. Rarely, some individuals show head coloration similar to pale South Polar Skua, but always have pale-barred rump and underwing-coverts; may lack darker breast-band.

6　**Juvenile, pale type** Sometimes shows paler creamy head against barred underbody, at distance creating underpart pattern similar to pale South Polar Skua. Note pale barring on underwing and undertail-coverts typical of younger *Stercorarius* skuas, but unlike uniform blackish of South Polar Skua.

7　**Juvenile, pale type** Note pale head. Pale extremes such as this are rare.

Pomarine Skua *Stercorarius pomarinus*

Almost circumpolar breeding in the Arctic. Winters generally north of the equator.

Immatures and adults

The largest *Stercorarius* species. Appears heavy and thickset, with broad elongated central pair of tail feathers; on older immatures and adult summer birds these are twisted at tip, creating blob-ended tail. Takes at least four years to attain full adult plumage. Note, however, that individual variation and progression of plumage development make accurate ageing difficult, and often impossible. The examples shown should be regarded as, for example, 'first- or second-summer types'.

1 **Immature (2-3 years), darker type** Until second summer, underwing is barred as on juveniles, including pale 'double patch'. Note shape and width of tail projection. Unlike Arctic and Long-tailed Skuas, retains bicoloured bill for several years.

2 **Immature and adult winter** Note barred uppertail-coverts and slight pale barring on mantle. Ageing of immature and adult winter not possible on upperside alone.

3 **First-winter/first-summer, in wing moult** Juvenile-like head and body (but with paler hindneck and normally paler belly). Aged in first summer by active flight-feather moult, worn plumage lacking regular upperpart scaling of juvenile; longer tail projection than juvenile, and bill appears less bicoloured than on juvenile.

4 **Second-summer, dark type** Note combination of adult-like head and body and juvenile-type barred underwing-coverts and undertail-coverts. From second summer, tail projection develops towards that of adult, but never as much as certain adult males; may show twisted tail-tip from this age.

5 **Second-summer, pale type** Aged by combination of adult-looking (but less clean) head and body and juvenile-type barred underwing-coverts and undertail-coverts. With immature birds, specific identification is based mainly on structure. Note also uniform dark cap contrasting with bicoloured bill (Arctic Skua normally shows pale colour surrounding bill), and clear pale 'double patch' on underwing.

6 **Third-summer** Similar to adult summer, but with some barred underwing-coverts and undertail-coverts and on average shorter tail projection. On second-summer and older birds breast band is dark, appearing spotted at close range.

7 **Adult summer, dark morph** (up to 10% of population) Appears uniform blackish-brown when fresh, often with a purplish tinge to body. Head dark, sometimes with narrow golden streaks on neck sides. Note diagnostic tail shape (blob-ended) and bicoloured bill. (Darker adults often show reduced pale wing patches.)

8 **Adult summer male, pale morph** All pale morph adult summers show fuller cap and deeper yellow tinge to neck sides than Arctic Skua. Note also bicoloured bill. Some males and all females show dark breast band (normally spotted, but sometimes dark grey). Adult males often lack the breast band, and show the cleanest underparts and the longest tail projection.

9 **Adult winter** Note combination of immature-like head, body and tail projection and all-dark adult underwing-coverts and axillaries. This plumage varies greatly, ranging from close to adult summer (but with pale barring on undertail-coverts) to juvenile-like; always aged by uniform dark underwing-coverts. Tail elongation frequently lacking.

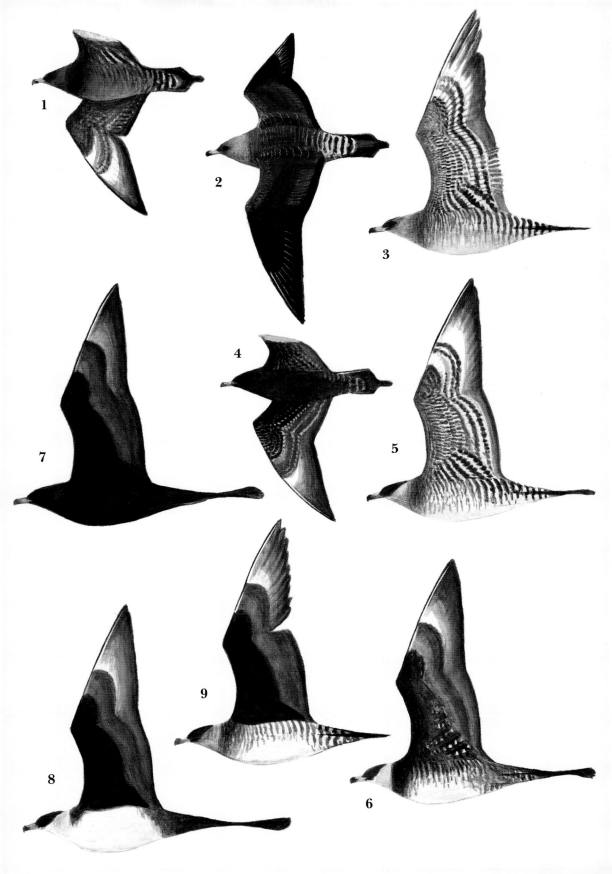

Arctic Skua *Stercorarius parasiticus*

Circumpolar breeding distribution in the Arctic. Winters chiefly in the southern oceans.

Juveniles

Arctic is a medium-sized skua, about the size of Common Gull *Larus canus*. Appears slender and long-winged, with moderately long tail; head smallish-looking, appearing triangular. Bill slender and bicoloured, this evident only at close range; at more than 200m, bill appears uniform as a result of its slenderness. Body slightly rounded, with centre of gravity around breast. Arm and hand of equal length and width. Tail elongation pointed, but less so than on older birds. Much plumage variation. Most birds have strong orange to rusty tinge to plumage with less contrast between body and underwing than on Pomarine and Long-tailed Skuas.

1 **Juvenile, pale type** This rare pale type shows almost whitish belly. Note tendency for dark bars on underwing and undertail-coverts to disappear on very pale Arctic Skuas. Traces of pale 'double patch' on underwing (see Pomarine Skua) illustrated; may appear on all types but typically much less conspicuous than on Pomarine Skua. Tail bicoloured, often distinctly so on paler types (as illustrated here).

2 **Juvenile, pale intermediate type** Common, strongly orange- to rusty-tinged type, typically appearing rather uniform on underparts owing to strong rusty tinge to underwing barring. Note dark cap contrasting with rusty neck band.

3 **Juvenile, pale type** Note orange head contrasting well with strongly rusty-tinged upperparts, vermiculated rump pattern, and rusty leading edge to inner wing. This individual shows conspicuous whitish primary patches similar to those of *Catharacta* skuas: among *Stercorarius* skuas, this is diagnostic of juvenile Arctic.

4 **Juvenile, intermediate type** Among the most easily identifiable juvenile skuas. Note pale shafts to most primaries, rusty neck band and leading edge to inner wing, and barely contrasting rump. Compare tail elongation with that of Pomarine and Long-tailed Skuas.

5 **Juvenile, intermediate type** Note strong rusty tinge to entire underparts (especially conspicuous in barring on underwing and undertail-coverts), lack of pale 'double patch' on hand shown by most Pomarine Skuas, and darker cap with contrasting rusty neck band. Hind-belly often appears paler than underwing barring (in contrast to typical juvenile Pomarine and Long-tailed Skuas).

6 **Juvenile, dark type** Typically appears uniformly dark, with slightly contrasting rusty neck band and barely visible barring on rump.

7 **Juvenile, dark type** Many dark (and a few intermediate) types appear all dark on underwing-coverts and axillaries, as on adult. Rare (but not exceptional) juveniles show almost uniform brownish-black head, body and coverts.

8 **Juvenile, pale type** Some appear creamy on head, as some Pomarine Skuas, and sometimes as coldish-tinged as Long-tailed Skuas. Note creamy tinge to underwing, head-and-bill shape, body shape and bicoloured tail.

9 **Juvenile, unusually greyish intermediate type** May approach coloration of Long-tailed Skua, but note lack of distinct pale patch on lower breast, barred breast band, triangular head, bill more pale than black, and rusty tinge to wing barring.

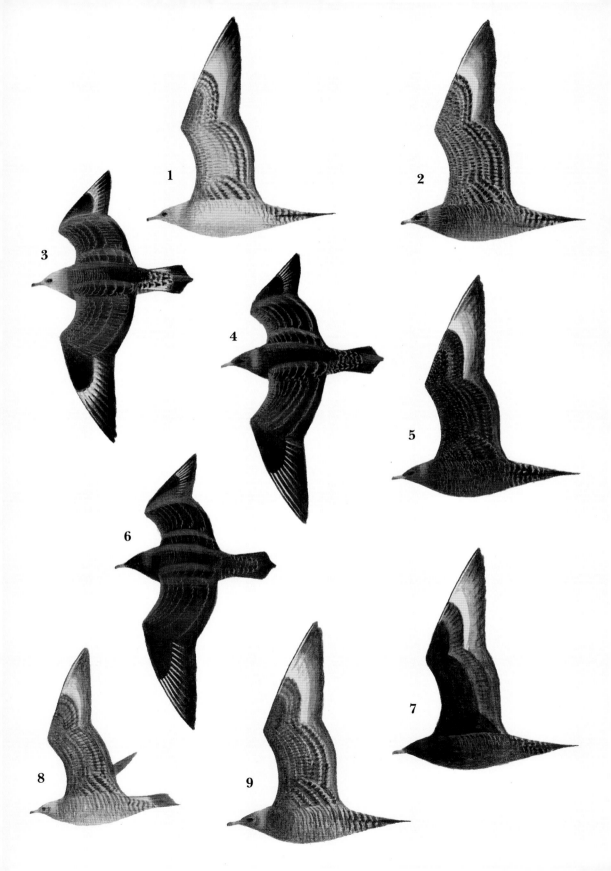

Arctic Skua *Stercorarius parasiticus*

Circumpolar breeding distribution in the Arctic. Winters chiefly in the southern oceans.

Immatures and adults

1 **First-winter/first-summer, pale type** Some become extremely worn and faded. Note active wing moult in summer, longer and more pointed tail projection than on juveniles, and strong creamy tinge to underwing. Very worn and bleached first-years may show dominant whitish plumage areas; wear more reminiscent of worn first-year gulls than that expected of a skua.

2 **First-winter/first-summer** Similar to juvenile, but note uniform mantle and (new) median coverts. Mantle feathers often show pale fringes in this and subsequent winter plumages.

3 **First-winter/first-summer, intermediate type** Superficially similar to juvenile, but typically worn and faded in summer, with a much-reduced warm tinge to plumage. Bill less bicoloured and tail projection longer than on juveniles. Pale birds show traces of dark cap and belly.

4 **Second-summer, dark morph** Similar to adult, but note juvenile-type underwing barring and shorter tail projection. Sometimes barred on undertail-coverts (distinct on paler types).

5 **Second-summer, pale morph** Head and body similar to adult summer, but with coarsely spotted breast band and barred flanks. This, together with bicoloured bill of many second-summers, creates head and body similar to Pomarine Skua, but note pale forehead blaze, shape of tail projection, and narrower head and body. Aged by combination of adult-like head and body and barred underwing.

6 **Third-summer, dark morph** As adult dark morph, but sometimes (as on this bird) with pale mottling on belly. Third-summer typically shows uniform underwing apart from barring on median or greater coverts, forming pale mid-wing panel (as illustrated).

7 **Third-summer, pale morph** Similar to adult (and advanced birds probably identical), but note pale mid-wing bar, narrow blackish scaling on lower breast, and sometimes pale barring on tail-coverts.

8 **Adult summer, dark morph** Dark greyish-brown with slightly darker cap. The darkest types show uniform blackish-brown head and body. Intermediates similar to dark morph, but typically with strong yellow tinge to neck sides, isolating dark hood. Pale primary shafts often reduced on very dark birds.

9 **Adult summer, pale morph** Note uniform grey breast band, paler than dark cap, pale forehead blaze, and lack of upperwing contrast (compare Long-tailed Skua).

10 **Adult summer, pale morph** Often lacks breast band. Note clean division between underwing and underbody, pale colour on underparts penetrating to undertail-coverts, and pointed tail projection.

11 **Adult winter, pale morph** Combines adult's dark underwing with immature-patterned head and body. On upperparts, shows pale fringes to mantle and pale bars on uppertail-coverts. Note contrast between fresh blackish-brown inner primaries and bleached, worn outer primaries.

Long-tailed Skua *Stercorarius longicaudus*

Circumpolar breeding distribution in the Arctic. Winters in the southern oceans.

Juveniles

Long-tailed is the smallest skua, the size of Black-headed Gull *Larus ridibundus*. Appears slim, with shorter, more rounded head and shorter, thicker bill than Arctic Skua but longer rear end, which looks triangular and slender. Body deepest at breast, with belly flat and gradually tapering towards tip of tail; compared with Arctic Skua, compressed at front and flattened at rear. Always lacks warm colour tones of Arctic, appearing greyish, and typically with better contrasting plumage than Arctic Skua. Other essential features to note are 2-3 (but rarely 4-5) pale primary shafts (usually 3-8 on Arctic and Pomarine Skuas), slightly rounded shape of tail projection, contrast between coverts and flight feathers on upperwing, and about half of the bill being black. White wing-flash on underwing generally narrower than on Arctic Skua. Tail projection often as long as the bill. Flight lighter, typically with shearwater-like glides even in light winds.

1 **Juvenile, pale type** The palest birds are whitish on head and body. Note distinct pale/dark underwing barring, lack of pale 'double patch' on hand, and coldish overall impression.

2 **Juvenile, pale type** Note clean-looking grey breast band separating pale head from whitish belly.

3 **Juvenile, pale type** Note conspicuous bicoloured upperparts, with pale coldish yellow head, distinct fine barring on mantle, and whitish barring on rest of upperparts; note also shape and length of tail projection. Some birds have distinct white edges to central pair of tail feathers.

4 **Juvenile, intermediate type** Note cold greyish neck band, conspicuous grey breast band, pale lower breast and central belly, barred flanks, and tail projection as long as the bill.

5 **Juvenile, dark type** Note cold dark brown head and body contrasting well with whitish barring on underwing and tail-coverts (sometimes restricted to undertail-coverts).

6 **Juvenile, dark type** Note blackish-brown overall impression, contrasting white bars on tail-coverts, and shape of tail projection. Darker birds appear blackish, but always show some white mantle barring.

7 **Juvenile, intermediate type** Note cold greyish-brown neck band, bicoloured wing pattern, and conspicuous pale barring on uppertail-coverts.

8 **Juvenile, dark type** Note conspicuous white barring on tail-coverts contrasting well with blackish overall coloration. Exceptionally, lacks barring on tail-coverts.

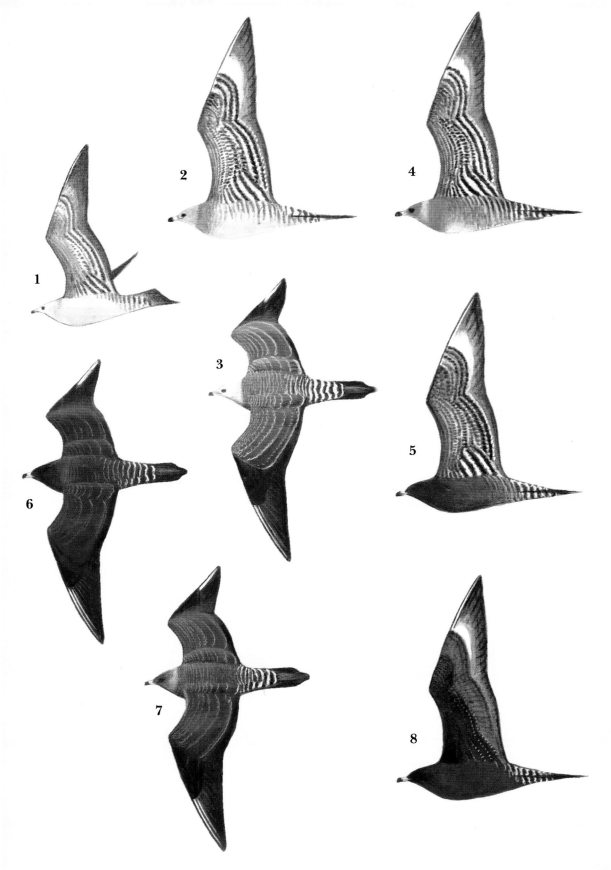

Long-tailed Skua *Stercorarius longicaudus*

Circumpolar breeding distribution in the Arctic. Winters in the southern oceans.

Immatures and adults

1   **First-winter/first-summer** New upperwing-coverts uniform greyish-brown, lacking pale scaling of juveniles. Frequently, shows pale barring on mantle (in late summer, fresh new feathers with black basal parts and whitish edges). Tail projection sharply pointed, at this age highly variable.

2   **First-winter/first-summer** Similar to juvenile, but with paler sides of head and belly. Note pale bases to retained juvenile primaries. Sometimes shows strongly developed dark cap at this age (probably unlike Arctic Skua).

3   **First-winter/first-summer** Certain birds acquire uniform greyish-yellow head and almost white underparts. New primaries dark, usually lacking juvenile's pale bases. Compare tail projection with figures 1 and 2.

4   **Second-summer** Head similar to adult, but body less clean, with mixture of pale, grey and barred areas. Underwing as on juvenile, but primaries lack latter's pale bases. Some develop adult-like body and underwing plumage at this age, and may be inseparable from adult.

5   **Second-summer** A darker type (probably having been dark in juvenile plumage) showing strong greyish barring on body and limited amount of pale barring on underwing. Upperparts of second-summer similar to adult but darker, thus less contrast between coverts and flight feathers, appearing similar to adult Arctic Skua, but with greyish tinge.

6   **Adult summer** Note bicoloured upperparts with narrow dark trailing edge to inner wing, only two white primary shafts, and black bill and cap. Tail projection typically much longer than on Arctic Skua.

7   **Adult summer, subspecies *longicaudus*** Note black bill and cap creating black 'helmet'. White of breast typically merges into dark grey of lower belly, producing predominantly dusky-looking underparts. Note uniform dark underwing of adult. In September-October, often lacks tail elongation and shows slightly darker grey sides of breast.

8   **Adult summer, subspecies *pallescens*** Note white of breast continuing to belly. See text for further details concerning geographical variation.

9   **Adult winter** Note uniform dark underwing combined with immature-like head and body. Upperparts barred on mantle and uppertail-coverts. Adult winter plumage as variable as in Pomarine and Arctic Skuas.

With perched or swimming juvenile *Stercorarius* skuas, look especially for overall coloration, head shape and streaking, bill pattern, and pattern of primary tips.

1 **Arctic Skua, juvenile intermediate type** Note strong rusty tinge to head, body and covert tips. Head shows narrow dark streaks, and rather pale feathers surrounding upper mandible (mirroring pale blaze of adult). Bill pale, with black distal 30%. Primaries show pale tips, typically as a row of arrowhead markings. Lesser and median wing-coverts with broad orange tips, creating pale leading edge to folded wings.

2 **Arctic Skua, juvenile intermediate type** Rare greyish variant, showing coldish tinge to head and body and traces of pale patch on lower breast. Note yellowish feather fringes to upperparts, and head streaks longer and more conspicuous than on Long-tailed Skua. Head pattern often better marked than on other species, with longer streaks and frequently pale 'lobster-claw' at rear of eye.

3 **Arctic Skua, juvenile intermediate type** With wear, shows stronger whitish hindneck and sometimes other parts of body. Compare bill coloration of figures 1-3, showing range of variation.

4 **Long-tailed Skua, juvenile intermediate type** Note rounded head, black covering distal 45-50% of bill, flat, long gonydeal angle, greyish overall tinge, and broad whitish edges to mantle and scapulars (creating distinct white mantle barring). Also clean greyish breast against pale spot on lower breast, distinct pale barring on undertail-coverts, and uniform primaries (at most with narrow whitish-grey feather fringes). Often appears dark-capped.

5 **Long-tailed Skua, juvenile pale type** Note white-headed appearance, distinct white upperpart barring, greyish breast band (with only very narrow pale edges), and pale patch on lower breast. Flank barring typically more distinct than on Arctic and Pomarine Skuas.

6 **Pomarine Skua, juvenile pale type** Similar to Arctic Skua, but head larger and more rounded, with fuller neck, stronger bill and body more thickset. Note bicoloured bill as on Arctic Skua (but contrast visible even at range of up to 200m), uniform head with darker shading in front of eye (creating angry look) and indistinct dark spots or scales (never strong streaking). Rear parts darker, as greater coverts normally lack pale streaks on webs and primaries dark, latter at most showing faint pale edges. Note dark bend of wing compared to Arctic Skua.

7 **Pomarine Skua, juvenile of commonest type** Note rather uniform greyish-brown head showing faint scaling and darker lores. Barring on breast similar to Arctic Skua. Bill pattern similar to Arctic Skua, but more striking bicoloured appearance due to broader bill; sometimes base of bill is broader than tip.

PLATE 12: JUVENILE NORTHERN SKUAS IN FLIGHT

Identifying flying skuas relies much on size, overall impression and manner of flight.

1 Arctic Skua Flight variable, with glides on angled wings alternating with quick, falcon-like flaps; frequent shearwater-like flight in strong winds. Note small, triangular head with narrow bill, poorly marked barring on rump, and rather uniform underparts, typically with belly the palest part. Tail projection short and pointed; normally visible at some distance. Most show diagnostic rusty to orange hindneck band and leading edge to inner wing.

2 Long-tailed Skua Flight similar to that of Arctic Skua, but with longer sequences of 'shearwatering' even in light winds. Note short, rounded head and bill but slenderer and longer tail compared with Arctic Skua. Typically more contrasting than Arctic Skua, with well-defined dark cap and breast band against paler throat and lower-breast patch, more distinct barring on underwing and rump, and more restricted pale primary-flashes below than on other skuas – typically showing as a white leading edge on the outer wing; pale rump barring may accentuate narrow tail-base. Tail projection longer and somewhat fuller than on Arctic Skua, typically as long as the bill and clearly visible even at distance (reinforced by its slightly rounded shape). Darkest birds have reduced rump barring and may appear sooty.

3 Pomarine Skua Largest and heaviest *Stercorarius* species. Flight lazy-looking, with steady direction, very similar to flight of larger gulls, and sometimes hard to tell from, especially, younger Lesser Black-backed Gull *Larus fuscus*. This is the only skua which could be overlooked as a medium to large young gull. Note full head and heavy bill, with colour contrasts of bill visible at range of several hundred metres and accentuated by dark face (Arctic Skua shows similar bill contrast, but visible only at closer range owing to slenderness of the bill). Also note lack of contrasting neck band, as well as conspicuous pale bars on uppertail-coverts and, below, good contrast between dark body and pale underwing barring. Pale 'double patch' on underwing well developed, and conspicuous at range when other characters are invisible (up to 2km). Tail projection short and broad, typically not visible even at close range.

4 Great Skua Even larger than Pomarine Skua, with bigger, more protruding head, much shorter tail, barrel-shaped body, and fuller hand. Heavier and darker than other skuas, appearing wholly dark apart from highly conspicuous white flashes on both wing surfaces. Flight active and low, similar to that of Pomarine Skua; rarely glides, regularly only in strong tail-winds, gliding with less W-shaped wings than *Stercorarius* skuas (hand angled only slightly backwards).

PLATE 13: ADULT *CATHARACTA* SKUAS

1 **South Polar Skua, intermediate adult** Individual with darker-than-average under parts. Note fuller pale blaze on forehead than congeners, hooded appearance, contrasting pale hindneck, and cleaner underparts than on Great Skua. Underwing-coverts generally more uniform than on Great Skua, typically appearing blackish and contrasting with pale belly. Worn birds may show pale-barred flashes.

2 **Chilean Skua, adult** Unlike congeners, shows broad rusty to dark orange fringes to underwing apart from greater coverts. Note dark cap and breast band (the latter often pale-spotted), warm tinge to entire underbody and bicoloured bill.

3 **Great Skua, adult** Note dark cap, heavily pale-streaked or blotched underparts, and narrow pale fringes or streaks to underwing-coverts, present on some individuals. Often shows irregular pale spots on head (especially crown) and, with wear, traces of pale feathers surrounding bill (but rarely creating strong pale blaze as on many South Polar Skuas). Worn birds may show pale-spotted flanks.

4 **Brown Skua, worn adult** Largest and darkest skua. Note dark hood, only poorly defined blaze on forehead, and irregular pale patches on underbody, most conspicuous on flanks. Bill of ssp. Subantarctic Skua *lonnbergi* larger and heavier than on congeners.

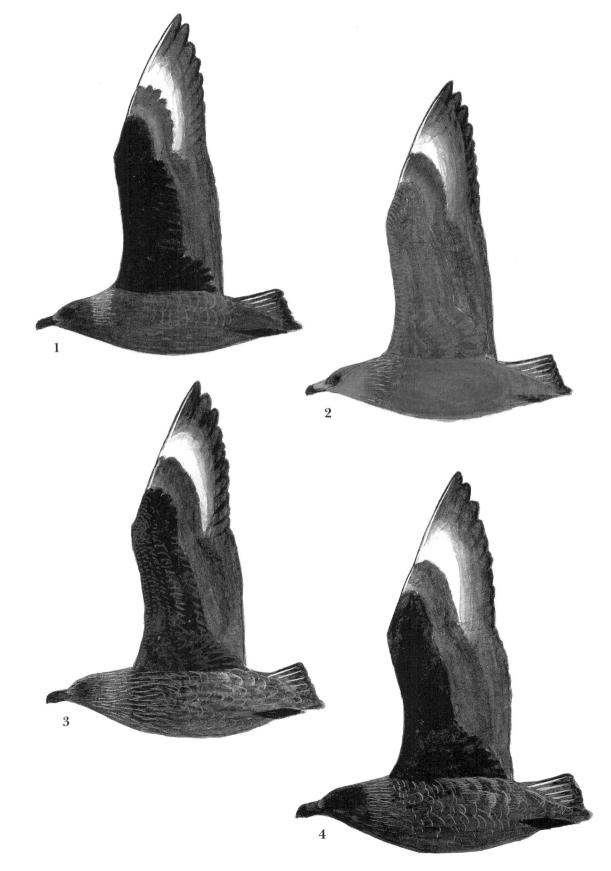

SYSTEMATIC
SECTION

1   GREAT SKUA
Catharacta skua

FIELD IDENTIFICATION Great Skua is the *Catharacta* of the northern hemisphere, being the largest and heaviest of the northern skuas. In flight it is barrel-shaped, with a large, protruding head and with a very short tail barely the length of the head; the tail appears triangular, as the central pair of feathers projects only slightly. The large, full head is frequently raised, when it is especially striking; at other times the species appears bull-necked.

The active flight is steady, with slow wingbeats (as in large gulls), and with only occasional very brief glides. Only in very strong tailwinds of more than 15m/sec is shearwater-like flight performed, but with less angled wings than in

Figure 1. Great Skua, adult. Note pale leading edge to wing and coarse blotching on head and forebody. Iceland, July 1994. *Markus Varesvuo.*

Stercorarius skuas, the hand slightly tapering backwards; even when passing waves the flight is normally active, recalling wave-passing by Northern Fulmars *Fulmarus glacialis* in moderate winds. Even soaring birds frequently flap their wings for long periods.

Perched or swimming birds are clumsy-looking, with a large rounded head, a heavy, strongly hooked black bill and thick, dark legs. On the wing, however, this impression disappears: in piratical flight, Great Skua chases large gulls and gannets with an agility comparable to that of Arctic Skua, forcing its victims down to the surface, and frequently killing seabirds. When penetrating seabird gatherings, all the birds are wary and immediately forced to take flight in panic.

The plumage is brown, with prominent white primary-flashes on both upperwing and underwing which are conspicuous even at ranges of several kilometres (as on other *Catharacta* skuas). The only *Stercorarius* with pure white flashes at the base of primaries on both wing surfaces is the much smaller juvenile Arctic Skua, which shows much narrower white patches on the upperwing. A few juveniles of all *Catharacta* skuas lack white flashes on the upperwing.

An identification pitfall is provided by large juvenile Pomarine Skuas, which have a smaller head and are better proportioned, with slimmer belly and longer tail (always longer than head). Even at some distance, pale barring on both underwing and rump is visible on all but very dark Pomarines. Only a few Great Skuas show so little white at the base of the upper primaries as to invite confusion with Pomarine Skua.

Adult Brown, with variable dark cap and paler streaks on hindneck and the sides of the head. Mantle and to a lesser degree upperwing-coverts have pale patterning, creating a coarsely grained or patchy appearance, contrasting with dark flight feathers; the upperparts thus appear bicoloured. Some show slightly paler lower back and rump, but not in clear contrast to the rest of the upperparts. A few are paler and colder brown with dark blotches.

Pale adults have a dark mask, with rest of head greyish-brown and concolorous with the body. They may easily be misidentified as South Polar Skua, but latter is greyer (never showing warm brown tinge in northern hemisphere), with more conspicuous pale hindneck, finer and more regular patterning on mantle and scapulars (sometimes creating pale mantle as extension of the pale hindneck) and uniform dark upperwing (apart from white wing-flashes and, on some pale birds, paler leading edge to inner wing).

Figure 2. Great Skua, adult. A colder-tinged individual. Note irregular pattern of entire upperparts, and white-peppered crown reducing dark cap to dark mask. Worn birds often show traces of paler forehead and pale spotting on flanks. Orkney, August 1991. *Rolland Kern.*

Worn Great Skuas normally show paler facial blaze and lores, but never such a conspicuous pale blaze as on some South Polar Skuas. When very worn (late spring/early summer) they may approach South Polar Skua in the pale coloration of head and underbody, but both underbody and upperparts have distinct, blotchy pale patterning and streaking, the coverts contrasting well with the dark flight feathers.

Adult winter is similar to summer, but has darker and more uniform head, at most with very slight contrast between dark cap and paler hindneck. The yellow streaks on the neck sides are less conspicuous than in summer plumage, and frequently absent. During body moult, there is a slight contrast between new and old feathers, making plumage even more patchy than in summer.

Juvenile Darker and more uniform than adult. Has a dark head, at distance creating impression of a dark hood against warm brown to reddish-brown underbody, which is slightly paler than the underwing. The upperparts are darker and more uniform than on adult, at most with short buffish subterminal spots on mantle, scapulars and some inner wing-coverts, but often shows pale leading edge to inner wing on both surfaces. The palest birds, moreover, show a rusty nape. The white primary-flashes are on average narrower than on adult, but normally still prominent, though they may be only half as big as on adults, and in rare cases reduced to broad white crescents or just pale shaft-streaks on the upperwing, similar to the pattern of Pomarine Skua. Almost blackish juveniles are known, but they are very rare: they are separated from similar dark South Polar Skuas by the slight rusty (not cold brown) tinge to underbody, and they always lack the pale frontal blaze of many South Polar Skuas; such individuals should, however, be observed at very close range for safe identification to be made. Conversely, very worn and bleached individuals in late spring have creamy head and underbody in good contrast to dark underwing-coverts; again, they lack the cold grey tinge of South Polar Skua.

First-winter Similar to adult winter, but has a different moult cycle (see Moult). Ageing is difficult because of similarity between adult and juvenile plumages (see Detailed Description).

Figure 3. Great Skua, adults. Pale-headed bird superficially similar to South Polar Skua, but shows strong rufous wash to head and body, irregular spotting on entire head and underparts, and pale pattern on upperparts penetrating onto upperwing-coverts. Iceland, July 1994. *Markus Varesvuo.*

VOICE Noisy at breeding sites, uttering several mewing or raucous screams when attacking intruders. Normally silent outside breeding season.

MOULT

Adult Moult from summer to winter plumage is complete, following breeding season. Primary moult starts with inner primary in August-early October, with inner 5-7 primaries renewed by November, and primary moult is completed between January and mid March/April; the moult is slow, with only 1-2 primaries growing at any one time (see South Polar Skua). Moult of head and body starts in June/July, generally before moult of flight feathers, but body moult is slow, continuing well into winter, with coverts being renewed October/November; head is moulted between June and October/November. Sequence of tail moult approximately t1-t2-t6-t3-t4-t5 (Cramp & Simmons 1983).

Failed breeders and non-breeders may start primary moult as early as July and finish in December/January.

Moult to summer plumage is partial, starting immediately after end of post-breeding primary moult, between January and March. The moult involves head, neck and sometimes parts of coverts and body, but not mantle and rump (Glutz von Blotzheim & Bauer 1982).

Juvenile Moult to first-winter plumage is complete. Primary moult starts with innermost primary in March-early April and is completed early June-late August, at the time of the start of the adult primary moult; whole primary moult takes 150-180 days, thus quicker than in adults (Ginn & Melville 1983). Tail is moulted in March-April. Head and body moult starts in December/January and is completed about March (when moult of flight feathers starts).

Moult to first-summer (summer of second calendar-year) is restricted to small amount of head and body feathers.

Moult to second-winter earlier than adult moult, starting with head, body and inner primary in May/June (Baker 1983). Moult of head and body is completed in August. Moult of flight feathers is slower

Figure 4. Great Skua, juvenile. Note traces of bicoloured bill and dark grey (not black) tarsus compared with adult. Skaffafjell, Iceland, August 1988. *Othmar Endelweber.*

than in adults, starting May/June, and is normally not completed before February/March. Baker (1983) notes that primary moult is probably completed by August/October (November).

Subsequent immature moults Similar to adult, but may be restricted to smaller areas of the plumage. Primary moult approximately one month earlier in third-year birds than in adults.

DETAILED DESCRIPTION

Adult summer (adult alternate) (March-September/October) Head variable: some have dark brown cap from base of upper mandible towards eye to crown and nape, contrasting with paler, yellow-streaked sides of head; others have paler greyish-brown head with dark restricted to mask around eye and ear-coverts, the rear ear-coverts being uniform pale. Normally shows irregular white, yellow or buff spots on head, especially on crown and lores, most striking with wear in late summer to early autumn. Lores, forehead and chin often slightly paler greyish-brown than rest of head, with wear (late spring and summer) creating slight pale blaze (but rarely conspicuous as on South Polar Skua). Nape, sides of neck, chin, throat and sometimes breast have narrow pale grey, pale yellow or golden shaft-streaks, creating 'hackled mane'. Head streaks normally narrower than streaking of upperparts. Mantle, scapulars and upperwing-coverts brown to dark brown with yellowish, buff or (rarer) whitish spots or short streaks, the palest-patterned individuals having whole central part of each feather pale, creating strong but often irregular pale streaking or spotting: most commonly, mantle and coverts are evenly marked, but on some the mantle is more strongly whitish-spotted/streaked than coverts (pattern thus closer to southern-hemisphere *Catharacta* skuas); some show contrasting darker inner coverts. On the darkest birds, pale markings are reduced to pale buff spots, broadening towards tip. Tertials, rump and greater coverts dark brown with variable, irregular pale edges, narrower than on lesser and median coverts; sometimes all dark. (Birds with the largest amount of pale patterning on upperparts also have the palest head and underparts, and dark-headed birds also have darker-than-average upperparts.) Flight feathers blackish: bases of primaries white, creating striking large white flashes, on upperwing covering 25-60mm of base on outer web of outer 2-4/5 primaries (30-40% of whole

Figure 5. Great Skua, adult. Note large protruding head, barrel-shaped body, very short tail and distinct pale wing-flashes, all typical of *Catharacta* skuas. Characteristic of adult Great Skuas are bicoloured upperparts showing contrast between paler coverts and darker flight feathers, dark cap and paler nape. Southeast Iceland, July 1973. *R.F. Dickens.*

feather) and 35-80mm on inner web of outer 2-5 primaries (usually more than 55%); division between white bases and dark outer part variable, but sometimes with some dark spots, rarely sharp (see Brown Skua). White extension on underwing similar, but slightly more diffuse, covering up to 80mm on primaries 3-5. Outer primary 6-13mm longer than second outermost. Tail blackish, with slightly elongated t1; fresh rectrices show narrow pale fringes. Underbody (chin to undertail-coverts) buff, pale brown, grey-brown or dark brown, sometimes even rufous (though rarely so on older adults); sometimes shows faint darker or paler spots or streaks, exceptionally as yellow shaft-streaks across breast and pale spots on flanks, rarely as broad but diffuse dark breast band; belly and undertail-coverts average darker than fore underparts, and may show slightly darker streaking, but less than on breast and flanks. Underwing-coverts dark brown, sometimes with cinnamon streaks on axillaries, lesser coverts and inner median coverts; primary coverts and greater coverts dark greyish with faint darker tips; marginal coverts sometimes pale-spotted, creating pale leading edge to

Figure 6. Great Skua, adult in aggressive display. Compare upperwing pattern with that of other *Catharacta* skuas. Shetland, June 1993. *Gordon Langsbury.*

inner wing. Bill blackish, with pronounced gonydeal angle (35-45% of whole length of lower mandible); nail sometimes slightly paler grey. Iris dark brown. Legs and feet black.

Sexes similar, but males average darker than females, with less distinct, more golden-brown hackles at neck sides and stronger cinnamon wash to pale spotting on body (Perry 1948; Furness 1987; own skin studies). Females generally show broader yellow hackles at neck sides, standing out more sharply against dark cap, and stronger pale flecking on body. Some females show all-dark outer web to outer primary (Cramp & Simmons 1983).

In autumn, adults may exhibit larger white wing-flashes (continuing towards bases of secondaries) when greater coverts are moulted, as pale bases of all flight feathers then become visible. A similar effect is seen on moulting dark-winged gulls.

Adult winter (adult basic) (September-March) Similar to adult summer, but head darker brown, with concolorous forehead, crown and nape, and much weaker pale streaking at sides of neck (frequently lacking); mask around eye sometimes darker. Feathers on head may show narrow pale fringes. Shaft-streaks of new upperpart feathers shorter and narrower, contrasting with paler retained feathers from summer plumage.

Juvenile Similar to adult, but cleaner, with more uniform and more strongly rusty-tinged plumage. Head dark brown, creating dark hood, but sometimes fading to greyish-brown on chin and throat; nape frequently grey-brown, ochre-brown or buff, but rarely in strong contrast to head; sides of neck may show short whitish shaft-streaks. Dark head typically contrasts with paler, warm brown and generally unpatterned underbody, but on darker-bodied birds head and underbody are concolorous. Upperparts darker and more evenly patterned than on adult: mantle and scapulars show some buffish terminal bars or U-shaped spots (shorter but more distinct than on adults), strongest on tips of mantle feathers, and sometimes broken by small black spots or complete dark shaft-streaks, the darkest individuals showing just rufous subterminal spot near feather tip; rump dark brown, often with narrow sandy to buffish spots (as on scapulars) or feather fringes. Upperwing-coverts dark brown with narrow pale feather edges; may show narrow, pale tips to greater coverts (creating wingbar). Tertials dark brown with irregular wavy marks and subterminal spots. Some individuals have almost unmarked dark brown upperparts, including back, scapulars and rump. Flight feathers similar to adult, but primaries generally with restricted white flashes: outer web of outermost primary usually black, with up to 25mm of visible white on outer web of outer 2-5 primaries (rarely, white lacking on upper surface) and 20-40mm on inner webs, and area of white can be as little as 50% that of adults; division between white primary bases and dark outer part more frequently shows dark spotting than on adult. Primaries pointed (not rounded as on adults). Tail as adult. Breast to undertail-coverts reddish-brown, rufous-cinnamon or medium brown, rarely paler brown, greyish-brown or blackish-brown; sometimes shows slight cinnamon or greyish mottling on breast, rear flanks and undertail-coverts, most striking with wear. Underwing as adult, but sometimes with more clear-cut rufous fringes to lesser coverts and axillaries; often shows rusty leading edge to wing and tips to lesser coverts. Bill dark grey to lilac-grey with blackish tip. Iris dark brown. Legs and feet black, usually with grey to yellow spots on tarsus; on some, legs and feet black.

Dark juveniles rare (2% of scrutinised skins). Show dark brown head and upperparts, with pale feather fringes restricted to upper body and lesser coverts; rest of upperwing uniform dark brown; underparts very slightly paler greyish-brown. The darkest extremes show restricted white on primary bases: just 1-1.5cm of white visible on outer 5 primaries (skin ZMO).

With wear, body and sometimes head become paler; in spring, many show worn pale greyish-brown areas on underbody, especially breast. With extreme wear (May-June), head and underbody may appear almost creamy, thus similar to pale-morph South Polar Skua, but never pure grey as on typical South Polar Skuas.

Sexes similar, but female has on average broader cinnamon marks on upperparts and shorter, darker upperwing-coverts than male.

Figure 7. Great Skua, juvenile. Dark hood, cleaner underparts and different mantle, scapular and covert spots important when ageing this species. Iceland, July 1994. *Markus Varesvuo.*

First-winter/first-summer (first basic/alternate) Similar to adult winter, but with juvenile feathers and normally some warm brown feathers admixed in body. Before moult, distinguishable by worn and pointed outer primaries and generally less white on the bases of juvenile primaries. Head more uniformly dark than on adult, lacking strong yellow hackles on neck and breast sides. Upperpart markings similar to juvenile; generally less heavily pale-marked, but from spring sometimes shows strong contrast between old and new feathers, the former bleaching to whitish, yellowish or golden-buff. Underparts retain clean, rather unpatterned look of juvenile, but in spring often

Figure 8. Great Skua, first-winter. Note dark hood and juvenile pattern to upperparts. With wear, underparts become blotchy. De Maasvlakte, Netherlands, February 1981. *René Pop.*

bleached to creamy on underbody and sometimes head. Tarsus may show traces of pale spots.

Second-summer (second alternate) Similar to adult summer, but with traces of winter plumage. Full adult moult cycle not yet fully adopted. Ageing in the field almost impossible, but second-years (third calendar-year) generally show less developed yellow neck hackles compared with adults (sometimes intermixed with whitish streaks) and on average less white at base of primaries, which generally do not follow adult moult cycle. This is sometimes combined with much worn winter plumage on head and fresh summer plumage in upperparts; upperparts (especially mantle and scapulars) show a mixture of rusty, yellow and whitish-patterned feathers. Tarsus normally has yellowish or blue-grey spots, which may still be present at an even later age.

With wear, head, breast and upperparts may become distinctly whitish-spotted.

Subsequent plumages Much as adult, but pale spots on tarsus probably a sign of immaturity.

Figure 9. Great Skua, probably immature. Unusually pale (leucistic) individual, showing creamy head, underparts and tail and unusual pale pattern on coverts on both surfaces of wing. Head and body similar to pale South Polar Skua, which shows uniform dark wings (apart from white wing-flashes) and tail. Underwing pattern approaches that of Chilean Skua, which is, however, strongly reddish-tinged with even clearer dark cap than Great Skua. Unst, Shetland, July 1975. *R.F. Dickens.*

Note A method for ageing of adults, using number of endorsal layers in the tibia, was described by Klomp & Furness (1992): the endorsal layers are absent in juveniles, but in adults (of known age) are found to accord with the number of years of age of the particular individual.

VARIANTS Partially albinistic birds are known to occur. These have white feathers on the upperparts.

An extremely worn juvenile (end of May) had creamy forehead, throat and entire lower underbody, contrasting well with dark cap and dark-spotted creamy breast; the feather edges on the upperparts were very heavily worn (skin ZMA). The individual showed no moult. Another very pale bird (probably immature) had pale creamy head, underbody and tips to all underwing- and upperwing-coverts, and also showed broad pale edges to all upperwing-coverts and rectrices (see figure 9).

Two cases of melanism have been described (Glutz von Blotzheim & Bauer 1982): each individual involved showed uniform blackish-brown plumage apart from white wing-flashes. In our view, these could well be representatives of the rare dark type mentioned above.

GEOGRAPHICAL VARIATION Scottish and Icelandic populations show slight differences in wing size: Iceland male 388-417mm (mean 401.2, n=12), female 404-423mm (mean 414.0, n=6); Foula male 393-433mm (mean 414.5, n=62), female 412-440mm (mean 423.5, n=62). Length of bill and tarsus, as well as weight, show no significant differences (Furness 1987).

MEASUREMENTS in mm. Own measurements; skins UZM, BMNH, ZMA, NNH, ZMO. North Atlantic and Western Europe.

Wing length

Adult male	376-425	(399.3)	92
Adult female	383-439	(408.8)	75
Juvenile male	367-406	(388.5)	24
Juvenile female	377-423	(397.5)	22
Second-winter	381-403	(393.1)	10
Immature (3-7 years)	395-428	(409.7)	11

Note: Furness (1987) gives adult male 382-433 (mean 407, n=198) and adult female 398-440 (mean 418.2, n=96), the larger measurements probably a result of measuring live birds.

Projection of t1 (tail-tip projection)

Adult	5-26	(13.7)	169
Juvenile	5-16	(10.0)	31
Second-winter	8-22	(12.6)	12

Note: Average for adult male and female identical.

Bill length

Adult male	45.5-53.1	(49.2)	93
Adult female	46.8-55.0	(49.8)	75
Juvenile male	43.8-50.6	(47.0)	14
Juvenile female	42.4-50.1	(46.9)	14
Second-winter	46.8-52.7	(49.2)	12
Immature (3-7 years)	46.4-52.3	(49.6)	10

Note: Furness (1987) gives adult male 45.4-53.0 (mean 50.0, n=105) and adult female 44.0-56.0 (mean 52.0, n=86).

Bill depth at gonys

Adult male	15.3-18.9	(17.3)	93
Adult female	15.3-19.0	(17.5)	75
Juvenile	14.0-17.5	(15.6)	30
Second-winter	15.6-18.0	(16.6)	12

Bill depth at base

Adult male	18.5-21.6	(20.0)	93
Adult female	18.0-23.3	(20.5)	75
Juvenile	16.0-20.2	(18.3)	30
Second-winter	18.6-20.6	(19.4)	13

Gonys length

Adult male	10.0-14.5	(12.2)	93
Adult female	10.8-14.0	(12.1)	75
Juvenile	9.5-13.3	(11.5)	30
Second-winter	10.7-13.7	(11.9)	13

Tarsus length

Adult male	59.0-71.2	(65.0)	93
Adult female	57.7-72.2	(65.9)	76
Juvenile male	57.9-67.2	(63.1)	14
Juvenile female	57.8-67.6	(61.7)	13
Second-winter	59.5-65.1	(63.1)	11
Immature (3-7 years)	59.8-74.0	(69.2)	11

Note: Furness (1987) gives adult male 63-73 (mean 68, n=77) and adult female 63-73 (mean 69, n=67), probably a result of measuring live birds.

WEIGHT in grams.
Shetland: adult male breeding 1180-1500, adult female breeding 1300-1650. Iceland: adult male breeding 1210-1410, adult female breeding 1360-1630 (Furness 1987).

Immature (3-7 years of age) 1140-1480 (Furness 1987). Weakened autumn/winter birds (all ages, Netherlands and Faeroe Islands) 770-1640 (skins ZMA, UZM). One weakened male weighed as little as 600 (Glutz von Blotzheim & Bauer 1982).

FOOD Opportunistic. During the breeding season, Northern Gannets *Morus bassanus* in particular are attacked and robbed of food, but Atlantic Puffins *Fratercula arctica* and Black-legged Kittiwakes *Rissa tridactyla* are also heavily persecuted, and the former often killed; also shows a preference for stealing eggs and young of Black-legged Kittiwakes, but all available seabird eggs are taken. In certain areas, most of the Great Skua population catch their own fish (especially sand-eels *Ammodytes*) or prey on small mammals. Outside the breeding season, when Great Skuas stay mostly offshore, they feed mainly by pirating food from birds up to the size of Northern Gannet (which is probably favoured when present); but, being an opportunistic feeder, this skua also kills weakened birds up to the size of large gulls or Brent Geese *Branta bernicla*, feeds on carcases, parasitises moulting flocks of Common Eiders *Somateria mollissima*, fishes for itself, and also gathers around fishing fleets, especially in winter.

Figure 10. Great Skua, adult. Note broad white spotting on mantle and unusually dark upperwing-coverts of this rather coldish-tinged individual. Dark cap, enhanced by pale, uniform patch behind eye, and lack of distinct pale frontal blaze are main distinctions from South Polar Skua. Southeast Iceland, July 1973. *R.F. Dickens.*

BREEDING About 14,000 pairs of Great Skuas bred in the North Atlantic around 1990, of which 5,400 pairs were in Iceland and 7,900 in Britain, mainly in Shetland and Orkney Islands (Tucker & Heath 1994). The British population has increased during the 20th century, probably linked to increasing population of sand-eels followed by heavy commercial fishing (for Herring and Mackerel, which prey on sand-eels), but development is less clear since decline in commercial fishing for sand-eels from the middle of the 1980s. Furthermore, increase in minimum mesh size of nets in commercial whitefish fishing could result in fewer small fish available, making competition with Great Black-backed Gull *Larus marinus* and Northern Gannet more serious, as these two species are better able to handle larger prey (Gibbons *et al.* 1993). The Icelandic population is stable, but showed range increase during 1970-90. The Faeroe population was estimated at 250 pairs around 1980 (Bloch & Sørensen 1984), following an increase from 4 pairs in 1897 to 550 pairs in 1961 (Bayes *et al.* 1964). From 1969, there has been a northward spread along the Norwegian coast to Svalbard, Bear Island, Jan Mayen and into Kola Peninsula, north Russia: the Norwegian population was 4 pairs in 1984, rising to 30-40 pairs in the first part of the 1990s, and the Svalbard population was 60-65 pairs in the early 1990s (Munkebye 1973; Furness 1987; Krasnov 1993; Gjershaug *et al.* 1994).

Figure 11. Great Skua, adult in agressive display. Rather dark individual, typically showing dense pale spotting on underparts and paler lesser upperwing-coverts. Note narrow pale spots on underwing-coverts. Southeast Iceland, July 1973. *R.F. Dickens.*

Great Skuas were not recorded by British naturalists in the 17th century and most of the 18th century, at a time when the species was common in the Faeroe Islands and in Iceland. The first known British breeding record dates from 1774, when a few pairs were noted from Shetland, on Unst.

Breeding takes place between May and August, the breeding grounds being occupied from middle to end of March. The Great Skua breeds in loose colonies on open ground in broken terrain, usually with short or taller grass and wet moorland with raised areas for lookouts. Colonies consist of up to several hundreds of pairs. Populations are densest in the vicinity of large seabird colonies, which are heavily preyed on. In many areas it coexists in a dominant role with Arctic Skuas, and has caused the latter to abandon its breeding grounds.

MIGRATION AND WINTERING Adults are short-distance migrants, leaving breeding sites in July-August. British adult population winters between the breeding area and south to the Atlantic off France and the Iberian Peninsula, which forms its main wintering area. Icelandic adults migrate east to winter in the Atlantic between Britain and Biscay, but also west to Newfoundland, with an equal number of recoveries from both coasts of the Atlantic (Furness 1987).

Juveniles and immatures up to 3 years of age perform a longer migration. Juveniles leave natal sites from August/September, migrating slowly southwards. The majority are present in the North Sea into September-November (with a general drift towards the east Atlantic as the autumn progresses). Some undertake a long migration in August, such as a Shetland-ringed juvenile recovered from Fuerteventura, Canary Islands (3,650km to the SSW) on 30th August. In December-January, the majority have reached Biscay and northwest African waters, where they remain during their first year unless continuing further south to reach the central and western Atlantic and northern shores of South America. The most southerly concentrations are found at upwellings off Senegal and Gambia (Urban *et al.* 1986). Icelandic juveniles winter mostly between Britain and Biscay, but with scattered recoveries from Newfoundland, North Carolina and the northern coast of Brazil (R. Dickens *in litt.*). Great Skuas spend their first summer in the wintering range, only a minority returning to their natal areas. Icelandic birds also move to the North Sea and eventually to Greenland and Newfoundland, with a number of recoveries in late August-September (R. Dickens *in litt.*).

In their second winter, Great Skuas perform their longest migration. The majority of the population winters in the eastern Atlantic, mostly between Portugal and northwest Africa, where the species is common in the zone of upwelling water between Cape Verde Islands and Senegal (Brown 1979). At this age, there is also a spread into the Mediterranean eastwards to Malta (Glutz von Blotzheim & Bauer 1982). Some Icelandic immatures also winter off the North American east coast northwards to Newfoundland and Greenland; a few Icelandic immatures have been recovered from Britain in April-May (R. Dickens *in litt.*).

In the second summer, British birds, too, spread across the Atlantic to summering grounds between Greenland and Labrador (June-September). Furthermore, small numbers disperse north to northern Norway and Svalbard. From their third winter, Great Skuas gradually move closer to their breeding range, although the main wintering area at this age is the seas around Iberia and North Africa, in the southern limits of the adults' main wintering area. In addition, a few Icelandic third-summer birds have been recovered from northern Norway and Greenland (R. Dickens *in litt.*).

Figure 12. Great Skua, adult. Pale-headed individual showing paler blaze and restricted dark head pattern. Note coarse spotting on head and underbody. Iceland, July 1994. *Markus Varesvuo.*

Of 582 recoveries of Scottish Great Skuas (all ages), the majority are from the eastern North Atlantic, but with others from Greenland (26), Canada and USA (4), Norway and Svalbard (23), Baltic Sea (5), inland Europe (26), Mediterranean (22), Guyana and Brazil (7) (Furness 1978). There are also scattered records from Belize and Nigeria (Urban *et al.* 1986; Tostain & Dujardin 1988; Bourne & Curtis 1994; Howell & Webb 1995). In the Mediterranean, this is a scarce passage and winter visitor east to the coast of Israel (Shirihai 1996). Furthermore, it straggles regularly to the Baltic, Central Europe, Kola Peninsula and Novaya Zemlya, mostly immatures in September-October (Il'icev & Zubakin 1990). Vagrants have occurred eastwards to Turkey and the west coast of the Black Sea (Dittberner & Fiebig 1986).

After the breeding season, concentrations of up to 11,000-13,000 gather in Skagerrak and the North Sea, accompanying passage of Northern Gannets (Malling Olsen 1992). In south Norway this skua is scarce, with most recorded in August, with day-counts of up to 49 at Utsira (Folkedal & Ness 1994). Along the southwest Scandinavian coastline, most Great Skuas are observed in strong westerly winds. Up to 642 have been noted along the Danish west coast in one autumn, with daily maxima of 143 on 17 August 1988 at Skagen and 118 on 28 September 1995 at Hanstholm (Malling Olsen 1992; Sørensen 1996). Totals of 50-200 are recorded annually along the Swedish west coast, daily maximum being 27 on 20 October 1983 (Hake 1984; Risberg 1988; Tyrberg 1994). Timing is similar along the British east coast, where up to 300 have been observed in one day in Norfolk and Kent. The species is scarce in Germany, with 119 records up to 1993, mainly from the west coast (Deutsche Seltenheitenkommission 1994), whereas the largest Dutch count was of 57 at Terschelling on 5 September 1992 (Dongen *et al.* 1995). Most North Sea birds probably head directly to the west to pass the western coasts of Britain: in Wales the largest numbers in one day were 198 on 3 September 1983 at Strumble Head; autumn migration at Cape Clear, southwest Ireland, peaks in August-September, the best autumn totalling 1,220 (Hutchinson 1992). At Gibraltar, up to 50 in one hour have been noted in strong westerlies (Finlayson 1992).

The largest known wintering numbers are 5,000 in the eastern part of the Bay of Biscay in January/February 1981 (Glutz von Blotzheim & Bauer 1982).

From 1990, an increase has been noted in winter numbers in southern Scandinavia, with 5-10 now annually on the Danish and western Swedish coastline (Risberg 1988; Malling Olsen 1992; Ekberg & Nilsson 1994; Christensen *et al.* 1996); this is, however, overshadowed by 56 passing Oostende, Belgium, on 2 January 1995 (Driessens 1995). In southern Scandinavia, there has also been an increase in numbers of migrants recorded since 1970, but whether this is a genuine increase or a result of more regular seawatching is not known (Durinck & Lausten 1990).

The Great Skua is only rarely noted in winter along the North American east coast, with most records from North Carolina (7 up to 1989). Seemingly, most birds stay well offshore.

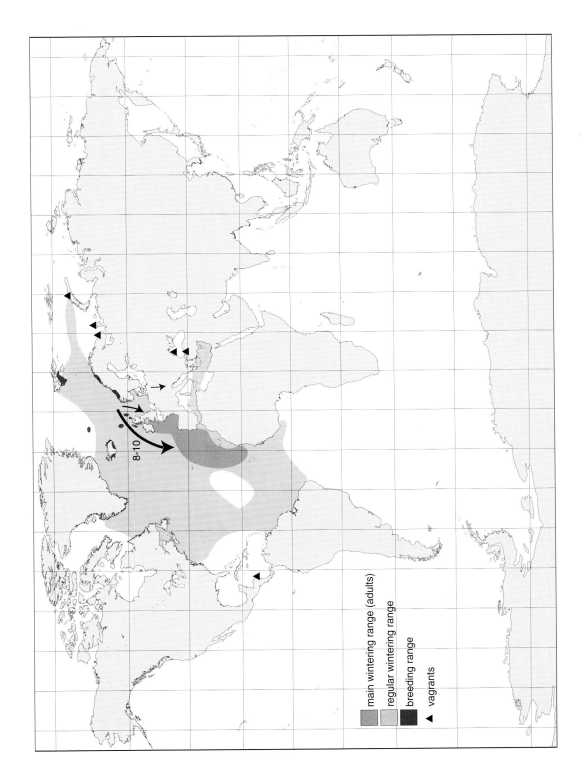

main wintering range (adults)

regular wintering range

breeding range

▲ vagrants

8-10

2 BROWN SKUA
Catharacta antarctica

Plates 2, 4, 13

FIELD IDENTIFICATION Brown Skua is the southern counterpart of Great Skua. It is treated here as a separate species, consisting of three subspecies: Subantarctic Skua (*lonnbergi*), Tristan Skua (*hamiltoni*) and Falkland Skua (nominate *antarctica*). Sibley & Monroe (1990) go one step further, regarding Tristan and Falkland Skuas as one species and Subantarctic Skua as another.

Subantarctic Skua, the most widespread of the subspecies, is the biggest of all skuas, becoming gradually larger towards the east of its range, New Zealand populations being especially big. Its aggressive behaviour is similar to that of Great Skua, but it is even fiercer: Subantarctic Skua has been named 'the lord of the far south' or 'the berserker among birds', and it seems to have a diabolical capacity for being a scourge. Murphy (1936) gives a detailed and vivid description of the feeding habits of Subantarctic Skua, which attacks all birds, but especially penguins and prions.

Brown Skua shares prominent white wing-flashes with other *Catharacta* skuas, these averaging narrower on the upperwing compared with Great Skua. The plumage is dark earthy-brown, the upperparts concolorous with or just a shade darker than the underparts; worn birds often have conspicuous but irregular pale blotching on the mantle, forming a pale saddle against much darker head and wings. Some have a slightly paler head and underbody, sometimes a dark crown or with scattered rufous feathers, and worn birds show irregular pale spots on the underbody, especially on breast and flanks. The bill is heaviest in eastern populations, where it combines with the flat crown to create a fiercer look than in any other *Catharacta*, comparable to the largest gulls (especially Great Black-backed Gull *Larus marinus*).

Separating Brown Skua from South Polar Skua requires care, but dark South Polar Skuas are scarce (most frequent in northern parts of their breeding range in Antarctica, where they overlap with Brown Skua). Compared with Brown Skua, South Polar Skua has a smaller, more rounded head, a less deep bill with shorter gonys, and shorter legs. Structural characters may be obvious in direct comparison, making South Polar Skua look less grotesque and 'malevolent' than Brown Skua. Typical South Polar Skuas are paler than any Brown Skua, with a strong greyish tinge to head and body, contrasting pale hindcollar, and normally broader and more conspicuous pale frontal blaze; unlike Brown Skua, they often show a contrasting dark eye mask. Most also show conspicuous contrast between pale head/

Figure 13. Brown Skuas of ssp. Subantarctic Skua *lonnbergi*, adults. Note variation in upperwing and flank patterns. Birds showing marked whitish saddle spots typically also show coarse pale spotting on breast and flanks; in flight, such birds show striking pale saddle against dark wings. Dark birds hard to separate from dark-morph South Polar Skua on plumage alone, but note darker hood with less pale streaking on neck sides, lack of pale frontal blaze and somewhat irregular pale streaking on upperparts. Torrett Point, Antarctica, December 1995. *Phil Palmer.*

underbody and dark upperparts, a feature immediately eye-catching compared with Brown Skua, which shows at most a slight contrast noticeable only at short range. Furthermore, South Polar has regular pale shaft-streaks on the mantle (irregular pale blotches on Brown Skua) and always lacks any indication of rufous in the body plumage (frequent on Brown Skua). Worn, pale-headed Brown Skuas are more difficult to separate from South Polar Skua, as features such as a dark mask, pale blaze and paler coldish head and underbody may appear with wear, but, fortunately, such birds show the most conspicuous irregular pale patterning on the upperparts. Furthermore, strong contrasts in head pattern are normal for South Polar Skua, but rare or lacking among Brown Skuas.

Adult (Subantarctic Skua) Cold blackish-brown, in breeding season with narrow and indistinct yellowish streaks on the slightly paler nape and neck sides. Otherwise, rather uniformly dark, but with wear mantle shows irregular white blotching, often penetrating around the bend of the wing to the flanks, thus isolating dark forewing. The head is dark and usually rather uniform, but sometimes with traces of an indistinct pale blaze and darker mask. The palest individuals show a slightly paler hindneck and underbody than hood and upperparts, but never strikingly so as on South Polar Skua. Bill and legs are black, but the bill sometimes appears slightly two-toned, with paler basal parts.

Juvenile Warmer and more uniform dark chocolate brown than adult, looking all dark at distance. There is often a reddish-brown tinge to the underbody, some underwing-coverts and few upperpart feathers; very narrow and indistinct pale feather edges to upperparts, as well as numerous pale shaft-streaks, are detectable only at very close range. The white wing-flashes above are generally narrower than on adult, and frequently lacking; they are almost invisible on the folded wing, whereas they can be seen on the folded wing of adults (Jehl *et al.* 1978). The bill is dark or slightly two-toned, with dark grey basal area and blackish tip. Legs and feet are dark grey, normally with pale spots on tarsus.

Juvenile South Polar Skuas are best separated by their medium grey head and underbody, as well as smaller size. Note that dark juvenile South Polar Skuas are probably very rare, but are the norm for Brown Skua.

Immature Poorly known. Probably intermediate between adult and juvenile, or as adult following post-juvenile moult.

VOICE Generally silent, apart from raucous calls when defending nest. Also more quiet, conversational calls like quacking of ducks.

MOULT Timing the reverse of that described under Great Skua, since Brown Skua breeds in northern-hemisphere winter.

Adult Subantarctic and Falkland Skuas are generally very worn in December-March, when moult of flight feathers has not yet started. Head and body moult starts with head, nape, breast and lower belly: small areas are sometimes moulted from January, and by February most show active moult, but some have not started by March; most of head and body renewed by late May. Primary moult starts late February to early April and is completed June-August/October (sometimes almost completed by April, though certain age of early-moulting bird not fully established: skins USNM, AMNH; Higgins & Davies 1996); in Pacific and Indian Oceans, primaries moult later, starting March-May and completed by October (Higgins & Davies 1996). With 1-2 primaries growing at one time, the moult strategy is slow as in Great Skua, unlike rapid moult of South Polar Skua (which see). Secondaries generally moulted before primaries (centrifugal, usually with two active feathers at one time: Higgins & Davies 1996). Head and neck moulted again before breeding season (September-October), when moult of flight feathers is completed (Higgins & Davies 1996; skins USNM, AMNH).

Juvenile/immature By one year of age (January) has almost completed primary moult, at a time when adults have not yet started. From a few skins studied, moult of primaries starts in September/January and ends March/June (probably immatures).

DETAILED DESCRIPTION

C. a. lonnbergi, Subantarctic Skua (South Georgia and Antarctic Peninsula across southern seas to New Zealand)

Adult Head dark brown to blackish, forming dark hood: lacks well-defined dark cap (apart from rare pale-headed birds); sometimes shows scattered white spots on forehead and crown. With wear (late breeding season), head may rarely become paler greyish-brown with darker mottling and solid dark mask around and behind eye, but head only exceptionally bleaches to whitish (as it does on pale South Polar Skua, some Great Skuas and Tristan Skua). Often shows traces of pale blaze, especially with wear. Nape, sides of head and neck slightly paler brown with narrow pale yellow to whitish (rarely golden- to reddish-brown) shaft-streaks, these sometimes continuing towards breast, but in all but extreme cases streaks narrower and colder-tinged than on Great Skua, and generally the least conspicuous among the *Catharacta* skuas; pale streaking most obvious with wear and increasing age (Higgins & Davies 1996). Upper-

Figure 14. Brown Skua of ssp. Subantarctic Skua *lonnbergi*. Often shows irregular spots on crown. Note cold dark brown overall coloration. Deception Island, Antarctica, December 1995. *Phil Palmer.*

parts dark brown, with irregular whitish to cold yellow (more rarely golden or rusty) streaks and 'hackles' on mantle and especially scapulars (lacking on very dark individuals): pale feather edges become colder and whiter with wear around end of breeding season, appearing as striking paler saddle, sometimes extending onto hindneck and inner wing or continuing towards breast sides, this pale colour probably being most conspicuous on very old birds, on which it may cover up to 20% of outer part of feathers on mantle and scapulars (Higgins & Davies 1996; skins USNM, AMNH); lower back, rump and uppertail-coverts blackish-brown, fading to medium brown with wear, pale-patterned birds often showing pale tips to these areas, matching mantle pattern. Tertials blackish-brown to brown, sometimes with irregular white mottling or streaks along edges or tips. Upperwing-coverts dark brown to blackish-brown, sometimes with narrow pale fringes or scattered white spots (but mostly inconspicuous in the field and confined to inner coverts), coverts becoming slightly browner with wear. (Birds showing palest head also show pale body/wing markings.) Flight feathers blackish-brown: bases of primaries show large white patches similar to other *Catharacta* species, although generally narrower on upperwing, with 10-50mm of white at base of outer web of outer (1)2-4 primaries and up to 40-60mm of white on inner web of outer 4 primaries (frequently inner webs of all primaries are dark, rarely so on Great Skua); division between white primary bases and dark outer part variable, may be sharp or slightly diffuse, often U-shaped, sometimes with indistinct dark spots. Outer primary 0-12mm longer than second outermost. Secondaries with narrow pale bases, in the field visible only during moult of greater coverts. Tail dark, with slightly elongated t1, generally longer and broader than on Great Skua; fresh rectrices may show narrow pale edges or

Figure 15. Brown Skua of ssp. Subantarctic Skua *lonnbergi*, adult. Dark individual with narrower, more irregular pale upperside streaking. Deception Island, Antarctica, December 1995. *Phil Palmer.*

mottling near tip; tail shafts often pale at base. Underparts dark greyish-brown to blackish-brown, normally with slightly rusty tinge, few reddish-brown feathers intermixed, and often with diffuse darker or paler mottling on breast and especially flanks, some individuals thus showing contrasting breast band; belly generally darker and more uniform than breast, in rare cases with a few yellowish streaks, sometimes contrasting slightly with darker underwing. Underwing-coverts blackish, sometimes with a few reddish-tinged feather edges (especially in fresh plumage) or pale spots; greater coverts dark greyish. Bill dark, sometimes with slightly paler grey base; gonys length covers 40-55% of lower mandible. Iris dark. Legs and feet black.

Sexes similar, but female generally larger and paler than male (Higgins & Davies 1996).

Juvenile Head dark greyish-brown to greyish-black; chin, throat and ear-coverts sometimes a little paler, creating slight capped appearance. Chin to underbody warm brown, varying from medium brown to blackish-brown, sometimes with a strong reddish tinge (lacking on adult), but this soon disappears with wear. Generally shows broader pale bases to feathers of head and underbody than adult; with wear large pale areas may become visible. Hindneck concolorous with head and mantle, lacking pale streaking of adult, but sometimes shows a few rusty streaks on hindneck and sides of neck. Upperparts blackish-brown, with narrow whitish or yellowish to reddish-buff hackles, shaft-streaks and U-shaped spots on mantle, lesser secondary coverts and (especially rear) scapulars, and narrow pale fringes to coverts, lower back and uppertail-coverts; rump uniform blackish-brown, probably never with rusty markings. Tertials lack irregular pale edges (frequent on adults). May show broader pale, sometimes rusty, tips to marginal, lesser and median coverts, creating paler leading edge to inner wing. About 10% of individuals much more uniform blackish-brown above, merely with faint grey fringes or shaft-streaks on mantle, back and scapulars, only at close range creating very weak scaling. Flight feathers as adult, but white wing-flashes generally narrower, sometimes restricted to 10-20mm on bases of outer 2-4 primaries, rarely even lacking (primaries thus similar to Pomarine Skua). Tail as adult, but t1 less elongated; very fresh t1 sometimes slightly pointed at extreme tip, but this soon disappears through wear. Underparts cleaner than on adult, lacking mottling or streaking, with markings restricted to faint paler scaling or shaft-streaks on breast sides and sometimes flanks; lower belly and undertail-coverts darker, normally being the darkest part of the underbody. Underwing as adult or more uniformly dark, but frequently with some narrow rusty to buff fringes to some coverts. Bill bluish-grey to lilac-grey with black tip. Legs on average greyer than adult's, with feet black; tarsus sometimes mottled black and white.

Longest primary, bill and tarsus fully grown about 50 days after hatching (Williams 1980).

Immature Similar to adult, but in second year (probably also in subsequent years before breeding) generally darker and more uniform, with no or fewer pale shaft-streaks at sides of head. Often shows a few scattered reddish-brown feather fringes in mantle and scapulars. Legs dark, sometimes with paler spots.

GEOGRAPHICAL VARIATION Three subspecies.

Subantarctic Skua *C. a. lonnbergi*

(Circumpolar, breeding from South Georgia and Antarctic Peninsula across southern seas to New Zealand) Described above. Geographical variation small; becomes gradually larger towards eastern part of breeding range. New Zealand birds have longer wings than other measured series: adult male 410-442 (mean 425.3, n=14), adult female 407-455 (mean 430.0, n=14) (own measurements, AMNH, UZM). Other measurements also average larger for New Zealand birds, especially gonys and tarsus length (own measurements; Mathews 1912; Hamilton 1934). Murphy (1936), however, notes that bill and tarsus of South Georgian birds are as large as in New Zealand; a specimen from Argentina has a longer bill than any other skua measured by him. Australian specimens slightly smaller than New Zealand birds: mean wing length of adult male 420.0, of female 419.8. Mathews (1912) noted that New Zealand chicks were darker and more uniform than in other populations. Few measured specimens from Kerguelen average larger than Antarctic birds.

South Shetland population averages smaller: wing of adult male 378-418 (mean 404.0, n=13), of adult female 392-419 (mean 406.4, n=5). South Shetland birds often have stronger yellow streaks on neck sides in breeding season than do populations from eastern part of the range (skins BMNH, ZMO).

Birds from Amsterdam Island and St Paul average smallest: adult male has wing 387.5, bill 52.3 and tarsus 71.3, respective means for adult female being 399.2, 51.6 and 72.8. Status of this population, in size closer to *hamiltoni* than to *lonnbergi*, is uncertain. Unlike other populations, it does not undergo post-breeding moult (Higgins & Davies 1996).

All measurements are combined in data listed below.

Tristan Skua *C. a. hamiltoni*

(Tristan da Cunha and Gough Island) Probably more closely related to Subantarctic than to Falkland Skua. Similar to Subantarctic Skua but slightly smaller, with proportionately longer bill and legs, and with more square head (in latter respect similar to Falkland Skua).

Adult Similar to Subantarctic Skua. Normally has very dark uniformly brown head and neck, but sometimes a rather well-defined dark cap (head pattern then intermediate between Subantarctic and Falkland Skuas). Neck sides show a few narrow golden to pale yellow streaks, sometimes warmer golden-brown than in other subspecies, and on some creating fuller pale necklace than on Subantarctic Skua. May show fine pale spots on forehead and crown. Upperparts generally with more conspicuous golden and rufous streaks on mantle, scapulars and upperwing-coverts, thus closer to Great Skua than to Subantarctic Skua, and,

Figure 16. Brown Skua of ssp. Tristan Skua *hamiltoni*, adult. Similar to Subantarctic Skua, but smaller with warmer tinge to hindneck and neck sides (and also mantle streaks). Tristan da Cunha, December 1993. *Anders Andersson.*

on some, bicoloration of upperwings approaches pattern of Great Skua. Outer primary 1-11mm longer than next outermost. Bill and legs blackish.

Juvenile Similar to juvenile Subantarctic Skua, having upperparts sprinkled with U-shaped cinnamon marks and underparts strongly reddish-brown (Devillers 1977). In general, underparts more heavily streaked than on Subantarctic Skua, with a warmer reddish tinge; sides of breast, hindneck, mantle, scapulars and lesser coverts sometimes show rufous feather fringes (skins ZMO; Harrison 1983). May show dark outer webs to all primaries and only 10-20mm of visible white on inner webs, thus creating less striking white wing-flash, matching darkest-patterned extremes of all juvenile *Catharacta*. Tarsus black with pale spots.

Falkland Skua *C. a. antarctica*

(Falkland Islands and Patagonia, southern Argentina) The smallest subspecies, but with a proportionately more powerful bill with stubby, bulbous nail and proportionately longer legs than Tristan and Subantarctic Skuas (although absolute measurements average the shortest). Rounded or square head shape shared with Tristan Skua, thus less fierce-looking than typical Subantarctic Skuas. Shows more prominent supraorbital ridges than other *Catharacta* skuas. Breeding range overlaps with that of Chilean Skua, but Falkland Skua is heavier, with jizz closer to Great Skua and plumage intermediate between Subantarctic and Great Skuas. This is the subspecies most resembling Great Skua, but typically colder and darker brown; plumage is more variable than in other subspecies and Chilean Skua.

Adult Plumage variation of head and underparts similar to that of Great Skua. Generally similar to Subantarctic Skua, but many show striking dark cap (not found on Subantarctic Skua), accentuated by stronger yellow streaks on nape and sides of neck, sometimes creating head pattern as well marked as on typical adult Great Skua. The palest individuals have dark markings reduced to dark eye mask; such birds also show the palest brown (sometimes vinaceous) markings on upperparts and underparts, as well as the strongest pale mottling on mantle, scapulars and breast. Others have yellow to rusty spots on central part of crown, mantle and belly, and often straw-yellow mottling on breast, being more strongly patterned on head and underparts than average Subantarctic Skua (which, not typically, shows paler-spotted breast contrasting with darker head). Rusty spots normally scattered, but on some dominant and producing rusty spotting on most of upperparts, stronger than on other *Catharacta* apart from Chilean Skua. The darkest birds have almost uniform dark brown head and underbody similar to Subantarctic Skua, with only very narrow and inconspicuous pale mantle streaks; others have a limited amount of diffuse pale mottling on upper breast and fore

Figure 17. Brown Skuas of ssp. Falkland Skua *antarctica*. Plumage intermediate between Subantarctic/Tristan Skua and Great Skua, with individual variation similar to latter. Dark individuals almost uniform blackish-brown and extremely similar to dark South Polar Skuas, but with coarser, more irregular pale patterning on crown and upperparts. Pale individuals have dark cap contrasting with paler neck sides and hindneck and are similar to Great Skua, but typically are cold brown with greyish (rather than yellowish or buff) patterning. Carcass Island, Falklands, December 1977. *Per Smitterberg.*

flanks, but sometimes more conspicuous spotting on flanks against dark brown ground coloration (more striking than the pattern of average Subantarctic Skua). Upperwing-coverts blackish-brown with indistinct pale edges and tips, but sometimes enough to form two-toned upperwing similar to that of Great Skua; rarely, shows pale spots at leading edge of inner wing. Underwing as on Subantarctic Skua, but underwing-coverts sometimes with a slightly reddish tinge (Devillers 1978). Flight feathers as in other subspecies; outer web of outer primaries with 5-30mm of white at base; generally shows less clear-cut division between white bases and darker tips than Subantarctic Skua and sometimes the white primary-flashes are more extensive. Outer primary 0-11mm longer than next outermost. Bill and legs blackish. Iris brown.

With wear (December-January), pale mottling on upperparts becomes whitish, creating saddle effect, and traces of whitish blaze may appear. Very pale-headed birds represent 8-27% of the population in different parts of the Falklands, but much rarer on mainland South America, where the population averages darker than in the Falklands (Devillers 1978).

Juvenile Has rather uniform dark head (creating dark hood); chin and throat often slightly paler brown. Underparts vary from dark brown to cinnamon or even reddish, thus similar to Chilean Skua; generally more rufous below than other subspecies, including frequent reddish tinge to dark brown underwing-coverts. Upperparts are dark brown with varying amount of U-shaped cinnamon bars on scapulars and coverts or narrow buffish feather fringes, creating very indistinct paler mantle (visible only at close range); rump dark brown, rarely with a slightly reddish tinge towards tip of uppertail-coverts. Bill dark grey with black tip. Legs dark, with pale tarsus spotting.

Immature Similar to adult, but generally darker and more uniform with no or reduced yellow streaks on hindneck, and restricted amount of pale blotching (or none at all, matching very dark adults) (Devillers 1977, 1978). A few individuals are quite reddish-tinged on underparts and in upperpart spotting. May show pale spots on tarsus up to age of 2 years.

VARIANTS An albinistic or leucistic Falkland Skua, showing normally pigmented bare parts and atypical broad white wing-flashes, is known from New Island, Falklands (Devillers 1978).

HYBRIDISATION Hybridisation between Falkland Skua and Chilean Skua is described under the latter.

Subantarctic Skua is known to hybridise with South Polar Skua where their ranges overlap in Antarctica (Parmelee *et al.* 1975), hybrids and back-crosses seemingly becoming more and more numerous during the late 20th century (C. Wilds *in litt.*). Where the two breed alongside each other, mixed pairs are frequent (up to 5% of population: Trivelpiece & Volkman 1982; G.T. Foggitt *in litt.*), in most cases male South Polar paired with female Subantarctic. Hybrids may be similar to South Polar Skua in showing dark hood and paler greyish-brown mantle, but blotching on scapulars and uppertail-coverts more pronounced, though more irregular, than on South Polar Skua (matching worn Subantarctic Skua); some have narrower pale feather edges than Subantarctic

Figure 18. Possible hybrid Falkland Skua *C. a. antarctica* x Chilean Skua *C. chilensis.* Characters of Chilean Skua are complete dark hood, unpatterned rear ear-coverts, strong rufous tinge to head and underparts, and traces of transverse barring on mantle. However, all-dark bill and dark cheeks and throat atypical for Chilean Skua and are probably indications of hybridity. Falklands, December 1977. *Per Smitterberg.*

Skua, thus similar to South Polar; underbody colder greyish-brown, typically in good contrast to dark underwing-coverts, and sometimes slightly barred (Parmelee 1988), with breast often contrastingly paler than chin and throat (not known in South Polar Skua). One specimen showed a yellow tinge to feather fringes on breast sides similar to South Polar Skua (skins AMNH; also mentioned by Higgins & Davies 1996, based on another skin). Parmelee (1988) describes hybrids as being similar to small Subantarctic Skua, but with feeding habits closer to those of South Polar Skua. Measurements intermediate between averages for those two taxa. Juvenile offspring looked more like Subantarctic Skua than South Polar Skua.

MEASUREMENTS in mm. Own measurements; skins AMHN, BMNH, NNH, NRK, USNM, UZM, ZMA, ZMO. Subantarctic Skua: South Shetlands, sub-Antarctic, Deception Island, South Africa, Iles Crozet, Macquarie, Kerguelen, South Australia, New Zealand. Tristan Skua: Tristan da Cunha, Gough Island. Falkland Skua: Falkland Islands.

Wing length

Subantarctic Skua *lonnbergi*

Adult male	378-442	(409.5)	54
Adult female	392-455	(420.8)	40
Juvenile	407-430	(413.7)	10

Note: Furness (1987) gives, for different parts of the range: adult male New Zealand 421-442, Iles Crozet 385-424, sub-Antarctic 385-405; adult female New Zealand 407-447, Iles Crozet 393-438, sub-Antarctic 400-440. Higgins & Davies (1996) give adult male 375-447 (mean 411.9, n=78), adult female 381-475 (mean 420.6, n=77). The largest birds are from eastern part of range.

Tristan Skua *hamiltoni*

Adult male	372-409	(382.8)	33
Adult female	378-423	(390.3)	28

Note: Wing averages largest in Gough Island birds (mean adult male Tristan da Cunha 387, Gough Island 397.9; mean adult female Tristan da Cunha 390, Gough Island 412.4).

Falkland Skua *antarctica*

Adult male	355-393	(375.8)	44
Adult female	372-402	(385.4)	38
Juvenile	375, 377		2

Projection of t1 (tail-tip projection)

Subantarctic Skua *lonnbergi*

Adult male	12-36	(18.3)	52
Adult female	9-36	(17.0)	41
Juvenile	7-19	(13.5)	5

Note: Largest projection found in New Zealand birds: 18-36.

Tristan Skua *hamiltoni*

Adult	9-26	(13.4)	18
Juvenile	13		1

Falkland Skua *antarctica*

Adult	10-29	(17.0)	41
Juvenile	10, 10		2

Bill length

Subantarctic Skua *lonnbergi*

Adult male	46.6-59.0	(52.9)	55
Adult female	46.2-61.0	(54.1)	48
Juvenile	52.3-58.5	(54.9)	6

Note: Furness (1987) gives, for different parts of the range: adult male New Zealand 51-56, Iles Crozet 54-61, sub-Antarctic 48-55; adult female New Zealand 48-58, Iles Crozet 53-59, sub-Antarctic 49-57. Higgins & Davies (1996) give adult male 43.5-61.5 (mean 54.7, n=79), adult female 44.0-62.0 (mean 55.3, n=79).

Tristan Skua *hamiltoni*

Adult male	49.2-56.0	(53.6)	30
Adult female	50.5-57.9	(54.2)	30
Juvenile	52.4		1

Falkland Skua *antarctica*

Adult male	41.1-51.3	(47.4)	33
Adult female	44.9-52.0	(47.6)	38
Juvenile	49,1, 50.2		2

Bill depth at gonys

Subantarctic Skua *lonnbergi*

Adult male	16.5-21.6	(19.9)	53
Adult female	16.7-22.3	(20.2)	46
Juvenile	17.4, 17.7		2

Tristan Skua *hamiltoni*

Adult male	15.5-18.5	(17.1)	30
Adult female	17.7-19.4	(18.4)	30
Juvenile	17.9		1

Falkland Skua *antarctica*

Adult male	16.4-20.2	(17.9)	34
Adult female	16.4-21.0	(18.2)	38
Juvenile	17.8, 18.2		2

Bill depth at base

Subantarctic Skua *lonnbergi*

Adult male	18.4-27.0	(22.2)	53
Adult female	19.8-27.7	(22.7)	46
Juvenile	19.5, 21.5		2

Note: Average in New Zealand birds largest: 26.8 for 3 females.

Tristan Skua *hamiltoni*

Adult male	18.1-20.1	(19.4)	30
Adult female	18.7-21.8	(20.1)	30
Juvenile	19.4		1

Falkland Skua *antarctica*

Adult male	17.7-21.2	(19.9)	33
Adult female	18.6-22.5	(20.1)	38
Juvenile	19.7, 20.3		2

Gonys length

Subantarctic Skua *lonnbergi*

Adult male	10.6-15.8	(13.6)	53
Adult female	10.8-15.8	(14.0)	46
Juvenile	13.4, 13.5		2

Note: New Zealand birds longest: adult male 13.2-15.8, adult female 13.0-15.8.

Tristan Skua *hamiltoni*

Adult male	10.2-12.7	(11.5)	30
Adult female	12.1-13.9	(13.1)	30
Juvenile	12.0		1

Falkland Skua *antarctica*

Adult male	10.4-13.3	(11.7)	34
Adult female	10.9-13.8	(12.0)	38
Juvenile	11.2, 12.2		2

Tarsus length

Subantarctic Skua *lonnbergi*

Adult male	65.0-84.6	(73.7)	52
Adult female	66.5-84.5	(75.9)	46
Juvenile	72.0, 72.5		2

Note: Furness (1987) gives, for different parts of range: adult male New Zealand 76-95, Iles Crozet 68-79, sub-Antarctic 65-71; adult female New Zealand 78-82, Iles Crozet 68-68, sub-Antarctic 69-72. Higgins & Davies (1996) give adult male 62.3-95.0 (mean 74.4, n=30), adult female 64.0-92.0 (mean 77.5, n=82).

Tristan Skua *hamiltoni*

Adult male	61.9-77.4	(71.9)	30
Adult female	64.7-79.0	(74.8)	30
Juvenile	69.7		1

Note: Furness (1987) gives adult male 71-77 (mean 73.0, n=12), adult female 71-79 (mean 75.4, n=12). Higgins & Davies (1996) give adult male 69.0-77.9 (mean 72.8, n=13), adult female 71.0-79.9 (mean 75.0, n=18).

Falkland Skua *antarctica*

Adult male	60.9-70.0	(66.0)	34
Adult female	62.3-71.0	(67.7)	38

Note: Devillers gives, for adults combined, 61.5-72.9 (mean 68.6, n=42).

WEIGHT in grams. Skins AMNH, NNH, USNM, ZMA, ZMO; Jehl *et al.* (1978); Higgins & Davies (1996).
Subantarctic Skua *lonnbergi*: adult male Iles Crozet 1250-1650, Antarctica 1600-1802, Chatham Island and South Georgia 1610-1960, New Zealand 1300-2108; adult female Iles Crozet 1560-1800, Antarctica 1708-2400, Chatham Island and South Georgia 1660-2180, 'South seas' 1940 and 2220 (skins ZMA), South Shetland 2540 (one skin NNH), New Zealand 1665-2220; juvenile South Georgia 1900.
Tristan Skua *hamiltoni*: adult male 1175-1600 (n=17), adult female 1175-1800 (n=16).

FOOD Brown Skua is an opportunistic scavenger and predator, feeding on a wide range of animals. Some populations hunt petrels and prions mainly at night on foot, digging them from shallow burrows (Fraser 1984; Furness 1987). When penguins are abundant, they are used as a main food source, including eggs, young, weakened adults and carcases. Brown Skuas are less prone to fish for themselves than South Polar Skuas normally are (Emslie *et al.* 1995); they show a preference for killing seabirds at sea (especially prions) instead of kleptoparasitism, forcing their victims underwater following plunge-diving, though they attack all birds

Figure 19. Brown Skua of ssp. Falkland Skua *antarctica*, adult. An individual showing broader paler edges to upperwing-coverts, creating upperwing contrast closer to that of Great Skua than to that of other subspecies of Brown Skua. Falklands, December 1995. *Phil Palmer.*

up to the size of albatrosses. On islands with introduced rabbits these form part of the diet, often alternated with seabirds, e.g. at Macquarie Island. Falkland Skua has a more varied diet than the two other subspecies, including petrels, fish and penguins.

The diet outside the breeding season is less well known. All populations probably feed mostly by scavenging dead fish, seabirds and marine mammals. Has been seen foraging on fields (Higgins & Davies 1996).

BREEDING A total of 15,500-17,500 pairs of Brown Skuas breeds in the southern oceans (Furness 1987). Of these, 10,000 are Subantarctic Skua *C. a. lonnbergi*, which breeds almost circumpolarly from South Georgia and Antarctica to southern parts of New Zealand; the largest populations are 2,000-4,000 pairs on Iles Kerguelen, 1,000 pairs on South Georgia and 550 pairs on Macquarie Island (Higgins & Davies 1996). The Tristan Skua *C. a. hamiltoni* population is estimated to number 2,500 pairs on Tristan da Cunha and Gough Island, South Atlantic. The Falkland Skua *C. a. antarctica* population is estimated at 3,000-5,000 pairs in the Falkland Islands with scattered populations in southern Argentina (Furness 1987).

Breeding takes place between September and March, although in Australia it has been noted in all months apart from October and December (Higgins & Davies 1996). The species breeds

Figure 20. Brown Skua of ssp. Falkland Skua *antarctica*, adult with chick. All *Catharacta* skua chicks are conspicuously pale. Falklands, January 1992. *Gordon Langsbury.*

mainly on offshore islets, low peninsulas and along protected coastlines, nesting among short tussock-grass and lush vegetation, sometimes also among rocks or on ground clothed with moss and lichens; Falkland Skua breeds in flat grassy areas or on heath with shorter vegetation than in habitats preferred by the other subspecies (which explains why its legs average shorter). In New Zealand this skua associates with tree-ferns (Higgins & Davies 1996), and in certain areas (such as Marion Island) it uses abandoned albatross nests as a windshield to protect the nest. Subantarctic Skua breeds in loose colonies, normally near colonies of seabirds such as penguins, albatrosses or petrels. When breeding alongside South Polar Skua, it lays about two weeks later than that species (Pietz 1987). Breeding sites are generally abandoned from March to May or early June, but juveniles sometimes stay well into June or even later (Murphy 1936; Higgins & Davies 1996).

MIGRATION AND WINTERING All populations probably stay close to their breeding range, where they are abundant all year (especially in less cold areas), but are partially migratory or dispersive, this being most marked in southernmost populations. Populations breeding in the vicinity of petrel colonies, however, are able to remain all year without the need of dispersal, as the winter presence of those seabirds provides a main food source. Birds from the antarctic islands straggle to between South Shetland and South Orkney, and from South Orkney to Elephant Island. Subantarctic Skuas ringed at Iles Crozet and Marion Island have been recovered between islands and from western and southern African coasts; one from Marion Island was recovered at Fremantle, Western Australia. The Kerguelen population probably winters around Australia, with two recoveries of Kerguelen birds there (Higgins & Davies 1996).

Figure 21. Brown Skua of ssp. Falkland Skua *antarctica*. Overall impression of paler individuals recalls coldish-tinged Great Skua. Close observation may reveal dark streaking on rear ear-coverts (uniform on Great and Chilean Skuas). Carcass Island, Falklands, January 1978. *Per Smitterberg.*

Subantarctic Skua exhibits some post-breeding dispersal northwards to coasts of South America, South Africa and Australia, especially between 30°S and 60°S, e.g. with large numbers occurring at about 47°S before arrival at breeding grounds (Lönnberg 1906); it is regular north to Rio de Janeiro, and is common off South Africa north to south Angola and south Mozambique between May and September. A bird at Iles de Saintes, Guadeloupe, is the northernmost record, having been ringed at Graham Land six years before its recovery (Blake 1977). An individual from Madagascar is the type specimen of the species, having been identified as a small male Subantarctic Skua

Figure 22. Brown Skua of ssp. Falkland Skua *antarctica*. Note coldish dark brown overall impression, pale frontal blaze and cold yellow hindneck streaks. Upperwing-coverts typically more uniform, with restricted pale patterning compared with Great Skua. Typically shows pale-spotted breast contrasting with dark head. Carcass Island, Falklands, December 1995. *Phil Palmer*.

(Brooke 1981); it is now known to occur regularly off the east coast of Madagascar.

In Australia, Subantarctic Skua occurs mainly between late March and October/November, most commonly in Tasman Sea and along southern Australian coasts and seas, with up to 50 together at Fremantle, Western Australia (Pizzey 1980; Higgins & Davies 1996); it is much rarer along the coasts of the northern half of Australia, with just scattered records from Queensland (Higgins & Davies 1996). It is widespread around New Zealand in the southern winter.

As a straggler, it has occurred in the Indian Ocean north to Kenya, Somalia and Oman (Urban *et al.* 1986; Beaman 1994): six records are known from Sri Lanka (de Silva 1991), at least two from the Maldives and one from Kerala, India, but additional claims from the Arabian Sea and Malaysia (Malacca Strait) have not been verified (Ash & Shafeeg 1994; Ali & Ripley 1969; Higgins & Davies 1996).

Falkland Skua has straggled to the coast off Buenos Aires, with records between end of April and end of August (Murphy 1936). A record from the Lesser Antilles, of an individual ringed at South Shetland, has been disputed, and could refer to South Polar Skua (Stiles & Skutch 1989).

Tristan Skuas normally stay close to their breeding sites, but with some dispersal, probably remaining within the South Atlantic between 35°S and 55°S. Nevertheless, two ringed Tristan Skuas have been recovered much farther north, from Pernambuco, Brazil (Sick 1993).

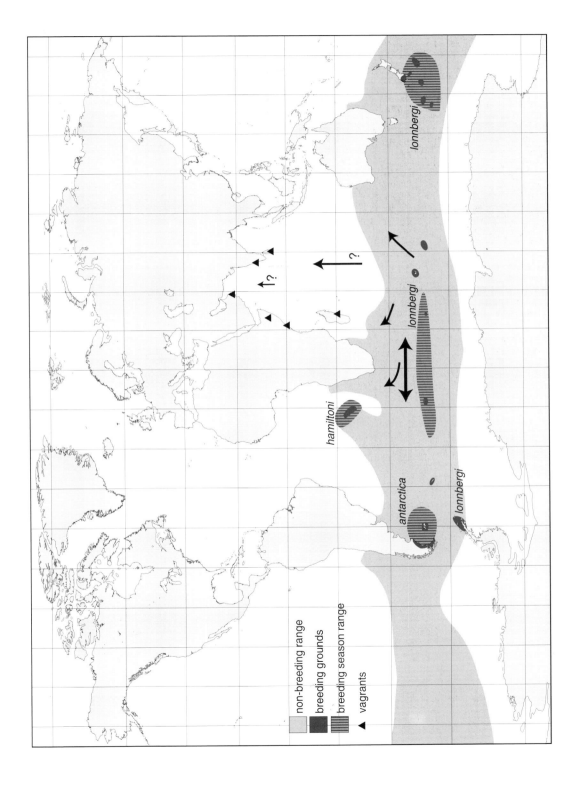

3   CHILEAN SKUA
Catharacta chilensis

FIELD IDENTIFICATION Chilean Skua is slightly smaller than Brown Skua, with a less heavy bill, slightly narrower wings and more slender tail. Most conspicuously, it has cinnamon to rusty underparts and underwing-coverts, creating predominantly reddish-brown underparts; this warm tinge is stronger than on any other skua apart from certain juvenile Arctic Skuas. Most also have a dark cap and bicoloured bill, and many adults furthermore show a dark breast band. The upperparts are spotted with rufous, on some creating a mantle pattern similar to that of juvenile *Larus* gulls.

With wear, the mantle becomes paler and forms a pale saddle contrasting with darker wings and cap. The underside loses some of its warm tinge and becomes greyish-brown with scattered rufous feathers. Such worn birds typically still show a warm rusty chin, throat and undertail-coverts.

Figure 23. Chilean Skua, adult. Note dark cap in good contrast to reddish head and underparts, strong yellow streaks on hindneck and neck sides, and slightly bicoloured bill. Beagle Channel, Argentina/Chile, August. *Ko de Korte.*

In size and jizz Chilean Skua is similar to South Polar Skua, which always lacks any warm rusty tones in the plumage, never shows a striking dark cap, and has uniform dark underwing-coverts.

Figure 24. Chilean Skua. Note bicoloured bill, dark cap contrasting with pale neck sides and hindneck, and spotting on breast. Ushuaia, Argentina, February 1996. *Graham Foggitt.*

This species is more of a scavenger than other *Catharacta* skuas. It often gathers in flocks at carcases, especially of penguins, and at refuse tips, although it also pirates food from terns and other seabirds up to the size of cormorants. Unlike other skuas, it sometimes breeds in dense colonies.

Adult Well-defined dark cap (similar to but less conspicuous than that of pale *Stercorarius* skuas) against pale orange to rusty hindcollar and neck sides, which in breeding season show conspicuous yellow or white streaks. The underparts are cinnamon to reddish-brown, often with a darker breast band which, although less conspicuous against the darker background than on pale *Stercorarius* skuas, is typically much more striking than the traces of a band rarely found on other *Catharacta* skuas; the breast band is, however, sometimes lacking. Mantle and scapulars are dark with brown spots or streaks; sometimes with dark bars forming pattern recalling young gulls, and in such cases diagnostic. The upper-wing pattern is similar to that of other southern *Catharacta* skuas, but generally with a paler leading edge to the inner wing, as lesser and median coverts often have broad pale tips. The bill is grey with a black tip (often looking quite uniformly dark). The legs are black.

Figure 25. Chilean Skua, adult. Note jizz similar to juvenile Pomarine Skua, and strong rusty tinge to lesser and median underwing-coverts. Chile, November 1978. *Per Smitterberg.*

Juvenile Similar to adult, but with a plainer and even stronger reddish-cinnamon tinge to the underparts. The dark cap is fuller, creating a hooded appearance, but sometimes looks more capped as on adult; lacks pale head streaks of adult. The upperparts are darker and more uniformly brown than on adult, with just narrow rufous tips to the upper mantle, light scaling on mantle and scapulars, and normally a contrasting cinnamon- or reddish-brown rump. The bill is similar to adult's, but probably always strikingly two-toned. Legs pale bluish-grey, with black feet.

Juveniles are separated from juvenile Brown Skuas by their reddish (rather than blackish-brown) under- wing-coverts, underbody, chin and throat. See Hybridisation below.

Immature Similar to adult, but lacks streaking on the nape and rufous mantle spots, and generally has fuller hood. Adult characters, such as dark breast band and paler edges to upperpart feathers, probably develop from second calendar-year.

VOICE Reported to differ in quality from that of Brown Skua *C. antarctica* (DeBenedictis 1997).

MOULT

Adult Has complete moult following breeding season. Primaries moulted between March/April and August/September; sequence of flight-feather moult similar to that of Brown Skua, with just 1-2 primaries growing at any one time. Head and body probably moulted in April, following breeding season, and again in August-October; no moult in skins dated January (USNM).

Figure 26. Chilean Skua, adult. Well-developed dark breast band and dark cap similar to adult pale morph Pomarine Skua. Chile, November 1978. *Per Smitterberg.*

Juvenile Moult unknown, but probably similar to that of other South Atlantic skuas. A bird moulting inner primaries in June (Murphy 1936) was probably a second-year bird, as the rest of the plumage was very worn and faded.

DETAILED DESCRIPTION

Adult Forehead, lores, ear-coverts and crown dark greyish-brown to blackish, frequently with paler forehead and narrow pale to rusty spots or shaft-streaks on crown (especially in middle and rear part): dark cap more extensive than on other *Catharacta* skuas, bearing resemblance to a diffuse hood of adult summer (adult alternate) Pomarine Skua. Rear ear-coverts uniform medium brown; hindneck and sides of neck rusty- to greyish-brown with yellow to white shaft-streaks. Upperparts dark blackish-brown to greyish-brown (rarely partly greyish): mantle and scapulars warm brown with rufous subterminal spots or bars and narrow grey edges (on some, similar to pattern of larger juvenile *Larus* gulls), and may show rufous or white shaft-streaks, creating pale saddle against darker upperwing and cap; rump and uppertail-coverts dark brown, sometimes with pale to cinnamon spots and streaks or broader pale edges, producing scaly appearance. Upperwing-coverts dark brown with narrow pale greyish-brown edges: greater coverts have broader pale fringes to grey-mottled edges, on some creating narrow pale wingbar (Harrison 1987, photograph 420), but frequently leading edge of wing and lesser and median coverts show broader pale edges creating pale leading edge to upperwing. Flight

Figure 27. Chilean Skua, adult, dark individual. Dark birds show less contrasting head and underparts than average birds, but note traces of dark cap. Tierra del Fuego, November 1994. *Howard Nicholls.*

feathers dark brown, with up to 4-5cm of white (rarely rusty) at bases of outer 2-4 primaries, gradually decreasing on inner primaries, with outer web of outer primary blackish; rarely, white on inner web of outer primaries may almost reach tip of feather, gradually decreasing on other primaries, but some have pale primary patch reduced to 1-2cm at base of outer feathers; division between white bases and dark outer part normally diffuse, but sometimes sharp. Outer primary (0) 5-16mm longer than second outermost. Tail dark brown, t1 slightly elongated (on most, 10-30mm) with rounded tip. Underbody from chin to undertail-coverts cinnamon-brown (on some, creating strong foxy-red underparts), less often predominantly greyish, but always with a few reddish-brown feathers intermixed, and always with cinnamon to rusty chin and throat as well as undertail-coverts (the latter often with dark feather fringes): breast mostly dark-spotted,

Figure 28. Chilean Skua, adults. With wear, underparts become greyer, but strong rusty tinge to chin, throat and undertail-coverts retained. Note strongly dark-spotted breast band on left-hand bird. As on other *Catharacta* skuas, crown is often white-spotted. Ushuaia, Chile, December 1995. *Phil Palmer.*

creating a narrow dark breast band, sometimes mottled pale greyish-brown (approximately 20% lack breast band, seemingly not related to sex: skins USNM, NMNH, BMNH, ZMO); upper breast and chest sometimes lightly streaked yellow or white; flanks may show pale rufous or dark streaks or spots, bleaching to whitish at end of breeding season. Lesser and median underwing-coverts blackish-brown, with broad cinnamon edges covering about 50% of the single feather and creating conspicuous brown impression; frequently, some underwing-coverts have darker brown centres or bars and paler (partly even whitish) fringes, arranged in parallel rows; axillaries often browner than median coverts, with narrower rusty to cinnamon tips or edges; greater underwing-coverts and primary coverts dark greyish-brown, especially near bend of wing. Bill dark grey to pale bluish-grey, with black tip covering outer 45%; on some strikingly bicoloured, on others rather uniformly dark. Iris brown to blackish. Legs and feet blackish to blackish-brown.

With wear (January-March/May), plumage loses most of the cinnamon tinge to underparts and becomes mottled with greyish-brown; may even show whitish areas, especially on belly. May with wear develop narrow whitish blaze, restricted to area just around base of bill; upperparts then become greyish-brown with distinct pale feather edges, and primaries acquire indistinct pale edges.

Juvenile Cap darker and cleaner

Figure 29. Chilean Skua, adult. Note diagnostic rufous underwing-covert pattern, rusty underparts, dark cap and breast band, bicoloured bill and more slender jizz than Brown Skua. Argentina, December 1993. *Anders Andersson.*

than adult's, sometimes as a complete dark hood. Upperparts dark brown to blackish, 50% of individuals having narrow cinnamon subterminal bars (Devillers 1978); some have narrow pale grey to rusty feather fringes to mantle and scapulars, and to a lesser degree wing-coverts, creating darker and cleaner upperparts than on adult; uppertail-coverts and rump deep cinnamon- or reddish-brown, this colour sometimes as transverse bars. Flight feathers and tail similar to adult; t1 generally shorter than on adult, and projection sometimes minute. Underparts (chin to undertail-coverts) uniform warm cinnamon-brown to brownish-red, deeper and cleaner than on adult, with much less brown patterning, mostly restricted to diffuse dark flank markings; normally lacks dark breast band of adult. Underwing similar to adult, but generally with broader and brighter cinnamon edges to coverts; sometimes, some underwing-coverts show only indistinct rufous tips (rarely lacking). Bill dark greyish-blue with blackish tip. Legs bluish-grey, with feet black.

Immature Following post-juvenile moult probably similar to adult, but second-year lacks dark breast band and strong yellow and white streaks on hindneck and neck sides, and has reduced pale edges to mantle feathers as well as brown streaking on flanks. Legs may show bluish-grey tinge or spots on tarsus.

GEOGRAPHICAL VARIATION
No clear variation (Devillers 1978).

VARIANTS Individuals with discoloured whitish areas on underparts also show a number of white underwing-coverts (Devillers 1978).

HYBRIDISATION Hybridises to a varying degree with Brown Skua of subspecies Falkland Skua *antarctica* on the coasts of Argentina (Harrison 1983). Measurements of two such hybrids: wing 385, 389, bill 49.0, 51.1, tarsus 68, 71 (Devillers

Figure 30. Chilean Skua, adult. Mantle and upperwing-coverts similarly patterned; mantle does not create conspicuous pale saddle as on other southern *Catharacta* skuas. Chile, November 1978. *Per Smitterberg.*

1978). Presumed (probably immature) hybrid Chilean x Falkland Skuas showed brown cap, cinnamon chin and cheeks, variegated brown and cinnamon underparts with most reddish to cinnamon on belly and breast, and dark underwing-coverts (unlike Chilean Skua); mantle and scapulars streaked with gold, cinnamon and whitish. Four further individuals similar to Falkland Skua, but with some reddish in underparts and narrow pale brown to cinnamon edges to some underwing-coverts; maybe within normal range of Falkland Skua plumage variation, but probably with Chilean Skua influence (Devillers 1978; skins AMNH). An individual similar to Chilean Skua, but with dark brown chin and cheeks as well as all-dark bill, is known (see plate 4 and figure 18).

MEASUREMENTS in mm. Own measurements; skins AMNH, BMNH, NRK, USNM, ZMO. Patagonia, South America.

Wing length

Adult male	368-405	(386.6)	35
Adult female	375-418	(398.9)	29
Juvenile	373-390	(381.3)	8

Projection of t1 (tail-tip projection)

Adult	8-35	(19.5)	44
Juvenile	3-10	(7.6)	10

Bill length

Adult male	45.6-51.4	(48.4)	30
Adult female	45.2-53.3	(49.5)	26
Juvenile	43.3-50.4	(48.6)	8

Note: Escalante (1970) gives adult male 49.4-56.1 (mean 52.2, n=18), adult female 51-56 (mean 53.3, n=10).

Bill depth at gonys

Adult male	15.6-18.7	(17.1)	35
Adult female	15.8-18.8	(17.4)	29
Juvenile	14.2-18.0	(16.3)	8

Bill depth at base

Adult male	17.2-21.2	(19.2)	35
Adult female	18.4-21.9	(20.0)	29
Juvenile	16.4-20.2	(18.6)	8

Gonys length

Adult male	10.7-13.8	(12.1)	35
Adult female	10.3-13.7	(12.5)	29
Juvenile	10.4-14.1	(11.8)	8

Tarsus length

Adult male	58.1-72.3	(66.8)	35
Adult female	59.4-73.0	(68.4)	29
Juvenile	66.7-67.5	(67.2)	8

Note: Escalante (1970) gives adult male 60.6-72.3 (mean 68.6, n=18), adult female 66-70 (mean 68.2, n=10).

WEIGHT in grams. Skins USNM; Furness (1987).
Limited information: two adult males 1193, 1224; two adult females 1433, 1431 (Tierra de Fuego).

FOOD Chilean Skua often gathers at refuse tips together with Kelp Gulls *Larus dominicanus*. During the breeding season, it feeds by scavenging and preys on invertebrates. At other times, it feeds mainly by kleptoparasitism, pirating food from birds up to size of cormorants, and is reported to prey on phalaropes (Escalante 1970).

BREEDING This skua breeds commonly along the coasts of Chile south of 37°S and southern Argentina, where it hybridises to a minor extent with Falkland Skua (Devillers 1978; Schlatter 1984). The total population has not been estimated, but probably consists of several thousand pairs.

Figure 31. Chilean Skua, adult, with Kelp Gull *Larus dominicanus*. Upperpart contrast similar to Great Skua, thus unlike most southern *Catharacta* species apart from certain Falkland Skuas. Note also dark hood against clean pale surroundings. Tierra del Fuego, February. *Alan Tate.*

Breeding takes place between November and March, often in dense gull-like colonies of up to 1,000 pairs in areas with short grass and herbs. This dense colonial breeding is unique among the skuas, although the species also nests in looser and smaller colonies.

MIGRATION AND WINTERING Chilean Skua is a short-distance migrant, wintering in channels, straits and fiords of South America. It normally stays close to the breeding sites, but with scattered records in the Falkland Islands, along the South American west coast north to northern Peru and along the east coast north to Brazil, mostly involving immatures (Devillers 1978; Harrison 1983). Claims from Japan, Mexico, Panama and western North America are now considered invalid (Devillers 1977; Howell & Webb 1995), being referable to South Polar Skua.

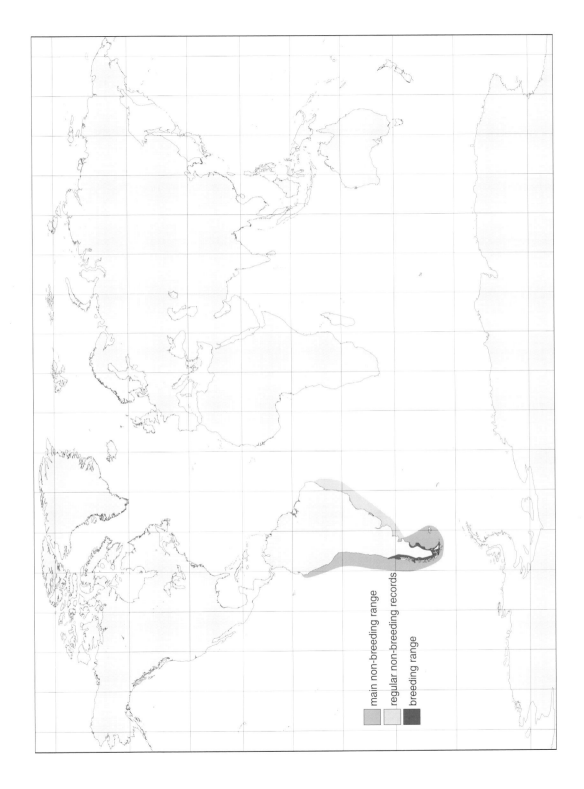

main non-breeding range
regular non-breeding records
breeding range

SOUTH POLAR SKUA
Catharacta maccormicki

FIELD IDENTIFICATION South Polar Skua is the greyest and coldest-tinged *Catharacta* skua, generally lacking any warm brown colour tones. Compared with Great and Brown Skuas, it is less powerful-looking, with proportionately smaller head, slightly narrower and less hooked bill, marginally narrower wings, and shorter, less heavy legs. On the smallest individuals, structural characters create a jizz intermediate between Great/Brown Skuas and juvenile Pomarine Skua, making typical individuals less heavy and 'malevolent' than Great and Brown Skuas. Note, however, that South Polar Skua's general size is similar to that of Great Skua and the smaller subspecies of Brown Skua, and that all juvenile *Catharacta* skuas have a smaller bill

Figure 32. South Polar Skua, adult dark morph. Note cold dark brown overall plumage, with only narrow pale streaks on hindneck and breast. Antarctica, December 1995. *Phil Palmer.*

than adults. Jizz and structure may be helpful, but should be used with extreme care when assessing birds outside their normal range, and should always be combined with the most reliable plumage characters. The latter make pale South Polar Skua the most easily identifiable *Catharacta*.

The flight is similar to that of Great Skua, but generally lighter and more agile. South Polar Skua feeds mostly by fishing, often making shallow plunge-dives, but it also attacks groups of shearwaters. It is less prone to kleptoparasitism than other skuas, and less successful in its attempts. When targeting victims, it normally behaves in a manner similar to that of Pomarine Skua, making short, but direct attacks.

Figure 33. South Polar Skua, adult intermediate morph. Note cold greyish-brown head and body, slightly paler mantle, and uniformly dark wing-coverts. Antarctica, December 1995. *Phil Palmer.*

Adult South Polar Skua occurs in three morphs, with clinal variation especially between pale and intermediates. On these two morphs, the head and underbody vary from pale grey to blackish-brown. Most show good contrast between pale head/underparts and blackish-brown wings/rear parts, particularly conspicuous on worn birds, which appear almost white-headed. Normally they show a striking pale hindneck (on some, stronger than on any other *Catharacta*), sometimes extending to include a paler saddle contrasting with dark upperwing and rear end. Many also show a pale frontal blaze, which may be conspicuous against a dark hood or mask. The cold greyish-brown head and body coloration has its parallel in juvenile Long-tailed Skua. Any cold greyish *Catharacta* skua with striking pale blaze and necklace as well as traces of a pale saddle is arguably a South Polar Skua. Note that a narrow pale blaze may occur on all worn *Catharacta* skuas, and that the pale saddle is often even more marked on Brown Skua (although appearing as irregular spotting, differing from the finer pattern of South Polar Skua). In the northern hemisphere, the very rapid primary moult, involving 3-4 primaries at one time (thus creating large gaps in the wing), is a reliable character; all other *Catharacta* skuas moult their primaries much more slowly, just 1-2 at a time.

Only very pale or worn Great Skuas are so pale as to invite confusion with South Polar Skua. They are separated from South Polar by showing a pale pattern to both mantle (irregular pale blotching) and upperwing-coverts (creating two-toned upperwing) and often irregular dark spotting on underparts (South Polar Skua sometimes shows darker transverse barring on the underbody). On dark-headed Great Skuas, the mantle is also dark, whereas the underbody is slightly paler; on similar dark-headed South Polar Skuas, the mantle is paler than the underbody.

The most problematic South Polar Skuas are the very dark, almost uniformly blackish-brown individuals, which are often impossible to separate from very rare dark Great Skuas and many Brown Skuas, the latter in most areas being even

Figure 34. Adult South Polar and Great Skuas; note especially wing pattern. South Polar often looks rather small-headed compared with other *Catharacta* skuas (but not evident at breeding sites when head feathers are 'fluffed out' as protection against cold weather).

larger and heavier than Great Skua (in direct comparison heavier, with larger, more powerful bill). The short gonys of South Polar Skua, extending 30-40% of total length of lower mandible (40-55% on Brown Skua), is helpful on perched birds. Other characters of dark South Polar Skua are golden streaks around the head, highlighting dark hood, symmetrical white shaft-streaks on mantle, and, if present, a pale blaze. Brown Skua does not show complete golden streaks around the entire head, has asymmetrical pale spots on head and mantle, and only worn birds show a conspicuous pale blaze, rarely matching that of South Polar Skua. Dark Great Skuas normally show a slight reddish tinge, never found on South Polar Skua, and they always lack the pale mantle of many South Polar (and Brown) Skuas.

An identification pitfall for the unwary is large juvenile Pomarine Skua, which is slightly smaller and less heavy, and more elongated, with more pointed wings. On flying birds, look for the white upperwing-flashes: Pomarine shows only a diffuse pale 'half-moon', as only the primary shafts are pale; South Polar shows the distinct white primary bases typical of *Catharacta* skuas (although, rarely, these may be lacking and it then resembles Pomarine). Furthermore, juvenile Pomarine has a paler patch on the uppertail-coverts (never shown by South Polar Skua), and a pale-barred underwing with pale 'double patch' created by pale bases to primaries and their coverts. South Polar Skua shows uniform dark underwing-coverts, typically darker than the body, whereas the reverse is the case on Pomarine Skua. The projection of the central tail feathers is similar on both.

Adult Adults occur in three different colour morphs, with a clinal variation from palest to darkest. All have black bill and legs.

Pale Morph Very pale greyish to biscuit-brown head, this colour often penetrating onto pale-tinged saddle. On pale-headed birds, the contrasting dark bill and isolated dark eyes are striking. The head and underbody contrast markedly with dark wings, rump and tail, creating a two-toned appearance - pale at front, dark at rear - especially in direct head-on light, when underbody is in shadow. With wear (May-July), may become almost white-headed.

Intermediate Morph The most frequent type has a dark hood against pale grey (sometimes noted as 'battleship-grey', but this may refer to juveniles) underbody and dark underwing-coverts. The majority have a pale frontal blaze, similar to most adult Arctic Skuas, but sometimes extending towards the lores (at most very indistinct on Great and Brown Skuas in worn plumage). The rest of the head is rather uniform, but some have a dark eye mask, a distinct dark cap as on most Great, Chilean and Tristan Skuas being exceptional. The hindneck is normally paler, contrasting well with the dark hood, and many also have a pale mantle, emphasising the upperpart contrast, although many others appear dark-backed.

Dark Morph Uniform blackish to dark brown ('plain chocolate'), apart from commonly a pale blaze and sometimes narrow, inconspicuous pale mantle streaks and traces of a paler hindcollar, often penetrating downwards to create a complete pale necklace. Slightly paler birds have cleaner and colder brown underparts than Great Skua, contrasting slightly with darker upperparts. 'Dark intermediates' are rare (there is a 'gap' in the cline between dark and pale intermediate types): such birds may show a uniform, paler head against a darker body, or a wholly dark head against paler body, and many have fine pale shaft-streaks on mantle and scapulars (most frequently on upper scapulars) creating a slightly mottled appearance, differing from the distinct yellow, whitish and brown mottling found on adult Great and Brown Skuas.

Breeding adults show narrow yellow streaks on nape and sides of neck (sometimes continuing across upper breast to form a narrow, but complete necklace, even on dark morph), reinforcing the pale collar. Streaks may be lacking in the non-breeding season.

Figure 35. South Polar Skua, adult pale morph, displaying. Note cold creamy head and underparts against all-dark-looking upperparts and wings. Deception Island, Antarctica, January 1978. *Ko de Korte.*

Figure 36. South Polar Skua, adult intermediate morph. Note conspicuous pale blaze, fine and regular pale streaks on mantle and all-dark wings. Peterman Island, Antarctica, December 1995. *Phil Palmer.*

Figure 37. South Polar Skuas, adult dark morph. Similar to Brown Skua (especially larger Subantarctic Skua *lonnbergi*), but note more rounded head, less heavy bill, short gonys and short legs, as well as more regular and narrower mantle streaks. Hope Bay, Antarctica, January 1982. *Per Smitterberg.*

Juvenile Similar to intermediate adult, but cleaner and even greyer, normally lacking any brownish tinge. The hindneck and underparts are uniform, lacking the pale nape streaks of adults. The upperparts are cold blackish, sometimes with indistinct pale scaling. Less frequently, juveniles have an indistinct darker crown or are darker brown. The pale blaze is weaker than on adults and frequently absent. The bill is bicoloured, with a pale blue base and an extensively blackish tip, although a few have an all-black bill. Legs and feet are pale.

Primary moult is generally later, and continues into September-October, at a time when adults have all flight feathers renewed.

Immature Similar to adult following post-juvenile moult, but pale streaking on hindneck and sides of neck is weaker or lacking in the first 2-3 years of life. The bill is normally still bicoloured on second-year birds (but less so than on juvenile), and the tarsus pale-spotted into the second year. Subsequent plumages as adult.

VOICE Noisy when feeding. Calls heard from feeding groups have been likened to the 'chatter' of farmyard ducks. Also several screams and shrieks similar to calls of larger gulls, being higher-pitched, faster and more harmonic than those of Brown Skua (Pietz 1985). Normally silent outside breeding range.

MOULT Timing the reverse of that of Great Skua. Moult descriptions from the northern hemisphere are probably based on immatures (Gantlett & Harrap 1992). The flight-feather moult is quicker than in other skuas.

Figure 38. South Polar Skua, adult intermediate morph. Note paler hindneck and all-dark underwing-coverts contrasting well with paler underbody. Rear end typically darker than rest of underbody. Antarctica, December 1995. *Phil Palmer.*

Adult Breeding birds normally very worn in February/March. Moults head and body between March and August/September, advanced birds starting in January with scattered feathers in these areas (those starting moult on breeding grounds are possibly non-breeders or immatures): in March to May/June, moults head, body, mantle and some median and lesser coverts; in May/June, shows good contrast between new and old feathers (Kuroda 1962). Primary moult completed in 45-60 days (Ginn & Melville 1983; skins AMNH, USNM), sometimes starting with innermost in late January in breeding range, but normally April/May, during last stage of northward migration or following arrival at northern 'wintering' grounds: advanced birds have renewed up to 5 inner primaries in May (rarely, all flight feathers by late May), but most moult inner 2-3(5) primaries quickly in June/July; most adults complete primary moult in late July-August (birds still showing primary moult in September-October are probably late arrivers or immatures). The very rapid flight-feather moult is found only among other extremely long-distance migrant seabirds, e.g. Great Shearwater *Puffinus gravis* and Arctic Tern *Sterna paradisaea* (Salomonsen 1976; Malling Olsen & Larsson 1995). Secondaries apparently moulted before most of primaries, sometimes fresh by late May. Tail moult starts with t1 in early March: in May, majority have renewed t1-5, but sometimes no traces of tail moult in May; tail moult completed by August (skins AMNH, USNM). In October, sometimes moults underwing-coverts (especially greaters), at a time when moult otherwise has been completed (Higgins & Davies 1996; photographs from Senegal).

During moult of greater coverts (mostly May-June, sometimes later, see above), white wing-flashes may be larger and 'expanded' towards inner part of wing, as they include exposed white secondary bases (A. McGeehan *in litt.*).

Adult has a partial pre-breeding moult in (September) October/November, including head, body and some coverts.

Juvenile Moults later than adult, as juveniles leave breeding sites later (late February/mid March). Earliest traces of moult from end March, when a few feathers in head and body are renewed. Greenland and Faeroe specimens from August-September have renewed the 6 innermost primaries (Bourne 1989). In two July Greenland specimens, 4 outermost primaries were growing at one time (Jensen 1982); one of these birds had extremely worn body and coverts, and had renewed t1-3. Two August Greenland specimens had renewed tail (apart from t5, which was growing), scapulars, and lesser and median coverts. Head and body much worn in August specimens, showing active moult on breast sides and flanks (Jensen 1982). A bird off western USA at end August had just shed inner 3 primaries.

Figure 39. South Polar Skua, probably immature. Note dark hood against paler hindneck, and slender outline. Head often looks smallish compared with that of Great Skua. Cape Hatteras, North Carolina, USA. August 1993. *Ed Kurater.*

Immature Similar to adult, but generally earlier. Specimens from 17th-22nd May (North Carolina) showed active moult of head and body, but worn primaries and rectrices (skins AMNH, USNM).

DETAILED DESCRIPTION

Adult breeding (adult alternate) Head and underbody vary according to morph (see below). Upperparts blackish-brown, with pale pattern restricted to small spots, streaks, shaft-streaks or paler overall tinge to mantle and scapulars, creating pale saddle effect or thin whitish line on scapulars; rump brownish-black, often with paler feather edges. Upperwing-coverts blackish-brown, rarely with indistinct pale fringes to lesser and sometimes median coverts; underwing-coverts blackish-brown, greater coverts paler greyish-brown. Primaries dark (may show narrow pale fringes, especially with wear), with white bases to outer 5 (6) covering approximately 20% of feather (thus similar to juvenile Great Skua), broadest on outer 2-4 primaries: outer webs of outer 4 primaries show 30-60mm of white on upper surface (outer web of outer primary sometimes all dark); up to 80mm of white on underwing, most on inner webs; division between white and dark on upper primaries forms 60-90° angle. Primaries slightly rounded, outer (0) 5-20mm longer than next outermost and with straw-yellow shaft. Secondaries black with paler shaft-streaks and bases (visible during moult of greater coverts). Tail dark brown above, paler below; shafts pale basally, with up to 3cm pale at base of t6,

Figure 40. South Polar Skua. Note uniformly blackish lesser and median underwing-coverts, contrasting well with underbody. White primary patches unusually small. Antarctic Peninsula, February 1996. *Graham Foggitt.*

gradually decreasing towards t1 (Higgins & Davies 1996); for projection of t1, see Measurements. Bill and legs black. Iris brown.

There is continuous scale of variation between pale and intermediate types, much affected by bleaching and wear. Less frequent are intergrades between intermediate and dark types. Males are generally darker than females (Ainley *et al.* 1985; Furness 1987; own skin studies). Bleaching affects the general appearance: in the final stages of breeding, pale types, and probably many intermediates, become markedly pale owing to extreme amount of ultraviolet sunlight, producing a striking dark-and-white pattern during moult as worn feathers may bleach to whitish. On darker birds this effect is much less striking, as the darker plumage better withstands ultraviolet light (Bourne & Curtis 1994).

Figure 41. South Polar Skua, adult pale morph. Note pale frontal blaze, coldish-tinged head and underparts, narrow yellow streaks on sides of neck, and uniform mantle. Also note stocky, short-legged appearance. Antarctica, January 1982. *Antero Topp.*

Pale Morph Head pale greyish to pale buff, often with a vinaceous-brown, in fresh plumage even orange-buff or maroon, tinge (especially to hindneck, which is normally the palest part of the head); sometimes with narrow pale feather edges, creating slightly scaly impression (especially on hindneck), or with indistinct darker mask around eye to ear-coverts. Feathers around bill normally paler (even whitish), creating pale blaze. In breeding season, shows faint pale yellow shaft-streaks on hindneck and sides of neck, sometimes continuing to upper breast to form complete yellow necklace (some adults have pale streaks on hindneck and neck sides throughout year). Mantle, scapulars and upperwing-coverts dark brown to greyish-brown, uniform or with narrow pale shaft-streaks and/or tips, these most obvious on mantle and upper scapulars (on well-marked birds creating pale saddle effect); occasionally, marginal coverts and lesser upperwing- and underwing-coverts have broader pale tips, creating paler leading edge to inner wing (Lansdown 1993b; skins BMNH). Sometimes shows pale shaft-streaks on coverts and pale fringes or tips to primary coverts and uppertail-coverts. Chin to undertail-coverts pale grey to pale buff, sometimes with inconspicuous darker grey feather bases to especially breast and flanks, creating indistinct mottling or short yellow streaks on chin and throat; on palest birds, pale tips to underbody feathers shade darker towards bases; normally becomes darker towards hind-belly and undertail-coverts. With wear, head, breast and flanks may bleach to creamy or greyish-white, on extremely worn birds (May-June) even whitish. Friedmann (1945) stated that older birds may become white-headed, but note that worn individuals, following the breeding season, are also very pale-headed.

Figure 42. South Polar Skuas, adult intermediate morph. Note variation in head and body: the darker bird is similar to dark morph, but body is paler and dark hood more contrasting. Dark cap on paler bird is rather rare in South Polar Skua. Hydrugga Rocks, Antarctica, December 1995. *Phil Palmer.*

Figure 43. South Polar Skua, adult dark morph. Note cold blackish-brown head and body apart from paler hindneck streaking. Hydrugga Rocks, Antarctica. December 1995. Phil Palmer.

Intermediate Morph Head pale greyish-brown (thus similar to pale morph) or medium brown to blackish-brown, on darkest birds creating dark hood (as on dark morph), but then contrasting with paler underbody. Often shows whitish or pale blaze, on best-marked individuals extending onto forehead (recalling male Eurasian Wigeon *Anas penelope*, although shorter: McGeehan 1991) or lores, but frequently indistinct and rarely lacking. Feathering around eye to cheek and ear-coverts often darker brown, creating indistinct dark mask; only exceptionally shows indistinct darker cap against paler ear-coverts. Sides of neck and hindneck paler grey to brownish-yellow (sometimes orange-buff, rarely rosy-tinged), with narrow pale yellowish needle-like streaks in breeding season giving silky, glossy sheen but bleaching to whitish after breeding. Pale hindneck contrasts well with head, and on some penetrates towards breast and mantle; crown and hindneck sometimes with fine pale spotting or mottling. Upperparts similar to pale type, but on average with narrower pale fringes to mantle feathers, scapulars and coverts, often just pale shaft-streaks on mantle and/or scapulars; rump often slightly paler, with narrow grey feather edges. Upperwing-coverts mostly uniform blackish-brown, concolorous with flight feathers. Underbody greyish-brown to dark grey ('battleship-grey'); on some blackish-brown, sometimes with indistinct darker or paler spotting, especially on breast and flanks, which may form transverse barring, but pale feather fringes narrower than on pale morph; hindbelly and undertail-coverts are generally the darkest part of underbody.

Many intermediate types occur (tending especially towards pale morph), and such individuals may show rather uniform dark head (often with paler tinge to ear-coverts) against paler body, pale head against dark body, or paler leading edge to inner upperwing. During moult, contrast between new and old feathers creates slightly blotched or barred underbody, but normally indistinct and visible only at close range. With wear, head and body become paler.

Dark Morph Head and underbody blackish-brown ('plain chocolate') to blackish, unpatterned apart from traces of white blaze (much narrower than on paler types, and lacking on more than 50%). Hindcollar and sides of neck have narrow orange-yellow to golden-buff streaks in breeding

Figure 44. South Polar Skua, pale morph. On breeding grounds often looks large-headed and small-billed compared with Brown Skua. Note paler head than all other *Catharacta* skuas, apart from some extremely worn individuals; pale creamy head with fine yellow streaks contrasts strongly with dark upperparts. Antarctic Peninsula, February 1996. Graham Foggitt.

season, but streaking narrower and generally restricted compared with other types (though sometimes continuing towards breast to isolate dark hood) and often lost following breeding. Upperparts uniform dark brown, at most with very narrow and restricted pale feather tips or shaft-streaks to mantle and scapulars; rump and uppertail-coverts often slightly paler, with very indistinct greyer edges, contrasting slightly with blackish tail. Upperwing-coverts uniform blackish-brown or with very narrow, indistinct pale edges. Belly frequently paler brown than rest of underparts, sometimes with slightly paler mottling, especially on flanks.

All but the darkest extremes normally show slightly paler head and underbody than wings and tail.

Adult non-breeding (adult basic) Similar to adult breeding (adult alternate) as described above, but some lack pale streaks on hindneck.

Juvenile Much less variable than adult (Higgins & Davies 1996; own skin studies). Similar to intermediate adult, but greyer (dark to medium grey), lacking pale streaks on hindneck and sides of neck. Head rather uniform, with pale blaze of many adults restricted or absent; may show narrow pale ring around eye or darker surround to eye (Higgins & Davies 1996), but paler hindneck of adult lacking. Primaries slightly pointed; outer primary 7-12mm longer than next outermost. White wing-flashes generally narrower than on adults, covering 30-50mm of base on outer 2-4 primaries above and up to 60mm below, but on some rather inconspicuous (as a white 'new moon'), or overshadowed by dark outer webs to all primaries. Upperparts similar to adult, but colder and greyer (Devillers 1977), with narrow pale feather fringes to mantle, scapulars and some coverts creating slightly scaly appearance visible only at very close range (but sometimes more obvious through bleaching), and lacking white shaft-streaks of adult; uppertail-coverts often slightly pale-mottled. Bill bluish-grey (sometimes yellowish-grey) with blackish tip, or dark with paler grey lower mandible - often restricted to grey stripe along sides of lower mandible; bill rarely blackish, but frequently appearing all dark in the field. Tarsus bluish with greyish to pinkish tinge (especially at front); feet bluish, sometimes darker grey or black.

Juveniles are all rather similar, although dark types seem to be more frequent than dark adults (skins AMNH, USNM, but material limited). Such birds may show a slight cold brownish tinge to head and underbody.

Immature Second-year similar to adult, but has two-toned bill similar to juvenile (McGeehan 1991), though pale colour may be restricted to nail; legs may show some pale spots, especially at rear of central tarsus. Lacks yellow streaks on sides of head and neck up to age of 1.5-2 years, or streaks much restricted compared with adult, but otherwise inseparable from latter. An individual aged 36 months was noted as being indistinguishable from older birds (Higgins & Davies 1996).

Figure 45. South Polar Skua, probably immature. Note conspicuous pale blaze and hindneck against dark mask. Note also simultaneous moult of inner three primaries. Hudson Canyon, New Jersey, USA. May 1976. *Alan Brady.*

Friedmann (1945) states that pale types become whiter with age, but see final comment under Adult above.

GEOGRAPHICAL VARIATION Clinal. In Antarctica, pale/intermediate birds predominate in most areas, representing 80-87%, with 13-20% dark types (Spellerberg 1970; Watson 1975; Furness 1987). At Cape Crozier, 58% were pale, 23% intermediate and 19% dark (Ainley *et al.*

1985). Pale birds are totally predominant from Cape Adare to Adélie Land and Ross Sea, where more than 99% are pale and intermediate types.

Dark birds dominate the Atlantic population in the northern part of the Antarctic Peninsula, King George Island and South Shetland Islands (Devillers 1977; Furness 1987; Higgins & Davies 1996). This area is at the warmer end of the breeding range, and is where the species overlaps with Brown Skua. This pattern, of darkest birds dominating in areas with the warmest climate and pale birds in coldest areas, shows similarity to the division of pale and dark morphs among Arctic Skuas.

The wing averages shortest in populations measured from Palmer Land: male 362-384 (mean 374, n=8), female 364-392 (mean 380, n=10) (Furness 1987).

HYBRIDISATION When breeding alongside Brown Skua, up to 5% of combined population may consist of mixed pairs (Trivelpiece & Volkman 1982). See Brown Skua.

MEASUREMENTS in mm. Own measurements; skins AMNH, BMNH, NNH, NRK, USNM, UZM, ZMA, ZMO. Antarctica (Ross Island, Palmer Land).

Wing length

Adult male	370-417	(390.2)	102
Adult female	377-421	(397.0)	100
Juvenile	368-400	(383.9)	6

Note: Spellerberg (1970) gives adult male 390-420 (mean 410), adult female 400-430 (mean 415), probably as live birds were measured. Average for 8 North American specimens 378.4, indicating immatures (Devillers 1977).

Projection of t1 (tail-tip projection)

Adult	9-35	(17.4)	189
Juvenile	6-20	(13.1)	7

Bill length

Adult male	43.0-52.5	(47.4)	101
Adult female	43.6-54.0	(48.0)	100
Juvenile	42.6		1

Note: Mean of 12 North American specimens 47.3, indicating immatures (Devillers 1977).

Bill depth at gonys

Adult male	15.2-19.0	(16.9)	102
Adult female	15.5-20.3	(17.1)	95
Juvenile	14.6		1

Bill depth at base

Adult male	16.8-21.5	(19.0)	102
Adult female	17.1-22.1	(19.3)	95
Juvenile	16.3		1

Gonys length

Adult male	9.9-14.2	(11.7)	103
Adult female	10.0-13.9	(12.0)	95
Juvenile	9.6		1

Tarsus length

Adult male	56.4-70.3	(62.2)	102
Adult female	56.6-74.4	(64.4)	98
Juvenile	65.2		1

Note 1: Spellerberg (1970) gives adult male 58.6-68.0 (mean 62.4, n=21), adult female 58-76

(mean 64.8, n=25). Average for 12 North American specimens 61.7 (Devillers 1977).
Note 2: Middle toe 50.0-59.6, on Brown Skua 61.9-75.2 (Higgins & Davies 1996).

WEIGHT in grams. Skins AMNH, USNM, ZMA; Spellerberg (1970); Furness (1987); Higgins &
Davies (1996).
Breeding adults, Antarctica: male 899-1502, female 920-1619. Juveniles at 49-59 days of age
1220-1560 (Young 1963a).

FOOD During the breeding season, South Polar Skuas feed mainly on fish and krill, normally
several kilometres from the colony, and frequently in flocks of up to 100 (Young 1963b). This is
especially true when breeding alongside Brown Skuas, which indulge less in active fishing, preferring penguins as a main food source (Trivelpiece & Volkman 1982). Where Brown Skuas are
absent, South Polar Skuas may feed on penguin eggs and newborn young, and several may
collaborate to take larger young and weak adults (Young 1963b). Inland breeders feed almost
exclusively on petrels (Higgins & Davies 1996). South Polar Skuas often gather at carcases, and
are reported to kill sick or weak individuals of their own species (Murphy 1936). They are less
prone to kleptoparasitism than other *Catharacta* skuas, but may attack petrels and shags, often
grabbing their wings, tail and belly (Maxton & Bernstein 1982; Spear & Ainley 1993). Outside
the breeding season, they mainly fish for themselves by plunge-diving, but sometimes follow
and attack flocks of medium-sized shearwaters and gulls; the Pacific migration is linked with
the migration of Pacific Saury *Cololabis saira* (Furness 1987). South Polar Skuas also feed at
refuse tips when available (Jouventin & Guillotin 1979).

BREEDING Some 5,000-10,000 pairs of South Polar Skuas are estimated to breed around Antarctica, the largest population being in the Ross Sea area. The population facing the Atlantic
consists of about 660 pairs (Devillers 1978; Furness 1987; McGeehan 1991). Certain studies
have shown that Subantarctic Skua preys on almost all seabird species available; in Antarctica its
diet included a small proportion of South Polar Skuas, but not sufficient to be considered a
threat to the South Polar Skua population (Higgins & Davies 1996). As with other *Catharacta*
skuas, the yearly survival rate of adults is more than 90% (Pietz & Parmelee 1994). South Polar
Skua does not normally breed until 7-9 years of age.

Breeding takes place between October and February, on bare, open ground with thin layers
of lichens and mosses, mostly in sheltered depressions free of ice and snow, with exposed rocky
outcrops (Eklund 1961; Young 1963a; Furness 1987). Most nest in loose colonies along coasts,
with nearby colonies of shags and penguins or, to a lesser degree, petrels (Young 1963a), but
sometimes 1-2km and exceptionally up to 250km from open sea (Higgins & Davies 1996). Nest
density is higher than that of Brown Skua where the two breed together (Pietz 1987).

MIGRATION AND WINTERING Adults probably stay close to their breeding grounds, as other
Catharacta skuas, although a bird ringed in 1968 in Antarctica was recovered in July 1986 in
Japan (Brazil 1991). The wintering grounds of adults are largely unknown, but they may lie in
the pack ice of the southern oceans around Antarctica (Eklund 1961). Breeding grounds are
abandoned between end February and mid April, but the species is often present in Antarctica
into early May.

Juveniles and immatures are long-distance migrants, some performing the longest known
migration between breeding and wintering grounds of any bird apart from Arctic Tern *Sterna
paradisaea*. The migration in the Pacific follows a clockwise route, peaking in Japan between
early May and late July (Kuroda 1963; Brazil 1991). Most appear off the coasts of British Colum-
bia and Washington in July-August, and the peak along the Californian coast is in September-
October, with a concentration in the middle of this period, when up to 15 have been noted in
one day; the earliest Californian records are in March, the latest end November (McCaskie
1971). Accidental at Hawaii. South Polar Skua is mentioned as regular between mid May and
early June in Mexico and south California (Unitt 1984; Mattocks 1989), and is recorded from

Figure 46. South Polar Skua, adult pale morph. Note striking two-toned appearance, with very good underpart contrast. Antarctica, January 1982. *Antero Topp.*

Costa Rica between May and October (Stiles & Skutch 1989), indicating a certain amount of wintering off Central America.

The species' occurrence in other parts of the Pacific is less known. It is rare in Australia and New Zealand between September and June, with some return migration along Australian coasts in September-November (Slater *et al.* 1986; Higgins & Davies 1996).

South Polar Skuas are much scarcer in the Atlantic. There are several recoveries of Antarctic-ringed birds from the coast between Brazil and the West Indies (Sick 1993; Bourne & Curtis 1994) and May-July observations from Trinidad and French Guiana (Manolis 1981; Tostain & Dujardin 1988), and the species is regular along the North Atlantic west coast between May and August, with a few remaining to September and an exceptionally late occurrence in Florida on 28th November. It is most frequent off Grand Banks, Newfoundland, where up to ten have been observed in one day, but numbers may be even higher as Great Skuas are also noted here at the same season. It is also noted from other Atlantic west-coast sites. Additionally, there are four July-August records from Greenland (Jensen 1982; McGeehan 1991), of which one, ringed as a chick in September in Antarctica and shot in July, set a new long-distance record for any ringed bird of more than 15,000km between ringing site and place of recovery!

The occurrence of this species in the West Palearctic is still poorly understood, the only definite record being of one collected at the Faeroe Islands in September 1889 (skin in AMNH), but there is an increasing number of claims (mainly August-October), including a bird showing the characters of South Polar Skua photographed off Cornwall, England, in August 1993 (Evans & Millington 1993) and another seen off Islay, Scotland in May 1994 (Curtis 1996). South Polar Skuas may well be regular but scarce in the eastern North Atlantic in late summer and early autumn. One was seen at Saõ Miguel, Azores, in

Figure 47. South Polar Skua. Note paler hindneck penetrating onto mantle, contrasting with dark wings. Pale primary patch small on this individual. Antarctica. December 1993. *Anders Andersson.*

September 1996 (own observation). Off Senegal, however, 160 were observed in two weeks in October 1995 and 198 on 11 days in October 1996 (R.F. Porter *in litt.*); before these astonishing observations, there had been just one record from Senegal (Bourne & Curtis 1994). South Polar Skua is rare off South Africa, with just two records from Cape Province (Urban *et al.* 1986).

A probable explanation for the species' irregularity in the West Palearctic is that migration from the northwest Atlantic heads directly southwards, or that this species, which must surely be extremely well adapted to endure adverse weather conditions, is less easily blown off course than other seabirds. On the other hand, dark-type South Polar Skuas probably turn up to a larger degree in the Atlantic than in the Pacific, as breeding populations facing the Atlantic are predominantly dark, and these are more difficult to identify.

There are scattered records from the Indian Ocean, including Antarctic-ringed birds recovered from the west coast of India (Ali & Ripley 1969) and reports from Sri Lanka (de Silva 1989). In the latter case, the measurements quoted or bill and

Figure 48. South Polar Skua, pale morph. Note coldish overall coloration, pale surrounding to bill and traces of dark mask, unevenly patterned plumage with darker flank bars. Peterman Island, Antarctica, February 1996. *Nigel Redman.*

tarsus seem too large for typical South Polar Skuas, and in our view may be referable to Brown Skua, which is also known as a vagrant to the area. There are further records from Somalia (one) and Eilat, Israel (two). It is suggested that the species may occur regularly in the Red and Arabian Seas and the Persian Gulf (Hollom *et al.* 1988; Shirihai 1996).

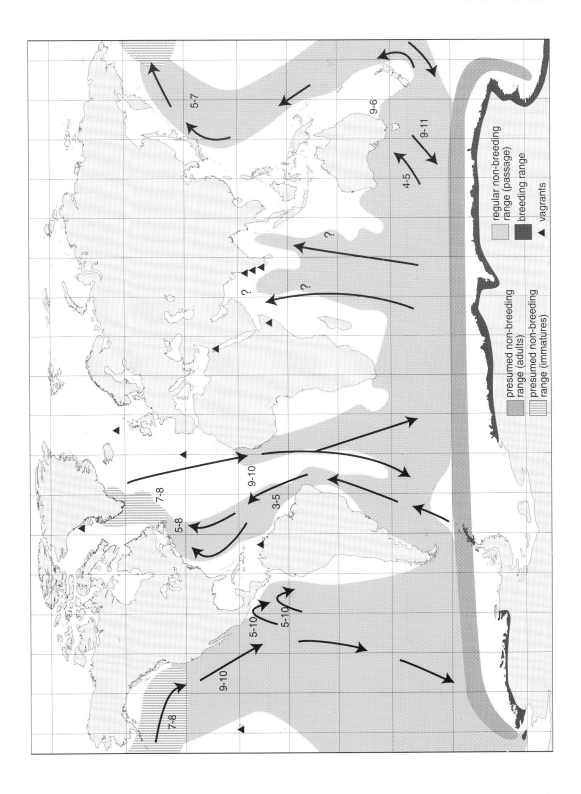

5-7

9-6

9-11

4-5

?

?

?

7-8

9-10

5-8

3-5

5-10

5-10

9-10

7-8

regular non-breeding
range (passage)

breeding range

vagrants

presumed non-breeding
range (adults)

presumed non-breeding
range (immatures)

5   POMARINE SKUA
(Pomarine Jaeger)
Stercorarius pomarinus

FIELD IDENTIFICATION Pomarine Skua is the largest *Stercorarius* skua. It is slightly smaller than a Herring Gull *Larus argentatus*, and has a fierce expression similar to that of a large gull. In the air, the first pointers to its identity are its steady active flight combined with heavy, full body, broad rounded head and heavy, bicoloured, gull-like bill. Typically, the centre of gravity of the underbody lies between breast and belly, on well-fed individuals creating a 'hanging belly' not seen on Arctic and Long-tailed Skuas. The arm is broader than the hand, which tapers towards the tip, often creating an S-shaped trailing edge to the outer wing. Even the lightest birds are heavier than any Arctic Skua, but note that the wingspan overlaps with that of the largest Arctics. When seen together with medium-sized gulls such as Common Gull *Larus canus* or Black-legged Kittiwake *Rissa tridactyla*, Pomarine Skua always looks larger, this being emphasised by its heavy, broad body.

Most important is the tail projection.

Figure 49. Pomarine Skua, adult summer, pale morph. Note gull-like jizz with heavy, hooked bill and rounded head. Upperparts blackish-brown, the darkest among the *Stercorarius* skuas. Barrow, Alaska. June 1995. *Alex Halley*.

Figure 50. Pomarine Skua, adult summer, typical individual. Note slightly paler tinge to head appearing with wear. Hudson Canyon, New Jersey, USA, September. *Alan Brady*.

Any smaller skua with clearly broad and rounded central tail feathers is a Pomarine Skua; if these two rectrices are twisted at the tips identification is straightforward, but even birds not showing this feature have proportionately broader central tail feathers than other small skuas.

Compared with Arctic Skua, the active flight is slower, more like that of larger gulls and *Catharacta* skuas, but also comparable to that of Cory's Shearwater *Calonectris diomedea*, Brent Goose *Branta bernicla* and large divers. The migration flight is steady and untroubled, following a direct line, with long series of stiff, slow wingbeats and just occasional short glides when passing wave-tops. Only in very strong winds, and in the case of lightweight individuals (especially juveniles), are frequent periods of passive shearwater-like flight - so typical of many

Long-tailed and some Arctic Skuas - exhibited. Large individuals approach the size of *Catharacta* skuas, and have a similar lazy flight action, but Pomarines never have striking white flashes on the upperwing (note that, rarely, some *Catharacta* skuas lack these) or an oddly short tail.

When gliding and soaring, Pomarine Skuas hold the hand depressed. In many cases, they glide with the hand held at a level well below the centre of the belly, this posture being rare for Arctic Skua, but more frequent for the much smaller and lighter Long-tailed Skua.

The piratical flight is slower and more laboured than Arctic Skua's, with much shorter, less enthusiastic attacks, as if the body were too heavy for quick changes in direction. Attacks are, however, frequently more direct and aggressive, and often the bird rather than its food is the victim: 'Pommies go for the player, Arctics for the ball'! Pomarine Skuas may kill birds up to the size of Black-legged Kittiwake, forcing them down to the surface (Divoky *et al.* 1977), and are noted to attack petrels in winter (Spear *et al.* 1993); they have even been observed directly attacking Great Black-backed Gulls *Larus marinus*, landing on the gull's back and briefly pecking at its eye. This aggressiveness bears more resemblance to the piratical behaviour of South Polar Skua than to that of Arctic Skua.

Especially on spring migration, Pomarine Skuas sometimes occur in dense groups, somewhat reminiscent of groups of migrating divers.

Field identification of adults is easier than that of younger birds, which in the case of juvenile could pass for an unusually dark immature gull - an impression never given by other skuas. Characters shared with Arctic Skua are 3-8 pale primary shafts in the upperwing and broader pale bases to the primaries below. Note that the exact number of pale primaries is difficult to judge in active flight, where the hand is depressed, and that a small percentage shows only two pale primary shafts.

Adult summer Pomarine Skua occurs in two morphs, the pale morph outnumbering the dark 9:1; intermediates are rare. Together with size and jizz, the main character is the long, projecting central pair of tail feathers, normally clearly twisted at the tip, producing a dark blob at the tail-tip. The projection may be as long as the rest of the tail, and looks much fuller than that of Arctic Skua. Against a pale background, e.g. pale sky, the tail shape is visible at very long range, creating the impression of a heavy rear end (as on large divers). When tail projection is less conspicuous, look for the width of the projection: always broader than on Arctic Skua, and not pointed as on latter.

Pale Morph Dark brown upperparts and pale body. The dark cap is fuller and more 'pulled down' than on Arctic Skua, and contrasts with the bicoloured bill. The sides of the neck are generally deeper brownish-yellow than on Arctic. Most have a dark, heavily brown-spotted breast band, normally matching the colour of the cap, and dark-barred or plain dark flanks. The most heavily barred individuals show the most conspicuous breast band, so that the white of the belly is restricted to the centre.

Adult males often lack the breast band and have a sharper demarcation between dark flanks/rump and pale belly, creating a cleaner impression. They also generally show the longest tail projection, sometimes matching that of adult summer Long-tailed Skua, but even more peculiar-looking owing to its shape.

Figure 51. Pomarine Skua, adult summer, pale morph. Note blackish cap almost reaching throat, bicoloured bill, coarsely spotted dark brown breast band appearing as dark as the cap, and conspicuous dark flank bars. Barrow, Alaska, USA, June 1996. *Alex Halley.*

Dark Morph Entirely blackish-brown (tinged purple up to midsummer, becoming browner with wear), often with a bronzy-brownish tinge to the head sides and neck, where the longer feathers are dark yellowish-brown. Some have a smaller number of pale primary shafts than on the pale morph, and most have a smaller area of pale colour on the primary bases.

Figure 52. Pomarine Skua, adult winter (or immature). From second year, immatures and adults show similar upperparts in winter, having pale-fringed mantle feathers, pale-barred uppertail-coverts and more diffuse cap than on adult summer. Ivory Coast, December/January 1982/83. *Ed J. Mackrill.*

Adult winter This plumage, normally acquired in the winter quarters, is variable, but the majority have reduced contrast between cap and hindneck, with throat and neck sides dark-patterned, uppertail- and undertail-coverts barred pale and dark, and tail projection shorter and normally not twisted at tip. The plumage variation is large, ranging from immature-like to almost like adult summer. Immature-type birds are aged by their uniform dark underwing-coverts and axillaries (pale-barred into second winter, apart from dark extremes). Moults back into adult summer plumage immediately before spring migration.

Juvenile Varies to a lesser degree than does juvenile Arctic Skua. The majority are dark greyish-brown with a plain-looking head, dark face, and pale/dark-barred underwing-coverts and axillaries contrasting with darker underbody. Typically, the pale tail-covert barring is the palest part of the upperparts. The central pair of tail feathers is short, broad and rounded (thumb-shaped), creating a triangular tail shape with the projection barely visible in normal field circumstances. Another reliable character is the pale bases to the under primary coverts which, together with the pale primary bases, create a pale 'double patch' on the underwing visible at long distances: if this is observed at a range when other characters are not, the bird is almost certainly a Pomarine Skua. Variation nevertheless exists, and some Pomarines do not show this 'double patch' (while a good number of Arctic Skuas do, though it is less striking). Other important points are:

Figure 53. Pomarine Skua, juvenile, rather pale-headed individual. Note dark face, no distinct pale neck bar, slight dark spotting on head and dark rear part of wing. IJmuiden, Netherlands, November 1985. *Arnoud B. van den Berg.*

1. Barred uppertail-coverts forming pale patch combined with uniform dark head is the rule for juvenile Pomarine Skua, but never found on juvenile Arctic (though frequent on Long-tailed Skua).

2. Head uniform, often darkening between eye and bill, accentuating fierce look and contrasting well with bicoloured bill.

3. Juveniles never show a conspicuous pale neck band: if the neck is pale, the rest of the head is pale, too.

4. At close range, look for small dark spots or bars on head, most conspicuous on neck sides and hindneck; Arctic (especially) and Long-tailed juveniles show clearer dark streaks.

5. General coloration is a rather cold medium brown, penetrating onto underparts; some are darker brown, a few paler buffish-grey, but never strikingly foxy-red or warm-tinged as many Arctic Skuas.

6. Underwing-coverts and axillaries are barred pale/dark, typically creating paler underwing than body; the opposite is typical for juvenile Arctic Skua.

Figure 54. Juvenile Arctic and Pomarine Skuas, dark individuals. Note differences in shape and underwing markings.

7. Even undertail-coverts are strikingly barred, not just vermiculated as on the majority of Arctic Skuas.

8. Bill bicoloured, pale with a black tip, thus recalling first-year Glaucous Gull *Larus hyperboreus*; although the same pattern is found on Arctic Skua, it is never as striking (as Arctic's bill is slender), and if bill contrast is seen over more than 200m the bird is almost certainly a Pomarine.

Figure 55. Pomarine Skua, juvenile, most frequent intermediate type. The same characters as outlined in figure 53 are evident in this individual. Compare pale edges of primaries with Arctic Skua. Schleswig-Holstein, Germany. November 1985. *Alex Halley*.

9. Upperwing-coverts never show pale leading edge as on Arctic and some Long-tailed Skuas: on perched or swimming birds, the bend of the wing typically looks darker than the breast sides (often paler or concolorous with breast sides on Arctic Skua).

10. Primaries uniformly dark or with only narrow pale fringes, never matching the line of pale primary tips of most Arctic Skuas.

11. Greater upperwing-coverts mostly dark, with just narrow pale tips, together with predominantly dark primaries creating dark rear end on settled birds.

Juveniles vary less than those of Arctic and Long-tailed Skua juveniles: 'If you have seen one, you have seen them all!' has been heard from experienced seawatchers. There is some variation, but 90% of individuals are related to the typical, dark greyish-brown type, whereas genuine dark birds (blackish-brown, including underwing-coverts and axillaries) and very pale-headed ones are rare. Pale-headed juveniles show a cold greyish-yellow head, creating an appearance closer to that of South Polar Skua: fortunately, such Pomarines also show conspicuous pale barring on underwing and tail-coverts.

First-winter Similar to juvenile, but with pale hindcollar following moult in winter quarters. Parts of the body plumage become worn and bleached. In the first summer, it is more irregularly patchy, often with active moult of the flight feathers, and appears much worn and bleached on the upperwing-coverts (especially greaters). Pale individuals show a paler hindneck and central belly and more conspicuous dark flank bars than juveniles. Some have a full dark hood. The upperparts are uniform, lacking the pale fringes of juveniles. The bill is similar to that of juvenile, but generally with darker basal area, and may appear uniform. Legs pale, with black tibia and most of foot.

Second-winter Pale birds are similar to juvenile, but upperparts uniformly dark apart from pale feather fringes on mantle, and the belly generally shows more conspicuous darker barring. Adult cap starts to develop. Underwing-coverts and tail-coverts are barred as on juvenile. Dark individuals appear adult-like apart from pale-barred underwing-coverts and lower belly. Bill similar to adult's. More than 70% of surface of foot is black, with tarsus pale.

Second-summer At this age combines adult-like head and body with barred, juvenile-like underwing. On pale morphs the dark cap is usually well developed, although less contrasting against pale, dark-spotted neck sides, which are rarely as strongly yellowish-tinged as on adults. The underparts are dirty-looking, with barring and spotting extending over entire belly. Both undertail- and uppertail-coverts are barred as on juvenile, but often more strikingly so owing to the whiter ground colour. Tail projection is generally half that of summer adults. In the second autumn, some lesser underwing-coverts and axillaries are often moulted to the plain dark of adult. Bare parts as adult, but tarsus often with pale spotting.

Third-winter Similar to adult winter, but with some pale-barred underwing-coverts and pale spots on dark tarsus.

Third-summer Similar to adult summer, but may show pale-barred greater underwing-coverts and some pale-barred tail-coverts. Tail projection generally shorter than on adult summer.

Figure 56. Pomarine Skua, second-winter moulting into second-summer. Note juvenile-like head, underparts and underwing. Broad white upperwing patch (similar to that seen on moulting dark-winged gulls), appears during moult of greater coverts. Ivory Coast, February/March 1983. *Ed J. Mackrill.*

Figure 57. Pomarine Skua, second-summer type. Note adult-like head (though with dark streaks on neck sides) but pale barring on undertail-coverts. Skagen, Denmark, August 1986. *Knud Pedersen.*

Figure 58. Pomarine Skua, second-summer. Certain *Stercorarius* at this age acquire conspicuous barring and mottling on neck and flanks, separated from dark cap by pale crescent below eye. Netherlands, December 1981. *Jan Mulder.*

Figure 59. Pomarine Skua, third-summer. As adult, but with some pale-barred coverts (especially greater) and generally shorter tail projection than adult summer. Skagen, Denmark, September 1979. *Knud Pedersen.*

Figure 60. Pomarine Skua, adult moulting from summer to winter plumage. Note winter-type rump barring and tail projection in otherwise adult summer plumage. Skagen, Denmark, September 1979. *Knud Pedersen.*

VOICE Silent outside the breeding season, although a low barking sound has been heard from a juvenile in November (M.S. Petersen *in litt.*). When accompanying trawlers, sometimes utters a sharp *which-yew, which-yew,* followed by a continuous *week, week, week...* (Higgins & Davies 1996). At breeding site, gives short calls similar to those of other skuas, though generally lower and harsher (see Cramp & Simmons 1983).

MOULT

Adult Moult from summer to winter plumage is complete. Head and body moult may start (July) late August to late September, but is normally limited in northern hemisphere (although frequent in years with no breeding, when most of head and body moult may be completed early autumn). Normally, most of the moult takes place immediately following arrival in winter quarters, by late November-December: sequence is cap, neck, mantle, throat, uppertail-coverts, followed by rest of head, belly, undertail-coverts and back; by late December-February most are in winter plumage, but some individuals moult only partly (own observations of skins, photographs and live birds mid Atlantic, Venezuela). Flight feathers moulted between (September) October and March/early April: by late November inner 1-4 primaries have been renewed, in December-January moult has reached inner 4-6 (8) primaries, and in January-March outer 3 primaries are renewed; in most advanced birds, all primaries new in February. Tail is moulted October-February, starting with t1 (moulted by a minority July-September); t1 may be lacking in winter, and is then probably moulted directly to summer feathers; sequence of tail moult t1-t2-t3-t4-t6-t5 (Higgins & Davies 1996).

Moult from winter to summer plumage is partial, including head, body and t1 late February-April, when still in winter quarters; starts when primary moult is almost completed. The last parts to be moulted are head, neck, mantle and flanks; underbody and tail-coverts may be new by beginning of March. Head moult is usually completed by early April, although a minority then still show winter feathers. t1 moulted first half of March, taking about 40 days to complete; sometimes t2 is also renewed (Higgins & Davies 1996). Parts of the winter plumage (especially rump feathers) may be retained in summer, presumably mostly by females (Cramp & Simmons 1983).

Juvenile Moult to first-winter/first-summer plumage complete. Head, body and tail feathers are moulted November-April. Flight feathers are moulted between December and July: in December-January most have moulted inner 1-4 primaries, in February-March inner 5-9 (on a few moult has reached only inner 8). Tail is moulted from February. Individuals remaining in northern Europe may have a very restricted moult (up to March), and may retain entire juvenile plumage to first spring, exceptionally to middle of summer, when the plumage is extremely worn and bleached.

Subsequent immature moults Basically as adult, but generally more irregular and incomplete, often retaining a small amount of winter-plumage feathers in summer; t1 from summer plumage may be retained in winter (up to 50% in some series examined). Primary moult similar to adult's, but timing more irregular; in second winter often delayed compared with adults, but may moult inner 3 primaries in autumn, starting in October. Probably, some moult t1 only once a year.

Moult of head and body may start in late June in immatures. Some probably acquire winter plumage in late August.

Figure 61. Pomarine Skua, first-winter. As juvenile, but note paler hindneck. Ivory Coast. December/January 1982/83. *Ed J. Mackrill.*

DETAILED DESCRIPTION

Adult Underwing-coverts and axillaries blackish-grey, greater coverts (especially bases of greater primary coverts) slightly paler. Flight feathers blackish, (2) 3-8 (10) outer primaries with paler shafts, most pronounced on outer 5-7. Undersurface of primaries shows up to 70mm of pale at base. Rectrices dark, with paler bases and pale shafts, pale most extensive on t6. Bill greyish-brown to pale yellowish-brown, with blackish covering outer 30%; pale part darker than on juvenile and younger immatures. Iris brown to dark brown. Legs and feet blackish.

Adult summer (adult alternate) (April-October) Tail with t1 elongated 48-115mm and twisted at tips (often bitten off or broken from summer, rarely leaving a single pointed feather).

Pale Morph (over 90%) Cap blackish (tinged brownish with wear), reaching base of lower mandible, rear ear-coverts and middle part of hindneck; rarely, shows a very narrow pale eye-ring. Throat and cheeks whitish; sides of head to hindneck (sometimes also upper breast) yellow to deep brownish-yellow, sometimes with browner shaft-streaks, fresh feathers on breast sides and hindneck often with scattered whitish fringes. Mantle to rump and upperwing-coverts blackish-brown. Breast to belly whitish, with variable dark breast-band consisting of heavy brown or black spots, more rarely clean dark brown to sooty-grey (when fresh, breast feathers may show buffish tips); flanks dark or dark-barred; undertail-coverts and sometimes centre of belly blackish.

Males generally cleaner-patterned, with breast band frequently lacking (20% in skins) and clean division between dark flanks/undertail-coverts and white belly; lack darker shaft-streaks on head and neck seen on most females. Tail projection averages longer on males. Females always show breast band and some dark barring on flanks. With wear (autumn), both sexes are sometimes paler greyish-brown on upperparts and with whiter sides of head and neck.

Dark Morph (5-8%) Whole plumage blackish-brown with purple tinge (up to middle of summer; with wear, browner). Sides of head and neck often tinged bronzy-brownish, with longer feathers tinged dark yellowish-brown. Wing and tail as pale morph, but sometimes with restricted number of pale primary shafts and generally smaller pale area on primary bases.

Intermediate Morph (less than 1%) As dark morph, but generally paler brown, with paler neck sides isolating dark cap. Some show dark/pale barring on entire underbody, sometimes conspicuous (K. Fischer *in litt.*).

Adult winter (adult basic) (late October-early March) Underwing-coverts and axillaries dark. Tail with t1 elongated 32-57mm, usually not twisted at tip, and frequently lacking; very fresh t1 may have slightly pointed tip (November-December, 4 skins NNH, UZM), which quickly wears off. Bare parts similar to adult summer; bill frequently greyish at base. *Pale Morph* Variable. Some similar to immature, but with uniform dark underwing-coverts and axillaries. Others closer to summer plumage, but with barred rump. Cap blackish-brown with paler fringes, especially towards rear; cheeks, throat and sides of neck pale to medium greyish-brown with dark or white spots or short streaks, frequently yellowish-tinged (paler than on spring adult). Thus, cap less contrasting than on adult summer (sometimes appears hooded). Upperside as adult summer, but mantle and scapulars have whitish, buffish or sandy feather fringes, sometimes forming

Figure 62. Pomarine Skua, adult summer, dark morph. Blackish-brown apart from pale primary patches. Note broad tail projection. North West Territories, Canada. June 1976. *Allan Kjær Villesen.*

paler saddle. Uppertail- and undertail-coverts barred pale and dark (barring sometimes restricted to a few feathers). Underparts less clean than on adult summer, with variable dark barring on belly; sides of breast sometimes with whitish or rufous barring.
Dark Morph Similar to summer plumage, but lacks yellow streaks on hindneck and sides of neck. Normally some pale patterning below, including on cheeks and throat.
Juvenile Upperparts dark brown with narrow pale feather tips, creating delicate scaly pattern. Flight feathers similar to adult, but generally with fewer pale shafts (percentage with 2 pale shafts 1.5%, 3=21.5%, 4=30.8%, 5=35.4%, 6=6.1%, 7=3.2%, 8=1.5%; n=85; skins NRK, UZM, ZMH, ZMO); outer part of primaries dark or with very narrow pale tips or fringes, generally most on pale juveniles. Rectrices dark with paler bases, rarely with narrow pale fringes; t1 broadly rounded (width 17-23mm) and slightly projecting. Bill pale grey (with brownish to bluish, rarely pinkish, tinge), with black tip. Legs pale greyish with whitish to bluish tinge; outer 65-75% of foot blackish.

Variation in degree of paleness clinal; pale/dark types bear no relation to adult summer coloration. Extremes are rare.

Figure 63. Pomarine Skua, juvenile of the most frequent dark type.

Pale Type (pale extreme rare: 0.2-1.3% in skin series examined) Head creamy, pale buff or greyish-brown, with dark patch in front of eye and indistinct dark spots on forehead, ear-coverts and crown (head generally colder brown than on Arctic Skua, never strongly orange- or reddish-tinged); chin and throat whitish with indistinct dark spots. Mantle, scapulars and upperwing-coverts brown with sandy to rusty fringes; greater coverts and tertials dark brown, with narrow pale fringes normally restricted to tip (although 5% show isolated pale fringe to outer web, especially on tertials); uppertail-coverts whitish with darker transverse barring, rarely diffuse darker wavy bars, and often with buffish tinge to distal part. Underbody pale brown, ranging from brownish-white to pale sandy-brown, usually with indistinct darker flank bars (especially on rear flanks); undertail-coverts pale with dark barring. Underwing-coverts and axillaries barred dark brown and whitish (rarely with faint rusty tinge); primary coverts usually pale basally, with darker tips.

Intermediate Type (90% or more) Head, chin and throat greyish-brown with narrow pale fringes to feathers of forehead and indistinct dark spots, especially on neck and sides of head; rarely, shows indistinct dark streaks up to 5-8mm long on ear-coverts; lores and spot in front of eye darker than on pale juveniles; crown concolorous with rest of head. Rarely, dark head forms dark hood against paler underbody. Hindneck as rest of head, or just slightly paler than crown, not creating pale neck-band of typical juvenile Arctic and Long-tailed Skuas. Upperparts similar to pale type, but generally with narrower pale feather tips; darker barring on uppertail-coverts generally broader than on pale types, and pale barring more frequently brownish-tinged. Tips of primaries only exceptionally pale. Breast to belly dark greyish-brown, often with slight rufous tinge (fresh feathers have narrow paler edges), entire breast with dense dark barring and therefore normally darker than throat and belly; belly and flanks with indistinct darker barring, generally most conspicuous on rear flanks; undertail-coverts barred dark and whitish, often with rufous tinge. Underwing as pale type, but some show broader dark barring on coverts and axillaries and darker-barred bases of primary coverts.

Dark Type (2-10%, but many intergrades with intermediate type) Head and body rather uniform brownish-black. Upperparts as intermediate type, but with on average narrower pale fringes to feathers of mantle, scapulars and coverts; may show limited amount of pale barring on uppertail-coverts. Underwing and axillaries similar to intermediate type, but pale barring averages narrower (on a few lacking, producing adult-like underwing).

Dark-type juveniles and immatures difficult to age owing to similarity between all plumages. Ageing is best based on bare-part coloration and projection of central pair of tail feathers.

First-winter/first-summer (first basic)
(January-August/September of second calendar-year) Similar to juvenile, but with paler, sometimes slightly yellowish-tinged hindneck and sometimes paler centre of belly. Shows traces of dark, white-flecked hood or cap against paler dark-spotted hindneck, sides of neck, chin and throat. Following moult, mantle, scapulars and upperwing-coverts are uniform brown with varying narrow pale fringes, especially on mantle. Rest of plumage similar to juvenile, but generally with more distinct brown and pale mottling on underparts, lacking warm tinge (although frequently showing pale brown feather edges to mantle, lower belly and tail-coverts). Dark birds similar to dark juveniles, but average colder brown, often with slightly paler belly. Barring of tail-coverts generally more contrasting than on juvenile. Tail with t1 elongated 10-41mm. Bill as juvenile, but frequently with darker cutting edges and in general more greyish-yellow tinge, rarely almost all dark. Legs

Figure 64. Pomarine Skua, first-winter moulting inner primaries and t1, reminiscent of juvenile. Note conspicuously barred uppertail-coverts as most distinctive feature of upperparts at this age. Ivory Coast, February/March 1983. *Ed J. Mackrill.*

pale, often with some dark spots (covering 30-90% of surface); 'knee' and whole of foot black.

Often moults flight feathers and tail in summer (opposite of adult). Those delaying moult become extremely worn and faded, especially on greater coverts, and typically look untidy.

Second-winter (second basic) (November/December-April) Generally similar to adult winter, but with pale barring on underwing-coverts and axillaries. Cap less contrasting; some are rather uniformly pale on head and neck. Dark individuals have dark head and body, but usually pale barring on lower belly and undertail-coverts. Tail with t1 elongated as on first-summer. Bill pattern as juvenile but usually less contrasting, with darker tinge to pale base and blackish cutting edges. Legs as first-summer, but frequently all dark.

Figure 65. Pomarine Skuas, two first-summers with probable second-summer. Note heavily worn plumage and hooded appearance of first-summer types; the 'second-summer' type is possibly of same age, but note head and body closer to adult. Immatures often appear strongly worn and bleached in summer. Qurm Nature Reserve, Oman, September. *Hanne and Jens Eriksen.*

Figure 66. Pomarine Skua, second-summer, dark type. Aged by predominantly pale underwing barring. Skagen, Denmark, September 1979. *Knud Pedersen.*

Figure 67. Pomarine Skua, third-winter. This individual is closer to adult summer than most birds in winter plumage. Ivory Coast, February/March 1983. *Ed J. Mackrill.*

Second-summer (second alternate) (March-October/November of third calendar-year) Tail with t1 elongated 20-70mm, as on adult winter and shortest-tailed adult summers, sometimes with twisted tip. Bill horn-grey with black tip and cutting edges. Legs dark with limited pale spotting, especially in middle distal part of tarsus (at most covering 20%); tarsus sometimes medium grey.

Pale Morph Cap dull brownish-black, diffusely separated from whitish hindneck, sides of head and throat by dark spotting on sides of head, especially below eye; sides of head and hindneck often yellowish-tinged, but less strongly than on adult summer; chin and throat sometimes with narrow dark transverse bars. On some, cap more concolorous with rest of head, creating hooded appearance. Upperparts blackish-brown, mantle feathers often with narrow whitish (rarely rusty) fringes; uppertail-coverts barred white and blackish, on average more striking than on juveniles owing to paler, often whitish ground colour (sometimes a few blackish feathers intermixed, but rarely predominantly blackish). Underbody variably whitish with dark bars and spots covering most of underbody; shows dark, adult-like breast band (and sometimes dark spot in centre of rear belly, some having lesser amount of dark barring, but never so clean as adult summer). Underwing as juvenile, but barring more striking as pale areas are whitish and dark barring blacker; a minority show more uniformly dark lesser coverts and axillaries, but normally with very narrow white feather fringes, from autumn of third calendar-year.

Dark Morph Head and underparts dark brown, usually with grey shading to lower belly.

Third-winter (third basic) (November-April) Similar to adult winter, but with predominantly pale/dark-barred axillaries and underwing-coverts and less clear-cut dark cap. Frequently, median and lesser coverts as well as axillaries are dark, as on adult, or with just narrow pale tips. Tail as adult winter. Bill similar to second-summer. Legs dark, with 10-30% covered by pale spotting.

Third-summer (third alternate) (April-November of fourth calendar-year) Tail similar to adult summer, but t1 averages shorter (see Measurements). Bare parts similar to adult summer, but may show a few pale spots on tarsus (up to 20% of tarsus may be pale). Some probably identical to adult summer.

Pale Morph Head and underparts as adult summer, but cap sometimes browner-tinged with some dark spots near border to pale neck sides; belly generally less clean, often with darker bars and spots. Uppertail-coverts usually at least partly barred. Underwing-coverts and axillaries as adult, but greater coverts and some tail-coverts usually dark/pale-barred and undertail-coverts frequently show paler edges; more rarely, a few barred lesser/median coverts and axillaries are present, even on birds showing uniform greater coverts.

Dark Morph Similar to adult, but often with indistinct pale feather edges on belly.

Fourth-winter (fourth basic) (October-April) As adult winter, but sometimes with a few pale/dark-barred underwing-coverts or narrow pale tips to dark underwing-coverts and axillaries. Bare parts as adult; tarsus sometimes tinged or spotted paler well into older immaturity (skin NRK).

Fourth-summer (fourth alternate) (March-November of fifth calendar-year) As adult summer, but a minority show some pale-barred feathers on underwing and (especially upper) tail-coverts. Males becoming pale-breasted normally still show dark feather tips in breast at this age. Tail as adult summer, but t1 averages shorter. Legs dark, but some show pale spots on middle part of tarsus.

GEOGRAPHICAL VARIATION Monotypic. Over whole breeding range, pale morph predominates. Percentage of dark morphs in different populations 5-20%, the highest being about 10% in Franz Josef Land, 15% on Baffin Island and 20% in Yamal Peninsula (Furness 1987). In different West Palearctic populations, 5-8% are dark (Malling Olsen 1986).

VARIANTS Albinism is much rarer than in Arctic Skua. A partially albinistic juvenile had white feathers at leading edge of wing and on lower belly (skin ZMA 27863).

MEASUREMENTS in mm. Own measurements; skins AMNH, BMNH, NNH, NRK, USMN, UZM, ZMA, ZMH, ZMO, ZMU. Different parts of range.

Wing length

Adult male	343-377	(359.7)	85
Adult female	341-382	(365.9)	64
Juvenile male	308-361	(344.5)	69
Juvenile female	335-364	(352.4)	59
First-summer	329-360	(357.2)	29
Second-summer male	329-360	(346.5)	27
Second-summer female	339-370	(354.0)	27
Third-summer male	339-358	(351.6)	18
Third-summer female	355-379	(366.1)	17

Note: For northwest Atlantic, Furness (1987) gives adult male 354-374 (mean 363, n=17) and adult female 363-382 (mean 373, n=11).

Projection of t1 (tail-tip projection)

Adult male summer	65-115	(91.1)	78
Adult female summer	48-111	(76.0)	62
Adult winter	25-57	(38.0)	15
Juvenile	5-22	(12.3)	164
First-summer	10-41	(25.2)	29
Second-summer	15-85	(43.8)	48
Third-summer	36-95	(68.4)	29
Fourth-summer	53-98	(75.5)	17

Note: Among juveniles and immatures males average larger than females, but complete overlap in extremes.

Bill length

Adult male	35.3-44.0	(38.6)	102
Adult female	35.7-44.0	(40.3)	98
Juvenile	33.4-41.0	(37.9)	154
First-summer	35.2-42.0	(38.8)	27
Second-summer	28.8-43.1	(38.4)	53
Third-summer	35.0-41.8	(38.2)	29

Bill depth at gonys

Adult male	11.5-13.6	(12.6)	78
Adult female	11.9-13.4	(12.5)	63
Juvenile	10.3-12.5	(11.1)	144
First-summer	11.7-12.6	(12.2)	27
Second-summer	10.9-13.4	(12.2)	51
Third-summer	11.3-12.9	(12.2)	27

Bill depth at base

Adult male	13.3-16.5	(14.9)	78
Adult female	13.7-16.2	(14.7)	63
Juvenile	12.4-15.0	(13.6)	145
First-summer	13.3-15.7	(14.2)	27
Second-summer	12.7-16.3	(14.4)	52
Third-summer	13.3-16.6	(14.3)	25

Gonys length

Adult	8.2-12.0	(9.7)	130
Juvenile	7.7-10.6	(9.1)	145
First-summer	8.9-13.9	(10.2)	27
Second-summer	8.0-11.4	(9.2)	73
Third-summer	8.5-11.6	(9.4)	29

Tarsus length

Adult male	47.1-56.0	(53.1)	100
Adult female	50.0-58.5	(55.0)	94
Juvenile male	45.0-56.4	(49.7)	84
Juvenile female	48.8-57.5	(51.5)	56
First-summer	46.0-54.0	(51.3)	27
Second-summer	47.2-53.4	(50.5)	63
Third-summer	44.8-56.4	(51.0)	29

Note: Among juveniles and immatures females average larger than males, but complete overlap in extremes.

WEIGHT in grams.
Breeding adults from Spitsbergen, Alaska and Yakutia: male 542-800 (n=86), female 576-830 (n=63). North Atlantic non-breeders, July-August: male 620-720 (n=12), female 690-810 (n=10) (Furness 1987; skins ZMA). Adult winter Mauretania, November-December: male 600-870, two females 725, 780 (skins NNH).

North Atlantic immatures (first- to fourth-summer) 500-810 (skins UZM, ZMA). Juveniles Netherlands (October-November) 385-685 (830) (skins ZMA).

FOOD During the breeding season the Pomarine Skua specialises almost exclusively on lemmings, other food sources making up only 3% (Maher 1974). At other times it feeds by scavenging and by kleptoparasitism, as well as killing weakened birds up to the size of medium-sized gulls. Small seabirds (especially Red-necked Phalarope *Phalaropus lobatus*) probably form the main diet in winter, as the largest concentrations of Pomarines are found in the main wintering areas for these species. This skua also feeds around fishing piers and boats, and where carcases are available.

BREEDING The total breeding population of this skua is unknown. It is highly nomadic, wandering around in large flocks in search of lemmings. The breeding range is almost circumpolar between western parts of northern Siberia and Baffin Island, but with a gap in distribution in the lemming-free areas between Greenland and the Murman Peninsula, north Russia (Cramp & Simmons 1983; Furness 1987); the most recent Greenland breeding records are from 1888 (Salomonsen 1967b). Pomarine Skuas

Figure 68. Pomarine Skua, juvenile. Note dark body contrasting well with barred underwing. Note also pale 'double patch' on hand. Schleswig-Holstein, Germany, November 1985. *Alex Halley*.

have been observed holding territory in Spitsbergen, but no confirmed breeding has been noted. It nests on high, open arctic tundra, always with plenty of lemmings, preferring low coastal tundra with lakes, pools and streams; it sometimes breeds far from the sea.

The density of the breeding population is related to the density of lemmings. In Alaska, it varies from 1.5 pairs/km² in poor rodent years to 7.8 pairs/km² in good years (Cramp & Simmons 1983); a wider fluctuation was noted by Furness (1987), who gave density varying between 0.1 and 13.7 pairs/km². Isakson *et al.* (1995) noted locally dense populations along the Siberian coast, whereas Pomarine Skuas were absent in other areas. This is the only skua not showing mate and site fidelity from year to year.

MIGRATION AND WINTERING

Figure 69. Pomarine Skua, juvenile/first-winter. As juvenile, but belly paler and hindneck often paler too. Note pale legs with black foot of juvenile. Ivory Coast, December/January 1982/83. *Ed J. Mackrill*.

Spring and summer The spring migration northwards starts around March. Off Senegal, 746 were recorded during 21-28 April 1991, with daily maximum of 282 (Marr & Porter 1992). The species is regular in the Red Sea between March and May. In spring 1993 41 were noted in South Yemen (Porter *et al.* 1996), and at Eilat, Israel, 100-300 are counted between March and May in average years, peaking late April to late May, with daily maximum of 64 on 30 May 1987 and the highest spring total 763 (Krabbe 1980; Shirihai 1996); another migration route heads through Suez and northwards from there. These populations probably arrive from the Indian Ocean southeast of the Red Sea. The species is rare at the Israeli Mediterranean coast (Shirihai 1996), more frequent in the Adriatic Sea in April and early May, and regular over a broad front between the Black Sea, Armenia, the Aral Sea and Lake Balkhash, where the birds arrive following an overland passage, which is known to occur both at Eilat and along the north coast of the Persian Gulf (Il'icev & Zubakin 1990; Shirihai 1996).

Pomarine Skuas arrive in the North Atlantic from April. Peak passage in Britain and Ireland is in May, with largest numbers in the northwest, and a highest count of 2,093 on 9 May 1992 in Shetland (Harrop *et al.* 1993). In Ireland several hundreds pass on peak days, the largest number seen from land being 265 on 5 May 1983 at Cape Clear, Co. Cork, and in England up to 120 have been noted in one day in Cumbria, in Sussex and at Dungeness, Kent (D.J. Davenport & J.D. Nielsen *in litt.*; Hutchinson 1992; Davenport 1992; James 1996). Migration in southern Britain peaks between late April and mid May, and in Ireland, Shetland and the Northern Isles between the latter half of May and the first week of June. Typically, Pomarine Skuas migrate in small to moderate-sized groups, the largest flock noted at Dungeness being of 28 individuals, in Sussex 51, in Shetland 78 and in Ireland 300 (Davenport 1975, 1981, 1984, 1992; Harrop *et al.* 1993). The biggest passage at Dungeness and in southern Ireland is associated with south to southeasterly winds, whereas large numbers in the northwest occur during depressions followed by strong northerly to westerly winds. Migration past the British Isles heads directly northwards.

Figure 70. Pomarine Skua, second-summer. Note combination of adult-type head and body and conspicuously barred underwing. From this age onwards tail projection may be as long as adult's. De Maasvlakte, Netherlands, November 1985. *René Pop.*

Along the eastern North Sea coasts, however, Pomarine Skuas are, by contrast, rare in spring; interestingly, the largest flock in Holland (17) and the largest day count in Denmark (eight) were on 9 May and 12 May 1992, corresponding with an unusually heavy migration past Britain. In the Baltic, an average of 40-50 is noted yearly in May in Finland and 30-55 in Sweden, mostly in the northern part (Malling Olsen 1986; Tyrberg 1994). Intense migration occurs along the Murman coast and Barents Sea in May, with up to 1,000 (exceptionally 3,000) recorded in one hour; largest count in Barents Sea on 16 May 1966, when 7,490 migrated west and 5,000 stopped off in the area (Glutz von Blotzheim & Bauer 1982; Il'icev & Zubakin 1990), indicating that enormous concentrations wander around in search of lemmings.

In North America, the species is most common along the west coast, with day counts of up to 100 off California in late April. Pomarine is the commonest skua in Japan during spring migration in April and May (Austin & Kuroda 1963; Brazil 1991).

In summer, concentrations may be noted almost anywhere in the high Arctic, many involving immatures. In Greenland, Pomarine Skua is a common summer visitor in flocks of up to 100, but last proved breeding in 1888; most of these are immatures (skins UZM; Salomonsen 1967a; Boertmann 1979). Summer gatherings of immatures are also known from New England and Canada (Wynne-Edwards 1935). Movements of flocks of adults have been noted in midsummer along the Siberian coast (Alerstam *et al.* 1995). Stragglers to western Europe at this time of year are mostly immatures, which represent as much as 35%, higher than in other long-distance migrants in the family Laridae, but matching the pattern of Arctic Skua (Malling Olsen 1993). At Eilat, Israel, Pomarine Skua regularly oversummers in groups of up to 20 (Shirihai 1996).

Autumn The migration from arctic Russian breeding sites partly turns west towards the Atlantic, but some populations head south overland or east to the Pacific Ocean. Smaller numbers (especially juveniles) migrate across northern Finland to the Baltic, following the routes outlined under Arctic Skua (which see).

Autumn migration is noted in the North Sea from around mid August, immatures first, followed by adults, peaking late September/first part of October, and finally juveniles, which begin to turn up in the first days of October. Pomarine Skua is usually scarce before late September, but large numbers of immatures are sometimes noted in August, such as 345 and 800 in Britain in 1989 and 1995, respectively, and 310 at Skagen, Denmark, in 1989 (Christophersen 1990). In south Scandinavia passage peaks in October, on average 3-4 weeks after the peak for Arctic and Long-tailed Skuas, and in influx years often in the first half of November. Annual numbers vary greatly, large numbers correlating with depressions tracking from the west. More strikingly, peak years have always involved a large number of juveniles, which can represent as much as 75-95% of the total autumn passage in south Sweden and

Denmark, compared with none at all in 'poor' years (Malling Olsen 1986; Nyrup 1992; Ekberg & Nilsson 1994). Recent influxes with large percentages of juveniles have occurred in 1976, 1979, 1982, 1985, 1988 and 1991, being a result of good breeding success on the arctic tundra in areas close to western Europe. These peak years correspond well with large autumn passages of other tundra-breeding species, such as Long-tailed Skua, Brent Goose *Branta bernicla*, Little Stint *Calidris minuta* and Curlew Sandpiper *C. ferruginea* (Malling Olsen 1986; Camphuysen & van IJzendoorn 1988; Breife 1989). In such years, large numbers of Pomarine Skuas pass through the Baltic (and to a lesser degree the great Swedish lakes of Vänern and Vättern), where adults are always scarce on autumn migration. Juveniles probably prefer more sheltered routes, rather than migrating directly to the North Sea. An unusually poor lemming population on the arctic tundra in summer 1992 took a year longer than normal to build up again, breaking the three-year cycle (J. de Korte pers. comm.), and no real peak autumn covering the whole of northwestern Europe has been noted since 1991.

In October 1992, Britain experienced a massive influx of some 3,000 Pomarine Skuas, of which 1,700 moved north during 9th-12th (including 1,090 at Seaton Carew, Cleveland, on 9th), and with a total of 845 at Hound Point, Lothian (Anon. 1992). In 1994, 1,150 were noted in Britain in October, mostly during 1st-3rd along the north and west coasts; the autumn 1994 migration in Sweden was better than average, but in no way exceptional (Tyrberg 1995).

The largest recent influx into northwestern Europe was in late autumn 1985, which combined favourable weather conditions with extremely good numbers of juveniles. In the North Sea, a first wave was noted in the second half of October (with equal numbers of adults and juveniles, though several hundred adults were seen at the Faeroe Islands: K. Fischer & J.K. Jensen *in litt.*); a second wave broke through in the first part of November, involving 2,000-4,000 along the Dutch coast (with up to 400 at one site on 6th-7th) and day counts of up to 90 in both the North Sea and the south Baltic (Malling Olsen 1986; Camphuysen & van IJzendoorn 1988). Traces of this magnificent invasion are evident in skin collections in UZM and ZMA! An influx was noted in North Jutland, Denmark, in autumn 1991, with 108 at Hanstholm on 18 October being the largest Scandinavian count ever (Andersen *et al.* 1992). Recent influxes are, however, eclipsed by the October 1879 events, when 5,000-6,000 Pomarine Skuas were driven onto the Yorkshire coastline (Glutz von Blotzheim & Bauer 1982).

Some individuals migrate south from the Baltic to pass through Central Europe, with 77 records in 1976 alone (Seitz & von Wicht 1980). Pomarine Skuas are regular in autumn in the eastern Mediterranean, in Italy and at the coast of Israel, with most in 1979 (up to 37 near Haifa on 2 November: Shirihai 1996), corresponding with an influx year in Scandinavia. Further south, observations are scattered: 3,800 were noted in 11 days in October 1996 off Senegal (R.F. Porter *in litt.*).

In North America, the migration is well spread. Up to 90 have been noted in one autumn at the Great Lakes, Ontario (mean about 30), and up to 39 in one day along the east coast. The species is more numerous off the west coast, with maxima of 190 on 23 August 1987 off Westmore, Washington, and 140 off California at San Diego, as well as yearly averages of 30-60 in Oregon (Unitt 1984; Mattocks & Harrington-Tweit 1987). The peak period along the northern Pacific coast corresponds with the pattern found in northern Europe. It is possible that some Nearctic populations migrate southeast to reach waters off West Africa, as suggested by Escalante (1972).

In the west Pacific, the largest concentration is of 250 birds in mid October 1985, seen from the Tokyo-Kushiro ferry in Japan (Brazil 1991).

Winter Pomarine Skuas generally winter north of the equator, north of the wintering range of Arctic and Long-tailed Skuas. The most important wintering grounds are upwellings off West Africa between Senegal and the Gulf of Guinea (especially between 8°N and 17°N), where flocks of up to 500 have been noted between October and March (Urban *et al.* 1986; Baillon & Dubois 1991), proving the species to be among the most numerous seabirds there. Fewer winter along the rest of the West African coast, between Morocco and Cape Province, but still several hundreds off Rio de Oro, northern Namibia and South Africa (Cramp & Simmons 1983; Urban *et al.* 1986). December-January records are known from the eastern Mediterranean in Israel and Egypt (Shirihai 1996; U.G. Sørensen *in litt.*). Pomarine Skua is very scarce in winter in the

North Atlantic, but it occurs regularly especially after autumn influxes of juveniles. Following the 1982 influx, 10-20 observations in Kattegat were the first evidence of wintering in Scandinavia apart from scattered records (Malling Olsen 1986); 12 were noted at Oostende, Belgium, on 2 January 1995 (Driessens 1995), associated with the largest winter occurrence in Britain of 50 in December 1994. Despite its winter scarcity in the North Atlantic, this species is still the most frequent *Stercorarius* there at that season.

The waters of the western Atlantic and the West Indies between Florida and the Caribbean coast form another main wintering area; hundreds were observed off Venezuela in January 1986 (own observations; Root 1988). There are additional records from French Guiana, Brazil and Uruguay and four records from the Antarctic (Escalante 1972; Tostain & Dujardin 1988; Sick 1993). Further small winter populations occur on both coasts of Central America, the western part of the Gulf of Mexico and along both North American coasts north to Oregon and North Carolina, as well as south along the Pacific coast between southern California and Chile and around the Galapagos Islands (King 1967; Furness 1987).

Figure 71. Pomarine Skua, adult winter. This individual is similar to younger immature, but with uniformly dark axillaries and underwing-coverts typical of adults. Florida, USA, January 1984. *Jan Hjort Christensen.*

In the Indian Ocean, the Pomarine Skua is scarce but regular in East Africa, but much rarer than on the Atlantic coast of Africa, the first two winter records being from Zanzibar in 1993 (Köhler & Köhler 1994). There is a significant winter population in the Arabian Sea between the Gulf of Aden and the Persian Golf, and regular wintering occurs off Pakistan and southern India (Bailey 1966; Ali & Ripley 1969; Bundy & Wear 1980; S.T. Madsen *in litt.*); an unknown number winter further to the southeast. Populations in these areas probably arrive after an overland migration from northern Russia.

Eastern populations winter between New Guinea and southeastern Australia. They arrive in the Tasman Sea in October, together with Short-tailed Shearwaters *Puffinus tenuirostris*. In the Tasman Sea, 40% were identified as dark morphs and 35% as juveniles. This percentage of dark birds is, however, far too high to fit any known pattern of morph ratios anywhere in the breeding range; it could reflect the presence of a large number of juveniles, as in Nyrup's (1992) analysis of records from North Jutland, Denmark, although Furness (1987) did consider that the dark morph might be more common in the eastern part of the breeding range. Up to 100 Pomarine Skuas have been noted off Sydney, New South Wales, where this is the most abundant wintering skua (Higgins & Davies 1996). Off Japan, Southeast Asia, other coasts of Australia and northern New Zealand it is scarcer (Sonobe 1983; Higgins & Davies 1996; M.K. Poulsen *in litt.*).

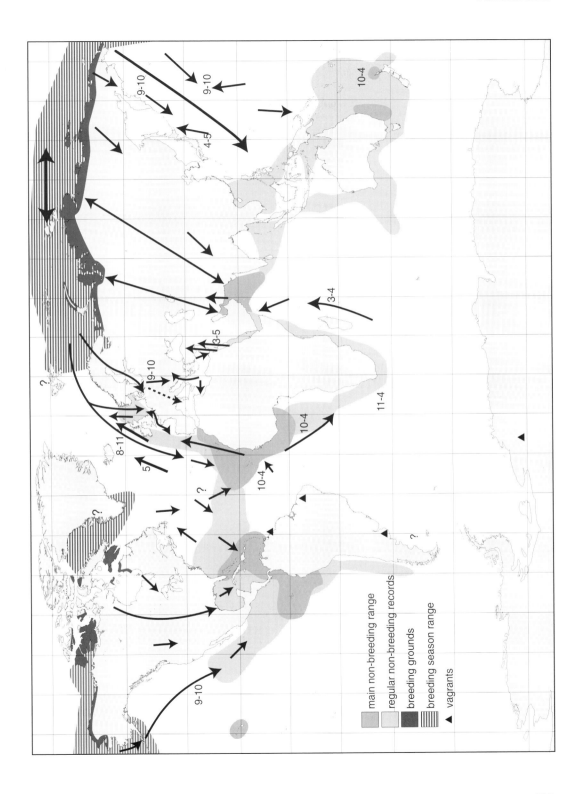

9-10

9-10

10-4

4-5

3-4

3-5

9-10

11-4

10-4

10-4

8-11

5

?

?

?

?

9-10

main non-breeding range

regular non-breeding records

breeding grounds

breeding season range

▲ vagrants

6   ARCTIC SKUA
(Parasitic Jaeger)
Stercorarius parasiticus

Plates 7, 8, 11, 12

FIELD IDENTIFICATION Arctic Skua is the size of Common Gull *Larus canus*. It has a small, triangular head created by a flat crown and slender bill, and the underbody is slightly rounded, with the deepest point at the breast. The wings are slender, with arm and hand being of similar length and width. The moderately long tail is highlighted by the pointed central pair of feathers, conspicuous on all but juvenile and moulting birds.

The active flight is unlaboured, with quick, almost falcon-like wingbeats alternating with glides in arcs when passing wave-tops. Shearwater-like flight is performed

Figure 72. Arctic Skua, adult summer pale morph. Note clean appearance and pale belly. Shetland, June. *R. F. Dickens.*

in moderate winds, but is more frequent in stronger winds. Arctic Skua is then separated from darker medium-sized shearwaters by its angled wings creating a W-shape, with arm and hand similar in length, its pale primary bases and its longer, pointed tail; the wingbeats are similar to those of smaller gulls. Shearwaters give quicker but more mechanical flaps (not dissimilar to swifts) and glide on similar-shaped wings, looking like a black cross; Sooty Shearwater *Puffinus griseus* has a pale grey panel on the underwing-coverts, at a distance superficially resembling the pale underwing of immature *Stercorarius* skuas.

The characteristic piratical flight of skuas is developed to its extreme in Arctic Skua, which chases terns and small gulls for up to several minutes until they deliver their food. The attack starts with low flight, suddenly rising to the final assault, with spectacular abrupt turns and dives; unlike Pomarine Skua or *Catharacta* skuas, Arctic rarely attacks the bird itself. Often two or three individuals hunt in cooperation. When landing among gulls this species normally keeps to the edge of the flock, whereas Pomarine Skuas regularly land in the middle of gull flocks.

Figure 73. Arctic Skua, adult pale morph. Note rather uniform appearance of upperparts. Atypically, this individual shows just two pale primary shafts (3-8 is the rule). Lofoten, Norway, July 1983. *Knud Falk.*

Flight and jizz are important in separating Arctic Skua from Pomarine and Long-tailed Skuas. Pomarine has a heavier head, bill and body (often with deepest point at belly) and a broader arm. Its active flight is low and sustained, as that of larger gulls or *Catharacta* skuas, 'shearwatering' being performed only for brief periods in very strong winds; its attacks on seabirds are rather laboured but often aggressive, going for the bird instead of its prey. Long-tailed Skua is smaller and more slender, with narrower wings, shorter rounded head, but more elongated rear end, the tail typically being longer than the width of the arm; the breast is deep and the belly flat, with a triangular outline to the rear end. In active flight it is more agile and tern-like, with long intervals of 'shearwatering' even in lighter winds; its attacks are more 'playful', briefer and less 'confident'.

Both Arctic and Pomarine Skuas have a diffuse pale 'half-moon' on the upperwing created by 3-8 pale primary shafts, but in active flight the visibility of this is limited owing to the folded position of the hand. Long-tailed Skua normally shows just two pale shafts, creating a narrower but complete pale line at the leading edge of the hand. On Arctic and Pomarine Skuas, the undersurface of all primary bases is pale, creating a pale 'half-moon' (unlike all but first-year Long-tailed Skua, which generally shows a narrower pale 'new moon'), but less striking than the white wing-flash of *Catharacta* skuas.

When perched, Arctic Skuas are relatively small- and slender-headed, with a narrow, longish-looking bill and slender legs. The shape is elongated, with deep breast but slightly pointed rear.

Adult Occurs in dark and pale morphs, with a number of intermediates, these tending especially towards the dark morph. All adults have dark underwing-coverts, bill and legs, and a pointed tail projection. All pale and intermediate and most dark morphs show a pale frontal blaze against the dark cap. The upperparts are similar in all colour morphs: dark greyish-brown with slightly darker flight feathers, even at close range appearing plain dark apart from a pale 'half-moon' created by pale primary shafts.

Adult summer

Pale Morph Dark cap, yellowish-tinged hindneck, and a whitish underbody sharply demarcated from the dark underwing and hindbody in a characteristically clean fashion. It has a dark breast band, varying from just a hint of dark at the sides of the breast to a full, clean grey band, that is always paler than the cap. Above, it often shows a slight contrast between dark greyish-brown coverts and blackish flight feathers (especially on worn autumn birds), but it never appears strikingly two-toned as does Long-tailed Skua.

Intermediate Morph Similar to the dark morph, apart from paler neck sides contrasting with a dark cap, and a slightly paler greyish-brown underbody. Pale intermediates (rare in western part of breeding range, more frequent in the Baltic) are similar to the pale morph, apart from 'dirtier' underparts with variable dark spotting or barring.

Figure 74. Arctic Skua, adult summer pale morph. Note slender head, clean pale underparts sharply divided from dark underwing and tail-coverts, and pointed shape of tail feathers. Varanger, Norway, June. *Hanne and Jens Eriksen.*

Figure 75. Arctic Skua, adult summer intermediate morph. Note pale neck sides in contrast to dark cap and, compared with dark morph, paler greyish-brown underparts. With wear, upperparts become slightly two-toned. Schleswig-Holstein, Germany, October 1988. *Kai Dallman.*

Dark Morph Ranges from uniform blackish-brown to greyish-brown, often with a slightly paler tinge to the neck sides. There is a continuous range of variation from intermediates to dark morphs, but the latter typically do not show a dark cap, the entire head being rather uniform. Dark morph sometimes lacks a pale blaze.

Adult winter Differs from adult summer in less well-defined dark cap, more dark spotting on underparts (including dark-spotted breast band), pale edges to mantle feathers, and pale-barred uppertail- and undertail-coverts. The tail projection may be lacking. Dark morphs are similar to adult summer, but with uniform dark hindneck and neck sides.

Figure 76. Arctic Skua, adult summer dark morph. In certain lights, basal part of upper mandible appears slightly paler. Note partial albinism as symmetric white spots on forewing. Shetland, June 1993. *Gordon Langsbury.*

Juvenile Highly variable, with a clinal variation from very pale on head and underbody to almost uniform blackish-brown. Most show a warm orange to reddish-brown tinge to the head and underbody. Juveniles have buffish scaling on the upperparts. Some show conspicuous white bases to both inner and outer webs of the primaries, appearing as white flashes similar to (but narrower than) those of Great Skua, a pattern unique among the *Stercorarius* skuas. The tail projection is short and pointed (less pointed than on older birds), normally being visible at up to 200-300 m. The bill is pale with a black tip, and the legs pale with black on the feet.

Recently fledged juveniles are fat and appear curiously small-headed, a good distinguishing character compared with Pomarine and Long-tailed Skuas. Juveniles may also look short-tailed, this in combination with a well-fed body creating a much clumsier look than at other ages, and sometimes closer to that of very small *Catharacta* than to other skuas.

Plumage variation is such that hardly any two individuals are identical (the same applies to Long-tailed Skua), making studies intriguing, but sometimes frustrating because of the large number of characters in common with the two other small skuas. A very warm reddish-brown juvenile *Stercorarius* is an Arctic Skua, but a minority have some parts of the plumage, especially head and

Figure 77. Arctic Skua, dark juvenile.

underbody, colder greyish-brown. Flight and jizz are most important. Even juveniles feed almost solely by kleptoparasitism. The following are the most important characters:

1. Smallish-looking, triangular-shaped head with long, slender bill; usually appears disproportionately small-headed.

2. Slightly pointed shape and projection to central tail feathers, visible at range of several hundred metres.

Figure 78. Different colour morphs in Arctic Skua, adult summer.

    a)   Pale morph; the palest variant, lacking breast band.
    b)   Pale morph, with incomplete breast band.
    c)   Pale morph, with complete breast band.
    d)   Intermediate morph; a rather scarce type.
    e)   Intermediate morph, dark type. Note contrast between cap and neck sides.
    f)   Dark morph; darkest birds give blackish-brown overall impression.

3. Hindneck often rusty- to orange-tinged (when creating a strongly warm-tinged neck band against dark cap, diagnostic); neck band lacking on juvenile Pomarine, greyish or coldish yellow on Long-tailed Skua.

4. Pale orange-brown leading edge to inner wing, created by pale fringes to lesser upperwing-coverts, sometimes conspicuous even at range.

5. Strong rusty tinge to upperpart feathering; when foxy-red diagnostic.

6. Uppertail-coverts as back or paler, with darker wavy patches, rarely distinct bars; pale uppertail-covert patch present only on pale-headed birds or those with pale neck band (but uppertail-coverts often dark as rest of upperparts, even on birds with pale neck band); dark-headed birds never have paler uppertail-coverts (pale patch the rule on Pomarine Skua, frequent on Long-tailed).

7. Warm brown tinge to pale underwing bars creates underwing concolorous with or darker than hindbody; normally, the opposite is the case with Long-tailed and Pomarine Skuas.

8. About 10% show pale primary-flashes in upperwing, as on *Catharacta* skuas but narrower; unknown in all other *Stercorarius* plumages.

9. Primaries have narrow, but distinct pale tips, diagnostic when arranged as arrowhead marks (similar to pattern on adult gulls): a good character on settled birds, but visible also in flight at very close range.

10. Head shows dark streaks, most conspicuous on ear-coverts and hindneck.

11. Often shows traces of pale frontal blaze, although not so conspicuous as on adult.

12. Bill narrow, with black tip covering outer 30%, may appear bicoloured at up to 200m range: pattern similar to that of much heavier-billed Pomarine Skua, whereas Long-tailed has outer 50% black (and often dark cutting edges), making contrast invisible even at close range.

13. Undertail-coverts less distinctly barred than on Pomarine and Long-tailed Skuas, and uniform-looking on darker juveniles; very pale juveniles also show almost uniformly pale undertail-coverts, never seen on Pomarine and Long-tailed.

These points should identify the majority under normal field circumstances. Most problematic are very dark individuals, which may be recognisable as juveniles only by bare-part coloration and short tail projection, although the plumage is normally deeper brown than at older ages.

Pale Types Creamy to pale orange head with dark staring eye, a pale underbody, and conspicuous barring on the underwing-coverts and axillaries; even the palest-headed birds show an orange or warm deep creamy tinge to the head. Orange to buff edges to the upperpart feathers, including leading edge of inner wing, are often conspicuous. Frequently, the bases of the under primary coverts are pale, and together with pale primary bases create a pale 'double patch' as on Pomarine Skua, although shorter (broadest on outer coverts) and less conspicuous than on Pomarine, and never visible at longer range than other characters as is the rule with Pomarine.

Figure 79. Arctic Skua, juvenile, paler type. Note unusually pale head, probably worn. With wear, pale fringes to upperpart feathers gradually disappear. Morocco, January 1996. *Christopher Randler.*

Intermediate Types Occur in a continuous range of variation, mostly towards the dark morph. They have a darker cap against pale hindneck and blaze, and the best-developed head streaking of all types. The ground coloration is typically warm brown, often diagnostically foxy-red on head and upperparts. Pale upperpart edgings and 'double patch' on underwing may be similar to those of pale types, but generally less conspicuous. Intermediate and darker types have a darker, closely barred breast and sometimes belly. The underbody coloration is mirrored in the pale barring on the underwing, making body and underwing appear concolorous at a distance.

Figure 80. Arctic Skua, juvenile, intermediate type. Recently fledged juveniles are well fed, looking curiously large bodied against small head (jizz reminiscent of Ruff *Philomachus pugnax*). Varanger, Norway, August 1994. *Dick Forsman.*

Figure 81. Arctic Skua, juvenile, dark type. Warm dark brown, but still with pale primary tips. Even darker birds may appear all dark apart from bicoloured bill and pale tarsus. Goedereede, Netherlands. September 1988. *René Pop.*

Figure 82. Arctic Skua, first-winter/first-summer. Extremely worn bird appearing white-headed and showing unusually bleached coverts. Juzur as Sewadi, Oman, November 1993. *Anders Blomdahl.*

Dark Types Vary from warm coffee-brown to almost blackish-brown. Pale feather fringes on upperparts and rump are narrow and warm brownish, difficult to see even at close range. Frequently, the underwing-coverts and axillaries are uniformly dark as on adult, but closer inspection should normally reveal narrow pale feather fringes; with such birds, checking of bare-part coloration is essential for safe ageing.

First-winter Similar to juvenile, but develops colder and even paler hindneck and belly from midwinter, when the warm brown juvenile coloration is gradually lost. As parts of the body are moulted, these early immatures become untidy. In the first summer, they are separated from juveniles by their colder brown upperparts, lacking pale fringes to coverts; the paler barring on rump and underwing-coverts is generally more evident owing to the whitish ground colour of the fresh feathers, and the tail projection is thinner, more spike-like, and slightly longer than on juveniles. The bill is still bicoloured, but the contrast is duller and the cutting edges (and sometimes lower mandible) are

dark. Black begins to appear on the 'knee', and the whole foot is black. The entire plumage is typically unevenly patterned, with a mixture of new and old feathers, and often active wing moult at a time when other ages have completed the moult.

Pale types develop an indistinct darker cap against pale greyish-yellow hindneck and paler belly; some are distinctively dark-hooded at this age. The flanks are extensively dark-barred. In late summer, many show whitish fringes to fresh mantle feathers. Dark types are more similar to juveniles, but lack any pale edgings and have a colder brown tinge to head and body.

In the case of pale individuals, an identification pitfall is provided by intermediate or pale-bellied juvenile Long-tailed Skuas, which are similarly patterned. Structural characters outlined under Long-tailed Skua are most important. Furthermore, Long-tailed has a greyer overall plumage, the outer half of the thicker bill black, distinct whitish feather edges to the mantle (creating transverse barring), slight contrast between paler upperwing-coverts and darker flight feathers, and often a striking pale spot on the lower breast against a complete, uniform grey breast band. Long-tailed Skua normally shows pale shafts on only 2 (3) outer primaries.

Second-summer Basically as adult, but with juvenile-patterned, heavily barred

Figure 83. Arctic Skua, second-summer with juvenile. Note dark spots on predominantly pale tarsus. Adult-looking head and body but juvenile-patterned underwing. Compare tail projection with juvenile's (lower). Skagen, Denmark, September 1977. *Knud Pedersen.*

underwing. Pale morphs never look so clean as adults, as the cap is duller, more diffusely offset from the lightly spotted neck sides, the underparts are barred, and there is often a heavily dark-spotted breast band; both uppertail- and undertail-coverts are distinctly pale-barred. Certain intermediates have a cleaner dark breast and flanks contrasting with pale central belly. Dark morphs normally still show distinct pale barring on all underwing-coverts. The tail projection averages shorter than on adults, but from this age overlapping with the shortest-tailed adult summer birds. The bill is bicoloured, but frequently only base of upper mandible is pale. Legs black, often with pale spotting.

Late in the second summer, the underwing-coverts begin to moult to dark, adult type, starting with lesser coverts and axillaries, but often a wholly juvenile-patterned underwing is retained into the third winter.

Figure 84. Arctic Skua, second-summer dark morph. Note combination of rather uniform, adult-looking head and body, and barred underwing. Faeroe Islands, July 1985. *Stig Jensen.*

In the second summer, pale morphs show a bill pattern and heavily spotted breast band similar to those of Pomarine Skua. Apart from the diagnostic pale blaze seen on most Arctics, there is a complete overlap in plumage characters between immatures of these two species. Jizz, flight and tail projection are essential in safe identification.

Third-summer Similar to adult, but normally retains some pale-barred greater underwing-coverts and tail-coverts; some pale birds still show dark spots or transverse bars on the breast. The legs are black, but may show a few pale spots. Some probably acquire full adult plumage at this age.

Separating second-years from third-years requires care, and these are better identified as 'second/third-year types' in the field. Furness (1987) mentions an individual with heavily barred underparts (although no details given on underwing and undertail-coverts) which was present for at least five years, with no loss of barring as it aged.

Figure 85. Arctic Skua, third-summer pale morph. As adult, but note pale mid-wing line created by pale barring on median coverts. Skagen, Denmark, August 1982. *Knud Pedersen.*

VOICE Call at the breeding site is a short *geeah*, similar to that of Black-legged Kittiwake *Rissa tridactyla*. Normally silent away from breeding grounds.

MOULT Similar to that of Pomarine Skua, but generally later, with even more restricted moult in northern hemisphere. Possibly, t1 is moulted only once a year (Cramp & Simmons 1983); t1 frequently lacking (June) August-September (own observations) in all age-classes other than juvenile.

Adult Moult from summer to winter plumage is complete, immediately following arrival on wintering grounds; of 3,000 in southern Scandinavia and western Europe (April-October), all were in summer plumage apart from a very small number showing a few fresh mantle feathers and, rarely, moult in inner primaries in September-October (own observations). Head and body moulted November-December, but (males) sometimes some small body feathers late August-September (de Korte 1972); head and body sometimes moulted before main moult of flight feathers; exceptionally, head, body and tail-coverts moulted from July and completed by mid October, probably failed breeders (skins BMNH). Primary moult starts with inner primary rarely from late August (5% in adults, southern Scandinavia, own observations August-early October); flight feathers generally moulted between (October) November and mid March/early April, on the most advanced having reached inner 6 primaries by mid December/mid January. Tail moult generally simultaneous with flight-feather moult (t1 sometimes shed during early part of autumn migration), the sequence being t1-t2-t6-t5-t3-t4 (Higgins & Davies 1996).

Moult from adult winter to summer plumage is partial, including head and body, and takes place in February-March immediately following conclusion of flight-feather moult before spring migration. A minority have traces of winter head in late March. Higgins & Davies (1996) note that moult of head and body may continue into April in birds still in winter quarters.

Juvenile Moult into first-winter/first-summer plumage from November (Glutz *et al.* 1982), rarely with minor parts by August (Baker 1983). Primary moult normally starts late December/January, with up to 3 inner primaries moulted at one time (Higgins & Davies 1996), reaching inner 3-4 primaries by late February and completed June/July, but much individual variation; the most advanced have completed primary moult in March, others have up to 5 outer primaries still juvenile by first summer; exceptionally, a bird in September of second calendar-year had just

Figure 86. Arctic Skua, first-winter moulting to second-winter. Note better developed cap and breast band than in figs. 82 and 97. The unusually late primary moult and the white bases to the juvenile primaries prove this individual to be of the age stated. Skagen, Denmark, August 1987. *Knud Pedersen.*

started juvenile primary moult. Secondaries are moulted between January and May. Head and body moult in winter, starting with minor parts in late December; in weak individuals, parts of the juvenile head and upperpart feathers are retained in first summer (rarely, whole plumage, which becomes extremely bleached and worn, especially head, primaries, tail and greater upperwing-coverts). Tail renewed from late February-March, starting with t1, which is sometimes renewed from late December (own observations, Morocco); t4-6 renewed between February and March, but sometimes still not completed in July.

Subsequent immature moults

Similar to adult, including limited moult near breeding sites, especially on mantle. Immatures, however, more frequently shed inner primaries and some tail feathers in late summer (especially t1; t3 and t4 sometimes moulted before t1 from late August), and are said to moult flight feathers on average 1-2 months before adults, most conspicuously in the case of younger immatures (Higgins & Davies 1996). Moult of flight feathers completed March-April (Baker 1983). Sometimes moult parts of head and body in July-August. Moult varies, however, and may be delayed in weakened individuals (especially those remaining north of the normal winter range); such birds may retain parts of the winter plumage into summer.

Figure 87. Arctic Skua, second-summer moulting into third-winter. Note new dark lesser coverts but otherwise predominantly barred underwing, heavy dark spotting on breast band and grey tarsus characteristic of second-summer. This individual atypically lacks pale frontal blaze (absence of pale blaze is frequent among immatures, almost unknown in pale and intermediate adults). De Maasvlakte, Netherlands, August 1981. *Arnoud B. van den Berg.*

DETAILED DESCRIPTION

Adult Underwing-coverts and axillaries brownish-black, apart from frequently slightly paler bases to primary coverts. Flight feathers blackish: outer 3-8 (10) primaries with pale shafts, gradually darkening towards tips (dark birds generally show restricted number of pale shafts, on less than 5% restricted to 2); undersurface of primaries basally pale. Tail feathers dark with paler bases, sometimes sharply divided from dark outer part, and with paler shafts grading to dark near tip; t1 elongated 60-105mm and pointed, creating narrow, evenly tapering tip to tail. Bill dull blackish, sometimes with paler olive-grey to brownish-grey base to, especially, upper mandible; very few show a pale bill-base as on adult Pomarine Skua. Legs and feet blackish.

Figure 88. Arctic Skua, adult summer pale morph, with complete grey breast band. Compare breast band and underparts with those of Pomarine Skua. Norway, July 1992. *Tomi Muukkonen.*

Figure 89. Arctic Skua, adult summer dark morph. Dark greyish-brown apart from darker cap and indistinct golden streaks on neck sides. Norway, July 1988. *Dick Forsman.*

Figure 90. Arctic Skua, adult intermediate morph. Note small, triangular head, and body being deepest at breast and evenly tapering towards tail-tip. Dark cap against pale hindneck and darkish-looking body typical of intermediate adults. Skagen, Denmark, August 1983. *Knud Pedersen.*

Adult summer (adult alternate) (March-November)

Pale Morph Cap blackish-brown, covering lores, crown, central ear-coverts and foreneck; forehead tinged paler, creating small pale blaze which merges into darker crown. Chin, throat, sides of head and hindneck pale with yellow to pale buff shaft-streaks. Upperparts dark greyish-brown to blackish-brown, usually showing no or very slight contrast with darker flight feathers (but contrast stronger with wear). Breast to belly whitish: many show uniform grey breast band, varying from dark patches restricted to breast sides to full band across entire breast (strength of breast band generally not related to sex: see below); flanks pale to greyish, undertail-coverts blackish-grey; may show some grey in centre of lower belly or a few dark spots on belly.

Of 79 pale adults from Scandinavia, 41 had complete grey breast band (25 males, 16 females), 23 incomplete (17 males, 6 females), and 15 lacked breast band (8 males, 7 females) (skins NRK, UZM, ZMO). In a Shetland breeding population, 49 males and 89 females were pale morph (O'Donald 1983; see also dark morph).

Dark Morph Head and body dark greyish-brown to blackish-brown; tail and flight feathers not contrasting with rest of upperparts. Cap blackish, showing little or no contrast with rest of head; pale frontal blaze frequent on all but the darkest birds. Many show dark yellow shaft-streaks on sides of neck.

In North Atlantic, dark morph is commoner among males (60-75%) than among females (Furness 1987); in another study (O'Donald 1983), dark birds included 146 males and 46 females (intermediates 183 and 224 respectively).

Intermediate Morph Most frequent type similar to dark morph, but with paler yellow sides of head and hindneck contrasting well with dark hood. Breast to belly generally paler greyish-brown than on dark morph, and on some slightly barred.

Paler intermediates (rare in North Sea, more frequent in the Baltic and probably at western part of arctic breeding range) similar to pale morph, but the underbody is dirtier, with grey spotting or barring (especially on flanks) and always dark (on some even sooty) breast band. Dark belly feathers have pale bases (O'Donald 1983).

Adult winter (adult basic) (October/November-March/April) Similar to adult summer, but with duller cap, barred tail-coverts, and more untidily patterned underparts. Tail with t1 frequently lacking or strongly worn, thus shorter than on adult summer.

Pale Morph Cap blackish-brown with narrow pale feather fringes, most prominent on central crown and hindcrown; rarely, chin, throat and neck sides also darkish (thus forming dark hood), but these areas and hindneck normally whitish with darker spots and streaks and varying amount of yellow (sometimes minute), rarely rufous tinged on, especially, hindneck. Upperparts similar to adult summer, but mantle normally with some blackish, white- or rusty-fringed feathers, sometimes divided by brown shaft-streaks (barring sometimes strong enough to create effect of pale mantle); uppertail-coverts often pale-barred, sometimes with rufous tinge, but central 2-4 feather pairs often uniform brown (Higgins & Davies 1996). Breast band grey, normally with darker spots or transverse barring (fresh feathers may be edged pale yellow to buff); breast to belly ranging from similar to summer to barred pale and grey, especially on rear flanks; undertail-coverts barred pale and dark.

Dark Morph Similar to adult summer dark morph, but sometimes with narrow whitish to rusty feather fringes and spots, especially on breast and flanks. Underbody usually with some darker barring, especially on flanks. Tail-coverts frequently pale-barred, most often on undertail-coverts, but on some individuals restricted to darker/paler shading. May show pale streaks or spots on hindneck and mantle; lacks yellow shaft-streaks on neck and sides of head of adult summer.

Figure 91. Arctic Skua, adult dark morph. Slightly paler greater coverts may be a sign of older immaturity. Norway, July 1992. *Tomi Muukkonen.*

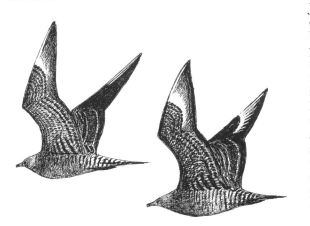

Figure 92. Juvenile Long-tailed and Arctic Skuas of similar plumage. Note difference in shape.

Juvenile (summer to February of second calendar-year) Flight feathers blackish-brown, primaries often with 1-2mm of yellowish to rusty at tips, on folded wing usually appearing as a line of small pale triangles, less frequently as narrow pale fringes similar to juvenile Pomarine and Long-tailed Skuas. (Even dark birds normally show pale primary tips.) Amount of pale primary shafts and bases as on adult, but approximately 10% show pure white to buffish bases to both inner and outer webs of primaries, creating pale upperwing patch similar to (although narrower than) that of *Catharacta* skuas, being 1-2 (4)cm broad, largest on 2nd-4th outermost primaries. Tail dark brown with paler, sometimes whitish or pale buff, base, often sharply divided from dark tip to create strongly bicoloured appearance: t1 8-22mm longer than others and 10-15mm broad, with tip pointed, although generally less sharply than on adults; t1 dark distally, rarely with indistinct pale tip or sides of webs. Bill pale grey (generally bluish-tinged, more rarely pink- or brown-tinged), with outer 30% black. Legs whitish to pale bluish-grey (rarely pinkish-grey), with outer 75% of foot black.

Plumage is notoriously variable, and division between dark and pale types clinal. Individual variation larger, with frequent pale and dark extremes. All but the darkest show pale feather fringes on upperparts, paler hindneck, short dark streaks on head and pale/dark-barred underwing-coverts.

Figure 93. Arctic Skua, juvenile, pale type. Note distinct head streaks, pale edges to lesser coverts and pale tips to primaries. Among *Stercorarius* skuas complete pale bases to primaries diagnostic of juvenile Arctic. Skagen, Denmark, September 1985. *Knud Pedersen.*

Pale Type (5-20%; very pale-headed birds 5-8%) Palest individuals have pale, orange-tinged brown head with dark spot in front of the eye. Forehead sometimes whitish; forehead, crown and sometimes rest of head may show short, dark streaks, most commonly on chin and throat (chin and throat sometimes with dark spots). Upperparts dark brown with rusty to pale buff feather fringes (a few feathers may show white edges, especially in scapulars and tertials), pale feather edges broadest on marginal and lesser coverts, scapulars and tertials (normally shows pale fringes on outer web on scapulars, tertials and coverts, generally connecting with pale edges); uppertail-coverts barred, broadly vermiculated or mottled dark and pale with rusty tinge. Breast to belly pale brown, even whitish-brown on belly, usually with a rusty tinge and slight dark barring, especially across breast and rear flanks; undertail-coverts pale with dark barring and mottling, this reduced to spots or lacking on very pale individuals. Underwing-coverts and axillaries barred dark and pale with rusty tinge; under primary coverts often pale with dark tip (but to a lesser extent than on typical juvenile Pomarine Skuas), but usually barred.

Figure 94. Arctic Skua, juvenile, pale type, Note typical silhouette, with slender, triangular head, centre of gravity at breast, and shortish-looking tail. On upperwing, note pale leading edge to arm. Also note paler neck band. Skagen, Denmark, August 1979. *Erik Christophersen.*

Intermediate Type (more than 50%) Head rusty-brown to medium brown, rarely greyish-brown. Crown normally darker, creating dark cap, and forehead frequently paler (but pale blaze weaker than on adults), both with narrow pale feather fringes. Crown, ear-coverts, chin, throat and hindneck show dark streaks, longest on ear-coverts (up to 10mm long and 4mm broad). Hindneck normally paler rusty- or orange-tinged, creating paler neck nand. Upperparts similar to pale type, but generally with narrower, deeper rusty fringes, although some show sandy fringes (rarely, a few white-fringed feathers intermixed), broadest on lesser and marginal coverts to form paler leading edge to inner wing; uppertail-coverts and rump rusty with dark mottling or wavy bars (a few show paler rump with stronger barring). Flight feathers similar to pale type, but generally with more indistinct pale primary tips. Breast to belly medium brown, rusty or foxy-brown, with denser dark bars over breast creating breast band, and darker mottling or barring on entire underbody; undertail-coverts dark with some pale barring (may lack bars; some show more distinct dark barring). Underwing-coverts similar to pale type, but generally more strongly rusty-tinged (thus looking more uniform in the field); a few percent show uniform dark underwing-coverts and axillaries (or with just narrow, indistinct pale bars, invisible in the field).

Dark Type (10-15%; wholly dark rare, less than 5%) Darkest individuals uniform brownish-black, apart from pale shafts and under-surface of bases of primaries and paler bare parts. More frequent types dark brown, with paler, deep rusty-tinged hindneck and belly. Head pattern similar to intermediate types, but on average darker with less conspicuous pale feather tips. Pale fringes to upperparts and pale barring on tail-coverts and underwing reduced compared with intermediates, but lesser upper-wing-coverts normally with rather broad rusty fringes. Most have uniform tail-coverts; pale barring or spotting strongly rusty-tinged. Primary tips rusty (but uniformly dark on some). Flight feathers and tail as on other types, but with on average less pale colour on primary shafts/bases and little or no pale on bases of rectrices.

Figure 95. Arctic Skua, juvenile, intermediate type. Rather worn individual with barely visible pale fringes to mantle feathers and unusually pale breast. Aged as juvenile on the basis of pale fringes to coverts, pointed shape to primaries, and clearly bicoloured bill. Dark tarsus spots rare on juvenile, but possibly developed in autumn. Santa Barbara, California, USA, November 1995. *Don Desjardin.*

Figure 96. Arctic Skua, juvenile, intermediate type. Note contrasting pale neck band, unmarked uppertail-coverts and pointed tail projection. Skagen, Denmark, August 1983. *Knud Pedersen.*

Note In the subsequent 3-4 years, pale birds gradually develop plumage similar to adult. This is also the case with dark individuals, but the general similarity of age-classes makes ageing more difficult.

First-winter (first basic) (December-October of second calendar-year) As juvenile, but scattered parts of head and body with more uniform pale patches. Gradually loses rusty or orange tinge and pale feather fringes through wear from end of November. Starts to develop black on tibia and 'knee' from midwinter.

In summer of second calendar-year as 'worn juvenile', lacking pale feather fringes on back and

Figure 97. Arctic Skua, first-winter/first-summer. More unevenly patterned and generally paler than juvenile. Note a few fresh, pale-fringed feathers in upper mantle, clean-looking pale nape, and black tibia. Skagen, Denmark, September 1979. *Knud Pedersen.*

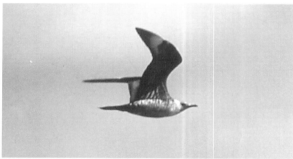

Figure 98. Arctic Skua, first-winter/first-summer. Note similarity to juvenile, but paler hindneck and underparts as well as colder-tinged plumage. Skagen, Denmark, August 1987. *Knud Pedersen.*

coverts as well as having more rounded new primaries. Upperparts greyish-brown, with (or without) a few darker, pale-fringed feathers, especially on mantle, sometimes continuing to leading edge of inner wing, and uppertail-coverts barred with whitish and blackish-brown; may retain a few juvenile feathers in this plumage (skins BMNH, ZMO). Head and underparts lose rusty tinge of juveniles, but in other respects similar to juvenile, but generally head and underbody paler, colder and less cleanly patterned, with darker bars, streaks or spots (e.g. in traces of dark cap): sides of head and hindneck dark-spotted, sometimes yellowish-tinged, hindneck normally pale with little dark mottling; central part of belly sometimes whitish against strongly dark-barred flanks. Underwing and undertail-coverts similar to juvenile, but barring on average more contrasting owing to whitish ground colour and more distinct dark bars; barring on greater underwing-coverts often less distinct. Tail with t1 more pointed than on juvenile and elongated 30-46mm. Bill pale with dark tip; generally more dirty yellowish than in juvenile plumage, with dark cutting edges or lower mandible. Legs pale, with blackish tibia and wholly black foot; tarsus with dark spotting (normally not more than 10% dark, but much variation, and exceptionally up to 90% of tarsus dark), sometimes medium grey.

Dark birds similar to dark juvenile, but duller and less warm-tinged, often with pale mottling on belly and a few rusty-fringed feathers on, especially, hindneck. Best aged by bare-part pattern. Some individuals with delayed moult become extremely worn and faded (greyish-brown) in first summer.

Second-winter (second basic) (November-March) Similar to first-summer or second-summer.

Second-summer (second alternate) (March-November of third calendar-year) Tail with t1 elongated 36-63mm and pointed. Bill greyish with black tip (outer third) and cutting edges; sometimes dark, with pale restricted to basal part of upper mandible. Legs dark, with up to 50% pale colour on tarsus (spots or pale tinge, especially in central part).

Figure 99. Arctic Skua, second-summer. Note bicoloured bill and dark-spotted breast band similar to Pomarine Skua, but also pale frontal blaze and pointed tail projection diagnostic of Arctic Skua. Juvenile-patterned underwings combined with adult-looking head and body typical of this age. Skagen, Denmark, September 1982. *Erik Christophersen.*

Pale Morph Basically adult-looking on head and body, juvenile-looking on underwing. Cap dull brownish-black, contrasting somewhat with whitish, pale grey or pale yellowish chin, throat, sides of head and hindneck; usually shows dark spots at division between cap and rest of head, as well as on chin and throat. Upperparts blackish-brown to greyish-brown, with narrow whitish feather fringes on scapulars (sometimes contrast between paler, worn second-winter feathers and darker, fresher second-summer feathers is evident, and may show light brown subterminal bars to some mantle feathers); uppertail-coverts whitish with darker barring (sometimes narrow, creating basically white rump). Breast to belly pale with varying degree of dusky barring and greyish-brown, black-spotted breast band; typically, shows distinct dark barring on flanks. Underwing-coverts and axillaries as juvenile, but barring more striking owing to lack of rusty tinge in white areas (pale barring frequently reduced, as on juveniles); may show a few blackish (lesser) coverts and axillaries.

Dark Morph Dark birds difficult to age, but those with dark head and body similar to adult combined with pale/dark-barred underwing are of 'second-summer type'.

Third-winter (third basic) (November–March) Both morphs similar to adult, but with a varying amount of pale/dark barring on underwing-coverts and axillaries and some pale on bill and tarsus.

Third-summer (third alternate) (March–November of fourth calendar-year)

Pale Morph Similar to adult, but usually with some dark/pale-barred greater and/or median underwing-coverts and generally less cleanly patterned plumage; may show some dark streaks on hindneck, making dark (and generally duller) cap less clearly demarcated from rest of head. Breast band similar to adult, but sometimes with darker spots or transverse bars, especially in lower parts. Tail-coverts dark, but frequently with a few dark/pale-barred feathers, especially below. Tail with t1 elongated 40–80mm. Bill as on adult, but sometimes with slightly paler upper mandible. Legs similar to adult, but with up to 50% pale on tarsus (especially as spots on central fore part).

Dark Morph Similar to adult, but aged by same criteria as described under pale morph. Often shows pale mottling on belly.

Fourth-winter/summer (fourth basic/alternate) As adult, but sometimes ageable by having a few dark/pale-barred feathers in otherwise uniform dark underwing. May show a few pale spots on tarsus.

Figure 100. Arctic Skua, second-summer, dark type. Skagen, Denmark, September 1981. *Knud Pedersen.*

Figure 101. Arctic Skua, third-summer. Shows few barred underwing-coverts and undertail-coverts. Hudson Canyon, New Jersey, USA, September. *Alan Brady.*

GEOGRAPHICAL VARIATION Monotypic. Considerable plumage polymorphism exists, however. Dark morph predominates in southwestern and southeastern part of the breeding range, the majority in populations from Britain north to southern Iceland, central parts of Norway, the Baltic, and again at Kamchatka and southern Bering Sea. Percentages of dark morph in breeding populations from Faeroes/Shetlands and Finland are 80% and over 95% respectively (Joensen 1966; Furness 1987; Wourinen 1992). Within southernmost populations, the smallest proportion of dark morphs is found in Outer Hebrides (50-70%) and in northern Iceland (60-65%). About 50% of the birds are dark in southern Greenland, northern Norway and southern Alaska, but in northern Greenland only 6% (Salomonsen 1967). There has been an increase in percentage of dark morphs since 1940: at Varanger, northern Norway, 45% before 1952 and 58% in 1976-78 (O'Donald 1983), with a similar but smaller increase within the Shetland population (Furness 1987).

Through the middle part of the breeding range (northern Iceland and Norwegian coastline) there is a clinal change towards domination by pale morphs, but east of northern Norway pale morphs are totally predominant. Dark morphs are virtually unknown in arctic Canada and Siberia east of Novaya Zemlya. In Spitsbergen, Bear Island, northern Greenland and high arctic Siberia, 92-99% are pale (Salomonsen 1967; Glutz von Blotzheim & Bauer 1982; O'Donald 1983; Furness 1987; Norderhaug 1989; Isakson *et al.* 1995).

VARIANTS Albinism is regular in the North Atlantic islands (as high as 2% in certain populations). Such birds show pale marginal and lesser coverts, creating a pale leading edge to the inner wing similar to that of adult female Marsh Harrier *Circus aeruginosus*, and many also have paler areas elsewhere, especially as a pale patch in the central and lower parts of the belly, but also as isolated pale coverts and distinct pale spots on the head. This partially albinistic type occurs in all age-classes (skins UZM; C.J. Camphuysen *in litt.*). A few cases of partially albinistic individuals with asymmetrical white spots on the upperwing are known.

Two cases of wholly albinistic birds are known to us. Both are juveniles and appear all white with pale yellowish bare parts (skin UZM; G. Andersen pers. comm.).

MEASUREMENTS in mm. Own measurements; skins BMNH, NNH, NRK, UZM, ZMA, ZMH, ZMO, ZMU. Several parts of West Palearctic breeding range; juveniles North Atlantic and western Europe, late August.

Wing length

Adult male	301-345	(319.9)	112
Adult female	310-347	(323.4)	136
Juvenile male	290-323	(306.7)	47
Juvenile female	294-323	(312.0)	43
Second-summer	308-329	(317.5)	23
Third-summer	305-344	(321.5)	21

Note: In a study from east Murman, Russia, average for 136 adult males 321.8, for 120 adult females 326.8 (Belopolskii 1961), these larger averages probably a result of measuring live birds. Two first-summer birds 311 and 321 (skins UZM, ZMO). Recently fledged juveniles by end August down to 245.

Projection of t1 (tail-tip projection)

Adult male summer	60-105	(81.4)	45
Adult female summer	54-90	(76.3)	54
Adult winter	21-68	(45.7)	16
Juvenile	8-26	(16.4)	90
First-summer	30-62	(43.8)	7
Second-summer	29-75	(49.1)	30
Third-summer	47-10	(65.3)	20

Bill length

Adult male	28.0-35.0	(31.2)	217
Adult female	29.0-38.8	(31.8)	227
Juvenile	26.7-32.0	(29.0)	88
Second-summer	27.7-31.9	(30.4)	30
Third-summer	28.1-32.5	(30.4)	24

Note: Juvenile bill averages 3.5 shorter when recently fledged.

Bill depth at gonys

Adult	7.8-10.1	(9.1)	311
Juvenile	7.5-9.0	(8.0)	83
Second-summer	8.3-10.0	(9.1)	41
Third-summer	8.7-10.0	(9.2)	35

Note: Average for adult male 8.6, for adult female 9.5.

Bill depth at base

Adult	9.5-11.7	(11.1)	316
Juvenile	8.2-11.0	(9.4)	87
Second-summer	9.1-11.5	(10.7)	40
Third-summer	9.4-12.0	(10.8)	35

Note: Average for adult male 11.0, for adult female 11.1.

Gonys length

Adult	5.9-8.3	(7.2)	313
Juvenile	5.6-7.9	(6.8)	83
Second-summer	6.3-8.3	(7.3)	39
Third-summer	6.5-8.3	(7.4)	35

Note: Adult male and female identical.

Tarsus length

Adult	37.3-50.8	(42.2)	325
Juvenile	36.6-45.4	(41.3)	90
Second-summer	38.2-46.0	(41.4)	40
Third-summer	38.3-46.1	(41.4)	35

Note: Tarsus identical for adult male and female; mean for juvenile male 40.6, for juvenile female 41.7.

WEIGHT in grams.
Breeding adults, different parts of range: male 301-568 (n=234), female 306-697 (n=229) (Belopolskii 1961; de Korte 1972; Furness 1987; skins ZMA). Non-breeders (Spitsbergen and Greenland) and wintering adults within the given ranges.
Juvenile 417-520; weak juveniles (Netherlands) 219-271 (ZMA). One first-summer 290 (skin ZMA).

FOOD In the breeding season the Arctic Skua is not especially bound to rodents, taking all available small invertebrates, fish (especially sand-eels *Ammodytes*) and plants (crowberries *Empetrum* frequently a major part of chick diet); does not, however, ignore rodents. Rarely fishes for itself, most fish being obtained by kleptoparasitism. Birds are freely taken, and may constitute more than 90%

Figure 102. Arctic Skua, juvenile pale type, chasing juvenile Common Tern *Sterna hirundo*. Note complete white bases to primaries, creating white wing patch similar to that of *Catharacta* skuas, and bicoloured tail. Skagen, Denmark, August 1983. *Knud Pedersen.*

of the diet in tundra habitats (Furness 1987); the largest species known to have been killed is Ptarmigan *Lagopus mutus* (Eisenhower & Paniyak 1977). In more coastal and southerly breeding areas, Arctic Skuas often nest in rather loose colonies close to seabird colonies, which are heavily exploited. In tundra habitats, they breed as solitary pairs or in loose groups. Densest populations are found in the vicinity of Black-legged Kittiwake *Rissa tridactyla* and Atlantic Puffin *Fratercula arctica* colonies in the North Atlantic, especially in the Faeroes and northern Britain. Puffins are sometimes robbed of sand-eels which they are carrying back to their nest in the bill, but direct physical attacks are rare (Taylor 1979). Solitary pairs consume rather more terrestrial food than colonial breeders.

Outside the breeding season, the Arctic Skua feeds almost exclusively by kleptoparasitism, especially on terns and smaller gulls, although rare cases of scavenging and feeding at sewage outfalls are known (particularly juveniles). It often chases birds up to the size of large ducks and gulls, and often attempts direct attacks on small shorebirds and passerines (especially passerines migrating over the sea). It sometimes takes food from the surface, but probably less frequently than do Pomarine and Long-tailed Skuas, and is less prone to follow trawlers than the larger skuas.

BREEDING This species has the widest distribution of the *Stercorarius* skuas, penetrating farther south and being less tied to tundra than Long-tailed and Pomarine Skuas. Several hundred thousand pairs breed circumpolarly from Scotland across the Swedish and Norwegian west coast and through Siberia to Alaska, Greenland, Iceland and the Faeroe Islands, with an isolated population in the Baltic Sea. The Russian population is estimated at 100,000-200,000 birds (Il'icev & Zubakin 1990). Sweden was estimated to hold 370-380 pairs in the mid 1980s, probably with some local increase in the 1990s; the Kattegat population has decreased slightly, at a time of increase in the Baltic population (Ahlén & Tjernberg 1992; Betzholtz & Swenzén 1992). There has also been an increase in Finland, following cessation of persecution by hunters, from 240 pairs in 1983 to 400-450 pairs in 1995 (Ulfvens *et al.* 1988; Koskimies 1992; Laine 1996). In Norway, the population was estimated to number 5,000-10,000 pairs in 1990; a decrease here was probably a result of poor food supply (Gjershaug *et al.* 1993). Other populations have been estimated at 3,350 pairs in Scotland, 1,200-1,500 in the Faeroes, 4,000 in Iceland, up to 10,000 in Greenland and Spitsbergen respectively, 40 on Bear Island, 30 on Jan Mayen, and maybe 200,000 in Canada and Alaska combined (Bloch & Sørensen 1984; Evans 1984; Furness 1987).

The Arctic Skua breeds on arctic tundra, moorland, low rolling country and sheltered grassy fields, preferably close to streams and small ponds and with large tussocks or rocky eminences, which are used as lookouts. Certain populations breed on small islands. While most breeding sites are near the coast and in the vicinity of seabird colonies, this species sometimes nests up to 10km inland. There are cases of Arctic Skuas breeding successfully for several years on golf courses in Shetland (R. Thorne *in litt.*). Breeding sites are occupied in the last half of April in the southernmost part of the range, eggs being laid in mid May on Fair Isle (O'Donald 1983).

MIGRATION AND WINTERING
Spring Spring migration starts in March, southernmost breeding sites being reached in April. The movement passes quickly, Arctic Skuas normally staying for some days in an area only if terns and smaller gulls are present, and showing less tendency to concentrate in flocks than do Pomarine and especially Long-tailed Skuas. Up to 64 have been noted in one day at the end of April in Senegal (Marr & Porter 1992). In the Red Sea, 67 were noted in spring 1993 in South Yemen (Porter *et al.* 1996), while farther north, at Eilat, Israel, 300-500 are counted yearly, peaking late April-May, with a total of 1,104 in 1983, mostly in late April; this passage heads in a northerly direction at a great height overland. More than 95% of the birds noted at Eilat are pale morphs, indicating a northern and eastern origin (Krabbe 1980; Shirihai 1996; own observations); from the end of April immatures gradually become more prominent, dominating the passage from late May. In the eastern Mediterranean (Bardawil, Egypt), Arctic Skua outnumbers Pomarine Skua

3:1 (U.G. Sørensen *in litt.*); most Mediterranean observations are of singletons.

The spring migration in Britain and Ireland is more regular but much less conspicuous than that of Pomarine and Long-tailed Skuas, usually occurring in small groups of up to eight, but mostly singly or in pairs (Davenport 1984).

Figure 103. Arctic Skua, juvenile dark and intermediate types. Even intermediates sometimes show uniform dark underwing-coverts, contrasting well with paler belly (never so on juvenile Pomarine and Long-tailed Skuas). Such birds aged by bicoloured bill and shape/length of central pair of tail feathers. Skagen, Denmark, September 1985. *Klaus Malling Olsen.*

In Scandinavia, the proportions of dark and pale morphs differ geographically. Along the Danish west coast dark morphs predominate, the migration peaking around mid May, with only 20-30% pale-morph adults, mostly in latter half of May (own observations, Skagen), and noted to be 39% in June (Nyrup 1992); a similar percentage of pale birds is found in south Sweden (Jönsson *et al.* 1990; Ekberg & Nilsson 1994). These percentages of pale birds are too low to indicate any heavy passage along western shores of south Scandinavia. In the Baltic and Finland, migration consists mainly of pale morphs, peaking in the latter half of May (Kapanen 1977). The time of peak migration in southern Scandinavia matches that of Common Tern *Sterna hirundo*, a pattern also seen at Eilat (Shirihai 1996).

In Pakistan and Japan, this species is regular in spring, but scarcer than Pomarine Skua (Ali & Ripley 1969; Brazil 1991).

Autumn In northern Europe, the first part of the migration consists mainly of immatures and non-breeding adults, peaking in July and the first part of August, when up to 30% are immatures (own observations); the same pattern was found by O'Donald (1983), who mentions that the first breeding adults leave the breeding sites by early August. Late summer sees a growing number of adults, whose numbers peak late August to first half of September. Up to mid September pale-morph and dark-morph adults are equally represented, whereafter pale morphs gradually predominate to reach more than 90% in October (own observations); an unusually heavy passage of several hundred individuals in Uppland, Sweden, on 18th September 1994 consisted of about 90% pale adults (Douhan 1995a, 1995b). The first juveniles are noted south of breeding sites in the latter half of August, juvenile passage peaking in the second half of September, in some years into mid October. In Sweden, Hirschfeld (1985) found adults to represent 80% before 1st September and just 10% after. In November, the Arctic Skua is much scarcer than Pomarine Skua in northern Europe.

Several routes are followed in Scandinavia. A major one crosses northern Finland and heads towards the central Baltic, with considerable passage sometimes noted in Uppland (see above). Migration is more scattered further north in Scandinavia, with 139 on 7th September 1994 in Västerbotten the largest day count; part of the north Baltic migration crosses overland towards the great Swedish lakes of Vänern and Vättern, where up to 100-150 Arctic Skuas are noted each autumn at certain sites, eventually reaching the Kattegat. Another route follows southern Finland southwards to the southern Baltic (Hirschfeld 1985), where up to 100 have been noted in one day along the south Swedish (north to Revsudden) and the Danish east coasts. The largest migration route in western Europe follows the North Sea, being noted on both Scandinavian and British coasts, and heading southwards towards the Bay of Biscay via e.g. the English Channel: there are yearly counts of 2,000-3,000 at Blåvandshuk, western Denmark

(Meltofte 1979), and autumn day counts of up to 200 in Denmark, more than 300 on Heligoland, 318 in Kent and 420 in Norfolk; fewer pass western parts of the British Isles, with day counts of up to 100 in Ireland (Hutchinson 1989).

Annual numbers in Scandinavia vary less than those of Pomarine and Long-tailed Skuas, but juveniles are normally most numerous in autumns when percentages of juvenile Pomarine and Long-tailed Skuas are also high, indicating good breeding success in peak lemming years. For example, 1994 saw 75% juveniles at certain Swedish inland sites, corresponding with good passage of juvenile Long-tailed Skuas (Darefeldt 1995; Tyrberg 1995).

Farther south, scattered individuals occur inland in most of Central Europe, where numbers are equal to those of Pomarine and Long-tailed Skuas (Seitz & von Wicht 1980), the inland migration of all three in Europe consisting mainly of the less experienced juveniles and immatures. In the eastern Mediterranean, the Black Sea and the Red Sea, Arctic Skua is regular but scarce; up to 15 in one day have been noted at Haifa, Israel, and 116 in August-September 1981 at north Sinai (Petersen & Sørensen 1981). In Senegal, Arctic Skuas are common in late August (Baillon & Dubois 1991).

Arctic Skua outnumbers Pomarine in the Gulf of Mexico, and is regular on the Texas coast, with migration heading both southwest towards the east coast of Central America (probably continuing to the Pacific Ocean) and southeast (Williams 1965). Up to 200 smaller skuas have been noted in one day along the North American east coast in autumn (mainly September-November). As with Pomarine and Long-tailed Skuas, the majority have probably arrived following migration overland, as indicated by the large number of single records of all three species in inland North America.

Few data are available from the Pacific, but the species is much scarcer than Pomarine Skua in Japan (Brazil 1991) and is accidental in Hong Kong. In California, the daily maximum of 27 is the lowest noted among the *Stercorarius* skuas. The easternmost Siberian populations probably move down the western Pacific, passing Sakhalin and the Kuriles and migrating rather directly to wintering grounds off Australia and New Zealand. Some probably follow a more westerly course to pass Java and Sumatra through the Sunda Strait before reaching Western Australia (van Balen 1991; Higgins & Davies 1996). The species has, however, been noted as scarcer than Pomarine Skua in Southeast Asian waters, with scattered records from Borneo, Bali, north Sulawesi and New Guinea.

Winter The main Atlantic wintering grounds of Arctic Skuas are between 30°S and 50°S. Ringing recoveries of British and Baltic breeders have proven wintering on both sides of the Atlantic (Furness 1987). Concentrations of several hundreds are found at the Benguela Current off Namibia and South Africa, and off Patagonia in South America. The species is scarce but regular in winter in the Gulf of Mexico, the Caribbean, and in the western Atlantic northwards to Florida and North Carolina (Root 1988; Stiles & Skutch 1989), although both Arctic and Pomarine Skuas winter in small numbers on the Great Lakes. In the northeast Atlantic, a few Arctic Skuas winter off Morocco (own observations) and in the Mediterranean, but further to the north Arctic Skua is much scarcer than Pomarine at this season; it is regular along the British North Sea coast (Lack 1986), but with only random observations in Scandinavia (Christensen *et al.* 1996).

Larger concentrations winter in the Pacific around southeast Australia, New Zealand and at the Humboldt Current off western South America (Murphy 1936; Glutz von Blotzheim & Bauer 1982; Higgins & Davies 1996), with up to 100 in certain places. Smaller numbers occur regularly in winter northwards on the Pacific coast of Central America to California (Small 1974; Root 1988; Stiles & Skutch 1989).

This species' winter distribution in the Indian Ocean is unclear, but it is probably regular eastwards to Papua New Guinea. It is rare in East Africa, with scattered records from Kenya, Tanzania and Madagascar in winter, but is likely to be regular (but overlooked) on spring migration.

Most immatures remain in the winter quarters in their first summer, but a larger percentage migrate north in their second summer. In Greenland, 38% of all recoveries of birds ringed as chicks were in their second summer (Salomonsen 1967).

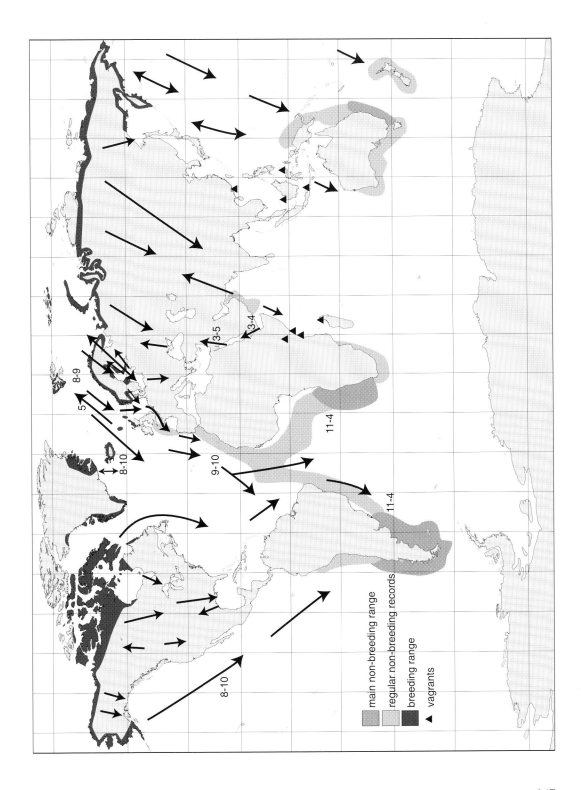

main non-breeding range

regular non-breeding records

breeding range

▲ vagrants

l

7　LONG-TAILED SKUA
(Long-tailed Jaeger)
Stercorarius longicaudus

Plates 9, 10, 11, 12

FIELD IDENTIFICATION Long-tailed Skua is the smallest and lightest skua. It is about the size of Black-headed Gull *Larus ridibundus*, although large individuals overlap with small Arctic Skuas. Differences in jizz are the pointer: Long-tailed Skua has a shorter and rounder head and longer and a narrower body and tail, appearing triangular and tapering behind the slender wings. The breast is deep and the belly flat, creating a typical 'body-builder' look. The tail is always longer than the width of the arm. The wings are narrower than those of Arctic, especially the hand, which is slightly longer than the arm. The

Figure 104. Long-tailed Skua, adult summer. With wear, feathers around bill sometimes become paler, creating pale blaze as on Arctic Skua, but less distinct. Skagen, Denmark, September 1987. *Knud Pedersen.*

short head is accentuated by the short, rather heavy bill, which is proportionately heavier than Arctic Skua's. Long-tailed shows just 2 (3) pale primary shafts in the upperwing, forming a narrow but complete pale line on the forewing, has two-toned upperwings and (apart from juveniles) lacks a pale primary patch below.

Figure 105. Long-tailed Skua of ssp. *pallescens*, adult summer. Note white breast and central belly. Kolyma, Siberia, Russia, July 1993. *Hanne and Jens Eriksen.*

The flight is lighter than that of Arctic Skua, with weaker wingbeats and much more gliding: even in moderate winds, Long-tailed Skua often uses shearwater-like flight for several hundred metres without flapping. Sometimes, it flaps for longer periods in low, tern-like flight, suddenly interrupted by short intervals of 'shear-watering', or in higher active flight reminiscent of the active flight of Black-legged Kittiwakes *Rissa tridactyla*. Shearwater-type flight is always adopted in strong winds, when Long-tailed Skua often in fact resembles a shearwater, but its true identity as a skua is suggested by the angled wings. The active flight is buoyant, with body moving up and down in time with the wingbeats. The light flight and the skeleton-slender jizz are often striking

when a Long-tailed Skua turns up on a seawatch dominated by Arctic Skuas. Soaring birds sometimes bear some resemblance to smaller falcons. Adults in particular have a tern-like jizz in flight.

Long-tailed Skuas attack victims in much the same way as Arctic Skuas do, but generally less eagerly. When watching a Long-tailed Skua for some time, the observer may be struck by the oddly 'playful' nature of its flight, which is interrupted by periods of snatching food from the surface in the manner of Little Gull *Larus minutus*, brief attacks on terns and gulls (opportunistic,

149

last-minute affairs, according to McGeehan 1995) and sometimes hovering. It also hunts insects at considerable heights, like Black-headed Gull or falcons. Juveniles often land on fields to feed on insects and worms. Weakened individuals are reported to eat carrion, including corpses of their own species.

On migration, Long-tailed Skuas sometimes occur in large, well-ordered flocks (up to 180 together noted in Shetland in May) with a nucleus at the front and the remainder trailing behind in a narrow line, recalling migrating terns (Davenport 1991).

Figure 106. Long-tailed Skua of ssp. *pallescens***, adult summer. Note white of breast penetrating onto belly, isolating grey flanks. Nome, Alaska, USA, June 1986.** *J.L. Dunn.*

Adult summer This skua occurs only as a pale morph. The concolorous dark cap and bill create a black helmet against pale neck sides and breast. The best characters on distant birds are the pale breast gradually shading into the grey belly, creating a pale breast patch against all-dark surroundings, as the underwing is uniformly dark (with just a pale shaft to the outer primary). The upperparts on the other hand are bicoloured, being pale grey to brownish-grey with contrasting black flight feathers and tail. The tail projection is normally much longer than on other skuas, somewhat recalling Arctic Tern *Sterna paradisaea*; in active flight, the central feather pair waves about in the wind. From summer, these feathers are often broken off, and on autumn migration they are often missing. The tarsus is mostly pale, unlike that of other adult skuas.

The existence of a dark-morph adult is still to be proven. Note, however, that about 30% of juveniles are dark, developing pale plumage when adult. (Any details which could cast light on the possible occurrence of dark breeding-plumaged adults will be much appreciated by the authors.)

Adult winter In winter, adults resemble immatures apart from their uniformly dark underwing. They have a variable dark cap (sometimes restricted to a mask around the eye) and pale underparts with dark spotting and/or barring on breast and flanks, often creating a dark breast band similar to that of adult summer Arctic Skua, or an 'untidy' greyish-mottled underbody (at distance sometimes darkish-looking). The upperparts are similar to summer plumage but generally darker, with contrasting pale-fringed mantle and scapulars sometimes creating a pale saddle. Uppertail- and undertail-coverts are often pale/dark-barred. The tail projection is much shorter than in summer plumage, and frequently lacking; rarely, the two central rectrices are slightly rounded, as on juveniles (see photographs of adult winters from Australia).

Figure 107. Long-tailed Skua, adult winter. Note uniform dark underwing, diagnostic of Long-tailed Skua. Winter plumage characters are grey head markings, dark breast band, and short (and in this case slightly rounded) tail projection. Wollongong, New South Wales, Australia, February 1986. *Alan McBride.*

Juvenile Juveniles are cold brownish-grey, never with the orange or rusty coloration typical of juvenile Arctic Skua. Compared with Arctic Skua, the tail projection is more conspicuous, being both longer and broader (slightly rounded at tips), and normally striking at distances when it cannot be judged on juvenile Arctic. In addition, juvenile Long-tailed Skua shows a short, rounded and 'compressed' head, a deeper breast and a much more slender and attenuated hindbody than Arctic Skua. The arm is narrower than the length of the tail, the latter being reinforced by the long central rectrices, forming a rounded spike when the tail is folded. The narrow base to the tail is emphasised by the pale barring on uppertail- and undertail-coverts. The wings are narrower than on Arctic Skua, although the wingtip may be slightly rounded up to early autumn. In gliding flight, the slender wings and long tail produce an almost skeleton-like impression compared with Arctic Skua. Differences in jizz between the two can be compared to the differences between Common *Sterna hirundo* and Arctic Tern (see Malling Olsen & Larsson 1995).

Settled birds are often confiding, unlike Arctic Skuas. When seen at close range, the bill differs from that of Arctic and Pomarine Skuas in that the gonys is as long as the inner part of the lower mandible, and never sharply marked. The outer 50% of the bill is black, making pale areas indistinct even at close range. The position of the nostril is also different: the distance between the loral point and the inner part of the nostril is shorter than the distance between the outer part of the nostril to the bill-tip; on Arctic and Pomarine Skuas, the reverse is the case (Ullman 1990).

Figure 108. Long-tailed Skua, juvenile, pale type. Note pale grey head against pale breast, and slightly rounded shape to elongated tail feathers. New York, USA, September 1989. *Anthony Tierno.*

Figure 109. Long-tailed Skua, juvenile, dark type. Typically, dark types with blackish-brown head and underbody still show pale barring on underwing- and undertail-coverts. Note length and shape of tail projection. Skagen, Denmark, September 1985. *Knud Pedersen.*

Figure 110. Long-tailed Skua, dark juvenile.

Juvenile Long-tailed Skuas are as variable as juvenile Arctic Skuas, generally with better contrasts in the plumage. They are greyish, always lacking any warm coloration. Pale birds appear almost white-headed or have a whitish belly, with strong dark and pale barring on both uppertail- and undertail-coverts and bicoloured upperparts. Intermediates typically have a darker cap against cold yellow to greyish hindneck, a broad dark breast band accentuated by a striking pale patch in the central breast, strongly barred underparts, and often conspicuous whitish mantle barring. Dark individuals are sooty-black, often with surprisingly distinct white bars on the undertail-coverts and narrow but still conspicuous white mantle barring. The majority of juveniles show clear dark and pale bars on the underwing-coverts and axillaries, usually creating a pale underwing contrasting with darker body. Further points to concentrate on are:

151

1. Tail projection up to 4cm, with slightly rounded tips (and sometimes white fringes), appearing striking even at range; typically, length of projection similar to length of bill (almost always shorter on any other juvenile skua).

2. Normally just 2 outer primaries show pale shaft.

3. Dark juveniles frequently lack visible barring on uppertail-coverts, looking uniform above apart from a slightly paler hindneck.

4. Mantle and upperwing-coverts show whitish fringes, even on otherwise dark birds; on Arctic Skua fringes are rusty to orange, with only scattered white-fringed feathers, not forming contrasting pale saddle.

5. The pale bases of the undersurface of the primaries are generally narrower than on Arctic Skua.

6. Under primary coverts barred as rest of underwing-coverts, only very rarely paler-based to form the pale 'double patch' common on Arctic Skua.

7. Underwing-coverts and axillaries strongly pale-barred on all but very dark individuals, creating paler underwing than body; on Arctic Skua, general pale coloration on underwing mirrors coloration on underparts.

8. Primary tips dark or with only very narrow pale fringes.

9. A juvenile skua appearing strikingly greyish with white head and/or belly is a Long-tailed (such birds give the impression more of first-year Common Gull *Larus canus* than of Arctic Skua); and a juvenile skua with grey head and breast against white belly is also Long-tailed.

10. Pale individuals may show whitish leading edge to inner wing, created by pale tips to marginal and lesser upperwing-coverts.

Figure 111. Long-tailed Skua, juvenile, intermediate type. Note dark cap and uniform grey breast band against paler hindneck and upper breast. Pale primary patch generally narrower than on Arctic Skua. Contrast between darker belly and paler underwing barring distinguishes it from most Arctic Skuas. Skagen, Denmark, September 1985. *Knud Pedersen.*

Figure 112. Long-tailed Skua, first-winter/first-summer. Tail projection barely visible as two spikes. Note pale juvenile primary patch. Nayanguing Point, Maine, USA, August 1981. *Michael Brown.*

First-winter/first-summer Similar to juvenile, but mantle and upperwing-coverts are plain greyish-brown, and underparts cleaner whitish, making breast band and sometimes dark hood more striking. Darker individuals develop a paler hindneck, but retain a predominantly dark head and underbody, the latter often distinctly pale-barred. The mantle often appears pale-scalloped. The tail projection has sharply pointed tips and is generally longer than on juvenile. The bill is duller, with dark tip and cutting edges. Begins to show dark tibia at this age.

Second-winter Similar to adult winter, but with barred underwing as on juvenile. The darker brown mantle feathers show whitish fringes, often creating strong transverse barring to form a pale saddle. Head and body plumage varies. The darkest birds are dark, with uniform underwing-coverts similar to adults (or with just very narrow pale barring, often invisible in the field), but often show a paler lower belly (Hario 1986).

Figure 113. Long-tailed Skua, second-summer. Note juvenile-looking head pattern combined with dark breast band, whitish belly and uniform dark underwing. Norrbotten, Sweden, July 1992. *Göran Pettersson.*

Second-summer Head and body similar to adult summer, but the cap is normally browner and duller, more poorly demarcated from sides of head and neck owing to the presence of short dark streaks or spots. The underparts vary a great deal, and some show a dark breast band or hindbody, although the belly is generally paler than on adults; the flanks usually show distinct dark barring. Underwing-, undertail- and uppertail-coverts are still predominantly pale-barred, but parts of (or all) underwing-coverts and axillaries may be uniformly dark. The primaries are adult-like, uniformly dark but with pale shaft to outer primary visible. Some also acquire adult underbody and underwing coloration at this age. The upperparts show a slight contrast between dark brown mantle and coverts and blackish flight feathers, the contrast at this and earlier ages being similar to that shown by adult Arctic Skua. The tail projection is generally shorter than on adult summer, but often strikingly longer than on any Arctic Skua.

Third-winter/third-summer Similar to adults, and the majority are probably identical. Some, however, show a few pale-barred underwing-coverts and, in summer, traces of a grey breast band and a paler belly than adults.

Fourth-summer Similar to adult, and the majority are identical. Some have a combination of shorter tail projection and dark patterning on the underparts (bars on flanks, spots on belly) and a few pale-barred underwing- and tail-coverts.

Figure 114. Long-tailed Skua, second/third-summer. Those showing as much dark on underparts as this individual probably had dark juvenile plumage. Note few barred rump feathers. Sweden, June 1971. *Michael Sundström.*

VOICE Most common call heard on the breeding grounds is a short series of *krit-krit-krit*, different from the mewing calls of Arctic Skua. In territorial disputes also a rattling *krr-krr-r-r-r-...* (Cramp & Simmons 1983, which see for detailed summary).

MOULT

Adult Moult from summer to winter plumage is complete. Head and most of body are moulted October-December, following arrival on wintering grounds (Melville 1985). A minority (probably failed breeders) start in July with minor parts of head and mantle; more frequently, some dark, pale-fringed mantle feathers present from late September. Sequence of head and body moult otherwise crown, neck, mantle, chest, flanks, tail-coverts, rest of head, belly and vent, and smaller scapulars. Moult of larger scapulars, back, rump, tail and wing between November and late February/March, generally later than in Arctic Skua (Higgins & Davies 1996; A. McBride *in*

Figure 115. Long-tailed Skua, adult, of nominate race in autumn, lacking tail projection.

litt.). Tail moult starts with t1, in a few moulted late June (skins UZM, ZMA), but in 50% still present during autumn migration in September-October, sometimes new t1 growing by early October; tail moult may start with t2; t4-5 are the last to be renewed. Moult of flight feathers starts after arrival in winter quarters (but in failed breeders from late July) and is completed by April; by December, primary moult has reached inner 4-6. Secondaries moulted in two series, ascendant and descendent, meeting centrally, sometimes before moult of primaries.

Moult to adult summer plumage is partial, including head, body and t1, in March-April, immediately before leaving winter grounds. Growth of t1 takes 30-40 days; may be growing end of March. May retain a few feathers from winter plumage, especially in mantle, scapulars, back, rump and undertail-coverts.

Juvenile Moult to first-winter plumage complete, on wintering grounds. The moult is later than in adults. Head and body are moulted October-February, flight feathers January-June, but often delayed to summer/autumn of second calendar-year, with t1 and outer primaries still growing by July/August; sometimes primary moult has just reached inner 5 by August. Probably, some head and mantle feathers are moulted again during spring. Tail moult starts with t1, followed by t2 or t4-5; a bird from Australia had not renewed t1 in early February when rest of the tail had been renewed (Higgins & Davies 1996).

Subsequent immature moults Moults directly from first-winter to second-winter, thus no genuine first-summer plumage. Moult to second-winter may start July-August, mostly starting with t1; flight feathers are moulted from late autumn on wintering grounds, generally later than in adults.

Subsequent moults are similar to adult moult. De Korte (1985) mentions that moult from second-summer to third-winter may start in June. Thus, plumage in autumn of third calendar-year may be a mixture of new and old feathers. Often, underwing-coverts and axillaries are moulted June-November. Primary moult starts November; two of four birds had changed innermost primaries and had new t1 in November (de Korte 1985). During immaturity, sometimes renews smaller amount of head and body feathers than adults in each moult.

DETAILED DESCRIPTION

S. l. longicaudus (West Palearctic to Siberia, east to Lena Delta)

Adult Flight feathers black with pale shafts on outer 2-3 (shaft of the third often intermediate in coloration between whitish outer and black inner ones), a few percent having up to 4 (exceptionally 5) outer primaries pale-shafted; outer and inner webs of primaries dark, rarely with up to 3-4 pale bases to inner

Figure 116. Long-tailed Skua, adult summer. Note good contrast between greyish upperparts and blackish flight feathers, only two pale primary shafts, and short dark bill. Norway, June 1985. *Gordon Langsbury.*

webs of outer 1-2 primaries. Underwing-coverts and axillaries blackish-grey; sometimes, a few median underwing-coverts show indistinct pale outer webs, invisible in the field. Bill dull blackish, often with dark olive to greyish-brown tinge at base. Tarsus and tibia pale grey with variable amount of dark spots, a minority (especially females: Cramp & Simmons 1983) having black tibia and tarsus; foot black; hindtoe black on more than 90% (de Korte 1985). Very old birds (probably more than 12 years old) may show all-dark legs (de Korte 1985); sometimes, one leg dark and the other with pale tarsus.

Adult summer (adult alternate) (March-October) Cap from base of upper mandible to hindneck black, glossy when fresh, with wear duller (rarely, brown-tinged with some pale at base of bill in autumn: fewer than 0.5% from late July to onset of moult to winter plumage). Chin, cheeks, sides of head and hindneck whitish to pale yellow, deepest on chin, but sometimes as complete yellow band on upper breast, contrasting with whitish breast. Mantle, scapulars and upperwing-coverts lead-grey to brownish-grey (rarely with narrow, indistinct dark shaft-streaks). Flight feathers and tail blackish, becoming browner with

Figure 117. Long-tailed Skua of ssp. *longicaudus*, adult summer. Note black cap and bill creating single complete black 'unit', bicoloured upperparts, and pale breast gradually merging into grey belly. Unlike other adult skuas, shows pale tarsus. Norway, June 1985. *Gordon Langsbury.*

wear. Tail with t1 elongated 125-246mm. Breast whitish, gradually shading to dark grey on belly and undertail-coverts; upper breast sides sometimes grey.

Sexes similar; female averages darker than male, but much overlap; 6% of adults show paler central upper belly (Cramp & Simmons 1983; see Geographical Variation). In general, males show stronger yellow tinge to breast than females, more frequently penetrating to breast and upper belly.

Full dark adult (said to be blackish-brown apart from 1-2 pale primary shafts) still requires documentation: in breeding populations, no dark individual showing a combination of all adult age-characters has been proven. Dark morph, if it exists at all, is extremely rare, and in our view could equally well be a melanistic variant. Dark birds from Greenland in summer (Salomonsen 1950) shown to be dark immatures (Glutz von Blotzheim & Bauer 1982). Specimen described in Cramp & Simmons (1983) as dark-morph adult is to our eyes a subadult, as it shows pale

Figure 118. Long-tailed Skua, adult winter. Same individual as in figure 107. Note bicoloured upperparts and pale barring on upper mantle. Wollongong, New South Wales, Australia, February 1986. *Alan McBride.*

mottling on belly (own observation, skin UZM), but in other respects is adult-type, with t1 elongated more than 150mm. A bird from Brazil with all-dark legs also showed uniformly dark plumage apart from faint pale barring on rump and flanks and pale grey feather tips on belly (Vooren & Chiaradia 1989); this could be a dark winter plumage. Other claims of dark-morph adults (Harrison 1983; Veit 1985) are probably referable to dark immatures.

Adult winter (adult basic) Cap brownish-black or greyish with pale feather fringes (cap less distinct than on adult summer), sometimes appearing pale-streaked. Cheeks, chin, sides of head and hindneck whitish with a variable amount of brownish spots and streaks. Some have dark eye mask and narrow dark cap on otherwise pale head. Hindneck may be uniformly pale, but sometimes with strong grey

Figure 119. Long-tailed Skua, adult winter (moulting greater underwing-coverts) and adult winter Pomarine Skua. South Australia, February 1983. *Alan McBride.*

or brown tinge, together with dark cheeks and throat creating hooded appearance; sometimes shows strong buff to orange streaks on hindneck, soon lost through wear. Upperparts darker grey than on adult summer, with less contrast between coverts and flight feathers, some showing whitish to pale buff or pinkish feather tips and edges to mantle (to a lesser degree scapulars); rump and uppertail-coverts barred pale and dark, but sometimes uniformly dark. Tail with t1 projected 40-100mm (on average 50% of length of adult summer), sometimes with whitish tips or sub-terminal spots; a minority show slightly rounded t1 (photographs, Australia). Breast and belly off-white to pale brown or medium grey with variable amount of dark spotting and barring, often creating dark breast band; flanks often darker greyish with strong transverse barring, this continuing onto lower belly and vent; undertail-coverts barred dark and white, sometimes uniform grey.

Juvenile Primaries blackish with 2-3, rarely 4 and exceptionally 5 pale shafts: normally, outer 2 shafts are whitish and third outer-most is intermediate in coloration; on birds showing 4-5 pale primary shafts, the inner of these is intermediate. Primary tips dark or with very narrow whitish to greyish-yellow fringes, exceptionally as whitish spots at tip; in general, inner primaries show broadest pale fringes. Undersurface of primaries pale as on juvenile Arctic Skua, but pale normally restricted to basal 20-30% of primaries (2-4cm at bases on inner primaries, 4-5(7)cm on outer), creating narrower pale area; on fully spread wing, may create a larger pale area (Hardwick 1993). Tail with t1 elongated up to 4cm and with slightly rounded tip, often with distinct pale fringes, and some-times with pale spots near tip or whole edge pale (with wear, tip becomes darker and

Figure 120. Long-tailed Skua, juvenile, intermediate type. Note coldish overall impression, dark cap contrasting well with pale hindneck, pale breast patch, and white transverse barring on mantle. Also note indistinct pale edges to pri-maries (distinct on Arctic Skua). Skipsea, East Yorkshire, England, October 1994. *J.M. Bayldon.*

slightly pointed, thus appearing arrow-shaped (Knolle 1994 and *in litt.*); rest of tail similar to adult, but with broader paler bases and sometimes scattered pale subterminal bars or spots (Higgins & Davies 1996). Bill pale grey (with bluish, more rarely brownish, greenish or pinkish tinge), with outer 40-50% black, often including cutting edges; gonys generally flatter and always longer than on Arctic Skua (see Measurements). Legs whitish to greyish with bluish or pinkish tinge; outer 62-78% of foot black; hindtoe white to pale pinkish.

Variation between pale and dark types continuous; no relationship with adult summer plumage, as approximately 30% of juveniles are more or less dark.

Figure 121. Long-tailed Skua, juvenile, pale type. Note position of pale breast patch, length of gonys, and colour division on bill. Weld County, Colorado, USA, October 1993. *David A. Leatherman.*

Pale Type (10-20%) Palest types have head and belly (on palest also breast) whitish-grey to pale yellowish-grey. Forehead and crown (sometimes also rest of head and neck) show indistinctly darker spots or short streaks; dark eye-crescent often prominent (probably more than on pale juvenile Arctic Skua: P. Knolle *in litt.*). On birds showing densest spotting on crown, hindneck contrastingly whitish to yellowish-grey, on extremes creamy. Mantle, scapulars, tertials and upperwing-coverts greyish-brown with distinct whitish feather fringes, creating scaly pattern, often covering whole of feather tips; sometimes shows dark tongue to near tip of especially scapulars; in rare cases, a few rusty-fringed feathers intermixed in upperparts. Marginal coverts often whitish or greyish-yellow, creating pale leading edge to inner wing; primary coverts and greater coverts darker, with narrower whitish to pale grey fringes and streaks on outer webs, isolated from pale tips. Uppertail- and undertail-coverts distinctly and evenly barred blackish and white. Breast to belly sometimes shows darker barring and variable degree of dark-shaded breast band. Underwing-coverts (including primary coverts) and axillaries barred dark and whitish, most conspicuous on axillaries and greater coverts;

on minority (1 out of 300) bases of under primary coverts are paler, creating indistinct pale 'double patch', but less conspicuous than on Pomarine Skua.

Intermediate Type (40-60%) Head, cheeks and throat greyish-brown with dark spots or short streaks (chin and throat may have grey streaks up to 10mm long); cheeks, throat and hindneck generally paler, on hindneck creating cold yellowish-grey to pale grey neck band contrasting with crown and mantle (pale hindneck often palest part of upperparts). Upperparts similar to pale type, but on average darker and with narrower pale feather fringes, contrasting less with dark flight feathers (though contrast normally visible under good field circumstances); uppertail-coverts distinctly white/dark-barred, contrasting well with rest of upperparts (in rare cases, a slight brown hue

Figure 122. Long-tailed Skua, juvenile, intermediate type. Note shape, greyish-brown overall impression, barred mantle, and dark streaks on hindneck. Helmsand, Germany, September 1985. *Alex Halley.*

has been noted in pale barring: Knolle 1994). Breast to belly greyish-brown to pure grey, breast band rather uniformly grey and with just extreme feather tips pale; central part of lower breast paler, often in good contrast to breast band; rest of underbody with variable darker barring, especially on flanks. Underwing- and undertail-coverts as on pale type, frequently with narrower pale barring.

Figure 123. Long-tailed Skua, juvenile, dark type. Note contrasting pale hindneck against dark cap and breast, cold yellowish mantle barring, and distinct white bars on undertail-coverts. Belgium, September 1996. *Michel Watelet-Cornet.*

Dark Type (25-35%) The darkest extremes (1-2%) are uniformly blackish-brown (apart from primaries, described above), including all-dark underwing-coverts, axillaries and tail-coverts, but still show very narrow whitish fringes to mantle and scapulars. More frequent dark types have white and blackish barring on underwing-coverts, axillaries and tail-coverts (especially undertail-coverts), but pale bars often narrower than on intermediate types, though still in good contrast to dark body, and frequently tinged greyish-brown; hindneck often slightly paler than head and body, tinged pinkish-buff to greyish-brown (exceptionally deeper yellow). Often lacks pale fringes to t1.

First-winter/first-summer (first basic/first alternate) (March-October of second calendar-year) Similar to juvenile, but back and upperwing-coverts uniform dark greyish-brown, apart from mantle and scapulars often showing narrow pale feather fringes. Head (especially hindneck) and body generally paler and less patterned than on juvenile; may show traces of dark cap (rarely adult-looking), cold yellow tinge to neck sides and dark breast band, generally more heavily spotted than on juvenile. Sometimes shows whitish, almost unspotted central belly. New primaries have uniform dark surface as on adults (a few show pale bases to outer

Figure 124. Long-tailed Skua, first-winter/first-summer. Note paler hindneck and belly than on adult, less bill contrast (owing to darker cutting edges), uniform wings, and fresh blackish, pale-fringed mantle feathers. Scania, Sweden, August 1984. *Magnus Ullman.*

primaries); primary tips more rounded than on juvenile. Tail with sharply pointed t1 elongated 10-80mm, often with off-white to pinkish-buff tip or edges. Bill similar to juvenile but duller, with brownish to yellowish-grey tinge and larger amount of dark at cutting edges; sometimes dark apart from pale basal part of upper mandible. Legs similar to juvenile, but 75-100% of foot black; hindtoe pale (6% show blackish hindtoe: de Korte 1985).

Dark birds show rather uniformly dark head and underbody, but usually have traces of pale hindcollar and pale mottling and barring on underbody, especially on lower belly. Some have rather plain grey head and breast in clear contrast to white belly; flanks usually with distinct dark bars (skins UZM, ZMA). Underwing similar to juvenile; may show a few uniform dark feathers intermixed with barred juvenile-type.

Second-winter (second basic) (November-March) Varies. Basically similar to adult winter, but with pale/dark-barred underwing-coverts and axillaries. The palest birds show pale greyish-

Figure 125. Long-tailed Skua, first-winter/first-summer. Some develop darker cap and breast band at this age. Skagen, Denmark, September 1986. *Knud Pedersen.*

yellow head and neck, whitish belly, and transverse pale bars on dark mantle. Tail-coverts barred as on juveniles. Dark birds have variably pale belly, sometimes in good contrast to dark head, but sometimes just with narrow pale bars. Upperwing-coverts dark brown with variable pale feather edges. Tail with t1 pointed and elongated 2-4cm. A few individuals seemingly develop basically dark (thus adult-like) underwing, and may be indistinguishable from adult winter.

Second-summer (second alternate) (March-November of third calendar-year) Much variation; generally shows combination of adult-like head and body but barred underwings, darker upperparts and shorter tail projection. Many have head and underbody similar to adult summer, but generally with duller,

less sharply defined cap (often with narrow pale feather fringes on forehead or with brownish-grey feathers intermixed in black cap) and short dark spots or streaks on sides of head and hindneck, less frequently on chin and throat. Some are dark-headed, with only faintly paler sides to neck. Upperparts darker greyish-brown than on adult summer, similar to adult summer Arctic Skua but generally colder-tinged; some mantle and scapular feathers blacker, with whitish fringes or spots (especially fresh mantle feathers); uppertail-coverts uniform or barred white and black (pale barring generally narrower than in younger age-classes). Breast to belly pale, less clean than on adult, with variable degree of dark-spotted or uniform

Figure 126. Long-tailed Skua, second-summer. Note bicoloured bill, traces of dark cap, heavily spotted sides of neck and breast, upperparts darker than adult's, and pale barring on lower belly. Skagen, Denmark, August 1985. *Knud Pedersen.*

grey breast band (frequently lacking), dark barring on flanks and dark spots on belly. In tail, t1 varies from as long as on adult summer to much shorter (see Measurements). Bill as adult, but frequently with paler nail. Legs pale with some dark spots; foot black, sometimes with small amount (up to 7%) of pale colour (de Korte 1985); hindtoe pinkish, in 21% black.

The darkest birds have dark head and underbody with indistinct paler wavy markings or barring, especially on flanks and lower belly; undertail-coverts dark or with variable pale barring (distinct on some birds). Underwing-coverts and axillaries still juvenile-patterned, but pale bars on average narrower, and a larger percentage than in Arctic and Pomarine Skuas have partly or wholly dark underwing; majority, however, retain some barred median/greater coverts and axillaries (barred underwing-coverts and axillaries moulted from late summer and replaced by uniform or less clearly barred feathers).

Third-winter (third basic) (November-March/April) Similar to adult winter, but with some pale/ dark-barred underwing-coverts and, more rarely, axillaries. May show several generations of feathers in head and body at this age, creating untidy look. Birds with wholly dark underwing generally inseparable from adult winter.

Figure 127. Long-tailed Skua, third-summer. Note traces of grey-spotted breast band, paler belly than on adults, and a few pale-barred median coverts. Skagen, Denmark, August 1986. *Knud Pedersen.*

Third-summer (third alternate) (April-November of fourth calendar-year) As adult summer, but often with duller, slightly pale-mottled hood, dark spots on chin and throat, and some grey barring on flanks, belly and undertail-coverts (may be traces from winter plumage); often also shows pale barring on (especially greater and median) underwing-coverts. May show dark bars or spots on breast, creating ill-defined dark breast band. Upperparts much as adult, but on average darker and more brownish-tinged. Projection of t1 much as on adult summer, but never exceeding 20cm; rectrices otherwise as adult, but sometimes with larger amount of white at bases and off-white spots at edges or tips (Higgins & Davies 1996). Bill as adult. Legs pale with a variable amount of dark spotting (dark probably increases with age); whole surface of foot black; hindtoe blackish, pale in 9% or fewer.

Distinction between second-summer and third-summer often problematic; many individuals are best assigned to 'immature type, second/third-summer'.

Fourth-summer (fourth alternate) (March-October of fifth calendar-year) Normally identical to adult summer; individuals showing combination of shorter-than-average tail projection, some pale barring on underwing- and tail-coverts, and slight dark barring on flanks and spots on belly are probably of this age (Hario 1986).

GEOGRAPHICAL VARIATION Two subspecies: differences very slight.

S. l. longicaudus (Scandinavia and northern Russia east to about Taimyr) Described above.

S. l. pallescens (Greenland, Nearctic and eastern Siberia to Kolyma Delta and Taimyr) Adult summer averages paler-bellied than nominate *longicaudus*, having grey on underparts partly replaced by whitish: 50% of adults show whitish breast and belly to undertail-coverts (just faint grey on lower belly and flanks), 44% have pale upper belly, and only 6% have dark belly as on typical *longicaudus* (skins UZM, ZMA; Cramp & Simmons 1983). Female averages darker than male, but much overlap (though pure white belly rare on female). In other respects identical to *longicaudus*, but yellow across lower neck and breast generally warmer and narrower, on many forming narrow but distinct band.

Intermediates between *longicaudus* and *pallescens* occur to an unknown extent in Siberia between Indigirka and Novosibirskiye Ostrova and also on Spitsbergen (Il'icev & Zubakin 1990; Cramp & Simmons 1983), and clinal variation is not clear; a certain proportion of dark-bellied birds from North America are similar to *longicaudus*, as are 30% of Greenland birds. With complete overlap in measurements, the valididy of *pallescens* seems arguable, and this form could well represent clinal variation.

Other plumages of *pallescens* are probably identical to *longicaudus*, but pale-headed juveniles are more frequent in North American populations (own observations).

VARIANTS No proven cases. A white-headed juvenile, described as 'partial albinistic' (Norman 1985), is probably no more than an extreme pale-headed individual.

MEASUREMENTS in mm. Own measurements; skins BMNH, MLU, NNH, NRK, UZM, ZMA, ZMH, ZML, ZMO, ZMU. Different parts of range. Measurements for *longicaudus* and *pallescens* similar, with complete overlap; combined in measurements below.

Wing length

Adult male	283-327	(307.2)	144
Adult female	294-334	(310.4)	135
Juvenile male	276-314	(297.2)	45
Juvenile female	282-306	(297.6)	32
First-summer	286-306	(294.3)	9
Second-summer	283-324	(301.3)	37
Third-summer	295-324	(310.6)	14

Projection of t1 (tail-tip projection)

Adult	125-265	(182.5)	193
Juvenile	(8) 15-38	(24.4)	88
First-summer	8-82	(37.0)	19
Second-summer	46-181	(97.3)	44
Third-summer	(18) 65-213	(138.3)	14

Bill length

Adult	24.0-32.5	(28.4)	294
Juvenile	23.8-30.5	(27.2)	187
First-summer	25.0-30.3	(27.1)	10
Second-summer	25.5-31.5	(28.2)	41
Third-summer	26.4-31.5	(27.9)	14

Bill depth at gonys

Adult	7.5-10.0	(8.8)	197
Juvenile	7.2-9.5	(8.4)	84
First-summer	8.2-9.9	(8.9)	10
Second-summer	8.4-12.5	(9.4)	35
Third-summer	9.0-9.6	(9.3)	14

Note: Average for adult male and adult female identical.

Bill depth at base

Adult	8.5-11.2	(9.8)	196
Juvenile	8.0-10.5	(9.5)	83
First-summer	9.5-12.0	(9.8)	10
Second-summer	9.4-11.4	(10.1)	37
Third-summer	9.8-11.4	(10.2)	14

Note: Average for adult male 9.8 (n=16), adult female 9.3 (n=14) (skins UZM, ZMA).

Gonys length

Adult	(6.4) 6.9-10.3	(8.4)	196
Juvenile	6.6-9.3	(8.0)	83
First-summer	8.1-9.2	(8.7)	10
Second-summer	7.1-10.2	(8.3)	50
Third-summer	7.5-9.3	(8.4)	14

Tarsus length

Adult	37.3-47.8	(42.3)	278
Juvenile	35.7-43.5	(40.2)	68
First-summer	38.4-40.1	(39.2)	10
Second-summer	36.0-43.6	(40.5)	38
Third-summer	39.8-43.1	(41.1)	14

WEIGHT in grams.

Subspecies *pallescens* (Greenland, Alaska): male 218-352 (n=115), female 258-444 (n=124); failed breeders generally less heavy (Furness 1987). Weakened immatures or adults from Brazil 218-236 (Vooren & Chiaradia 1989). Australian males 234, 360.

Juvenile 165-257 (Glutz von Blotzheim & Bauer 1982; Cramp & Simmons 1983; skins UZM, ZMA); 4 weakened juveniles from Netherlands 163-214 (skins ZMA; C.J. Camphuysen *in litt.*). second-summers 245-355 (17 skins NRK, UZM, ZMA). Starving immatures, Australia, 178, 207 (Higgins & Davies 1996).

Nominate *longicaudus* probably similar: in July, 4 adult males 260-295, 2 females 352 and 365 (ZMA).

Figure 128. Juvenile Long-tailed Skua 'dip-feeding'.

FOOD Although a rodent specialist in the breeding season, this skua also takes all available smaller prey such as insects and passerines, as well as vegetable matter (berries), during that period (Maher 1974; de Korte 1976).

Outside the breeding season, it exploits a wider range of food sources than Arctic Skua. While it feeds mostly by kleptoparasitism during the autumn migration, it also regularly hovers, catching insects or fish by direct hunting. Juveniles are often recorded feeding on worms and smaller animals on newly ploughed fields in autumn, a habit unknown for Arctic Skua. In winter, most Long-tailed Skuas probably feed by fishing for themselves, although they frequently attack terns and smaller gulls and have been seen to rob Wilson's Storm-petrels *Oceanites oceanicus* during migration (Lambert 1981; Brady 1988). They regularly pick food from the surface.

BREEDING Tens of thousands of pairs of Long-tailed Skuas breed from central parts of Scandinavia across arctic Siberia, Alaska and Canada to Greenland; there are scattered breeding records from Scotland and Spitsbergen (Furness 1987; Norderhaug 1989). Estimates of the breeding population include (in pairs) Sweden 10,000, Finland 1,000, Norway 1,000-5,000, Greenland up to 10,000, and tens of thousands in Russia, Alaska and Canada respectively (Furness 1987; Koskimies 1992; Gjershaug *et al.* 1993; del Hoyo *et al.* 1996). A rough assessment put the Russian population at 200,000-250,000 individuals (Il'icev & Zubakin 1990).

Breeding sites are occupied between late May and early August, a shorter period than among other skuas. This species breeds on the arctic tundra, from the coastline to the fringes of the wooded tundra. Generally it is more of an inland breeder than Arctic Skua, preferring dryer ground with lookouts such as rocks and boulders. In upland zones it breeds at up to 1300m and often far inland, making daily feeding flights of several hundred kilometres in the breeding season (Cramp & Simmons 1983).

MIGRATION AND WINTERING Most of the migration passes well offshore at both seasons, and is thus observed more irregularly from land-based seawatching points than the passage of Arctic and Pomarine Skuas. This is the most pelagic of the skuas in winter, too.

Spring The wintering grounds are left in April and the first part of May. The majority migrate far out at sea, well out of sight from land. At Eilat, Israel, this is the scarcest of the *Stercorarius* skuas in spring, with yearly totals of 5-30, but an exceptional 95 in 1983. Off Senegal, 24 passed during 21st-28th April 1992, often associated with Sabine's Gulls *Larus sabini* (Marr & Porter 1992). Spring passage in the North Atlantic peaks in a short period in the latter half of May.

Most of the movement passes through central parts of the Atlantic, where hundreds or even thousands have been noted in late May (Wynne-Edwards 1935; Block & Sørensen 1984), with land-based observations recorded mainly at the Faeroe Islands and off western Britain. Particularly large numbers have been counted in the Outer Hebrides, the peak time coinciding more or less with the later part of Pomarine Skua passage (Davenport 1981, 1984, 1991): the largest day count was 1,268 in North Uist on 18th May 1992 (Murray 1994), with flocks of up to 180, the largest flock at sea being of 244 northwest of North Uist on 15th May 1992. As with Pomarine Skua, Long-tailed is rare and irregular on spring migration in western south Scandinavia and the Baltic.

Figure 129. Long-tailed Skua, adult winter. Distinct barred tail-coverts and dark-spotted breast band differ in comparison with figures 107 & 118. Note much longer tail projection than in figures 118 & 135. South Australia, January 1983. *Alan McBride.*

There is little information from the Pacific. The species is noted as regular but scarce in Japan at the end of May, on average two weeks after the peak for Pomarine and the scarcer Arctic Skua, and as regular off California and probably the American east coast (Austin & Kuroda 1953; Brazil 1991).

In summer, Long-tailed Skua is scarce throughout areas between the breeding and wintering grounds, but a small percentage of immatures turns up at breeding sites (Hansen 1984; de Korte 1985). According to de Korte (1985), 2-year-olds do not hold territories, pairing at the age of 3 years. Small but regular numbers of immatures are seen during the breeding season at Eilat (Shirihai 1996) and also scattered in southern waters, e.g. around Tristan da Cunha, and in the tropical Pacific off Ecuador. The regular, but sparse, observations from southern Scandinavia between June and mid August are mostly of immatures (Bertel 1994).

Autumn Autumn migration starts at the beginning of August. The timing is similar to that described under Arctic Skua; numbers are generally lower, but show a much wider yearly variation. In north-

western Europe juveniles normally outnumber adults (Nyrup 1992), probably because breeding adults migrate directly to the west after breeding and move into the central Atlantic before turning south, a major proportion of the more experienced adults thus dispensing with any pre-migration dispersal. In northern Europe, the largest passage occurs along the British east coast, especially in the north (Sharrock 1974; Dymond *et al.* 1989). The North Sea is probably preferred as being better for feeding in hard weather conditions than the rougher Atlantic (Sharrock 1976), but it also attracts large gatherings of terns and gulls which the skuas exploit for feeding; the largest day counts here consist of 126 (see influx years below). An unprecedented migration of adults was noted during 6th-11th August 1995, with 850 passing the Highlands and Humberside, seeking a short cut to the Atlantic. The species is scarcer along the British west coast and Ireland, where up to 15 have been recorded in one day.

Figure 130. Long-tailed Skua, juvenile, dark intermediate type. Sometimes shows combination of pale hindneck band and almost unbarred uppertail-coverts. Note distinctly pale-barred undertail-coverts. Skagen, Denmark, September 1982. *Knud Pedersen.*

In Scandinavia, Long-tailed is the scarcest of the *Stercorarius* skuas in autumn. It generally follows the routes mentioned under Arctic Skua, although it is relatively scarcer in eastern Denmark than at the Swedish lakes and the Baltic. Day counts of more than 5-10 are the exception, although larger numbers have been noted during influxes of juveniles. The most recorded in Sweden is 240, in autumn 1994 (Tyrberg 1995).

The largest passage in the southern part of the English Channel is of 131 passing Oostende, Belgium, in autumn 1994, with day counts of up to 24 (Driessens 1995). Until its removal from the Dutch rarities committee list in 1992, 93 records had been accepted for the Netherlands (Wiegant *et al.* 1994).

Figure 131. Long-tailed Skua, juvenile. Very dark type, with just faint barring on undertail-coverts but uniform underwing-coverts. Note tendency for tail to appear wedge-shaped when tightly closed. Scania, Sweden, September 1991. *Hans Larsson.*

Massive influxes into the whole of north-western Europe were noted in the autumns of 1988, 1991 and 1994 (cf. Pomarine Skua). In 1988, 2,333 were recorded in the North Sea area, of which 714 were in Denmark and 1,224 in Britain, atypically involving both adults and juveniles; numbers peaked at the end of September to the first part of October, with the maximum in Denmark (74) on 8th October at Blåvandshuk (Dunn & Hirschfeld 1991; Malling Olsen 1992). In autumn 1991, over 5,000 were noted in the British Isles (3,000 of these along the north-east coast) and 350-400 in Denmark: this influx, consisting mainly of juveniles, was most conspicuous in September, with a peak in the first week, when 300 were counted on 5th-6th at Møle, western Norway, and about 2,000 in Britain during 5th-8th (largest number 245 at Cullercoates, Tyne & Wear, on 7th); several smaller waves followed. The 1991 influx was also noted in southern Sweden and Germany, although numbers were lower (Risberg 1990; Ekberg & Nilsson 1994; Deutsche Seltenheitenkommission 1994). A smaller invasion occurred in autumn 1994, in Britain totalling 970, of which 500 were in September, with a maximum 126 on 1st at Sheringham, Norfolk (Golley & Millington 1994): this influx was also noted in southern Scandinavia, especially in the south Baltic in September, with 50 at Revsudden, Kalmar Sound, the highest seasonal total; more than 90% of the Baltic birds were juveniles (G. Gustafsson pers. comm.; own observations).

In all the peak years mentioned above, presumably large breeding numbers in northern Europe were combined with favourable weather for observing skuas during the migration period. Lemmings were present in the southern part of arctic Scandinavia in 1996, but this did not lead to any significant influx being recorded, as winds during the autumn were for a long period most unfavourable for seawatching in southern Scandinavia. The annual numbers seen in recent years in Britain range from 161 to 5,350 individuals.

Along the south coast of the Baltic and in Central Europe, Long-tailed Skua is both more frequent and more numerous than Arctic Skua (Seitz & von Wicht 1980; Glutz von Blotzheim & Bauer 1982). In Polish collections, there are 52 skins of autumn Long-tails compared with 15 of Arctic Skua (Tranda 1961). In autumn 1976 alone, 40 Long-tailed Skuas were reported in Central Europe. In the Bodensee (Lake Constance) area of Switzerland/Germany, there were 269 records between 1961 and 1981, compared with 138 Arctic Skuas (Schuster *et al.* 1983), but in other parts of Central Europe Long-tailed is considered the scarcest of the skuas (Glutz von Blotzheim & Bauer 1982). Juvenile Long-tailed Skuas are probably more prone to migrate overland than juveniles of other species, but larger numbers of Long-tailed Skuas inland may also be explained by their particular habit of landing in fields, as well as their tameness, making them easy goals for hunters. In the Mediterranean and the Black Sea, there are only scattered observations in autumn, the most being seven in north Egypt in May 1981 (U.G. Sørensen *in litt.*).

In autumn 1990, 104 were recorded at Cape Verde, Senegal, the largest daily number being 69 on 30th August (Baillon & Dubois 1991). Migrating Long-tailed Skuas are hardly ever seen further to the south, but have been noted in many areas as vagrants, including several well inland in Africa.

The timing of migration in North America is similar to that in the West Palearctic, but the migration is less known. On the west coast, 5-35 are noted off Oregon each autumn, but larger numbers in 1988 included 193 and 100 off Westport, Washington, on 27th and 20th August respectively (Mattocks 1989); in California, day counts in September peaked at 46 off Monterey and 57 in Humboldt Bay. Along the east coast, there are scattered records southwards to Florida. As with Pomarine and Arctic Skuas, several stragglers have been found inland in North America.

Winter Most Long-tailed Skuas probably winter in the same areas as Arctic Skuas, mostly around 35°S. In the Atlantic, the largest concentration recorded was 220 at the Benguela Current between Angola and

Figure 132. Long-tailed Skua, first-winter/first-summer. Same individual as in figure 124. Scania, Sweden, August 1984. *Magnus Ullman.*

South Africa (Lambert 1980; Urban *et al.* 1986), but this area is seemingly used irregularly, with more frequent observations at the Agulhas Bank and Agulhas Current south of the Cape (Ryan 1989). In the western Atlantic, a large movement of up to 1,500 individuals daily was noted during 4-7 November 1920 off Argentina (Cramp & Simmons 1983). Most of these birds were believed to have been immatures. Probably, most winter off both sides of South America, especially off Patagonia and at the Falkland Current between 39°S and 45°S; up to 500 have been observed 250-400km east of Argentina between these latitudes (Veit 1985; Lee 1989). Further to the north there are only scattered records, e.g. from Brazil (Sick 1993).

Figure 133. Long-tailed Skua, second-summer. Note uniformly dark underwing combined with poorly developed head markings and pale belly. Percentage developing adult underwing at this age is probably higher than in Arctic and Pomarine Skuas, though the majority still show distinctly pale/dark-barred underwing. Tail projection similar to adult. Skagen, Denmark, August 1985. *Erik Christophersen.*

In the western Pacific, Long-tailed Skua winters regularly off southeast Australia (Higgins & Davies 1996; A. McBride *in litt.*), arriving by September and leaving in April/May, with most records from January. An influx of a few dozens occurred off northern New Zealand in January 1983, probably related to the exceptionally severe El Niño of 1982/83 (Melville 1985); in the same year, an influx was noted in eastern Australia, mostly at Sydney Head, New South Wales, but with records also from Queensland and Northern Territory. This species is rarely recorded in Southeast Asia, with only a few records from Hong Kong, Indonesia and Papua New Guinea.

It is possible that Long-tailed Skuas concentrate at upwellings in the South Pacific between 40°S and 50°S, an area hardly ever visited by ornithologists (Furness 1987).

Figure 134. Long-tailed Skua, third-summer. Note pale rump barring and worn upperparts. Skagen, Denmark, August 1986. *Knud Pedersen.*

Figure 135. Long-tailed Skua, adult winter. This individual shows dark cap present on many adult winter *Stercorarius* skuas. Note dark markings on breast, pale-barred undertail-coverts, and white mid-wing line created by pale bases to secondaries (visible during greater-covert moult). Wollongong, New South Wales, Australia, January 1985. *Alan McBride.*

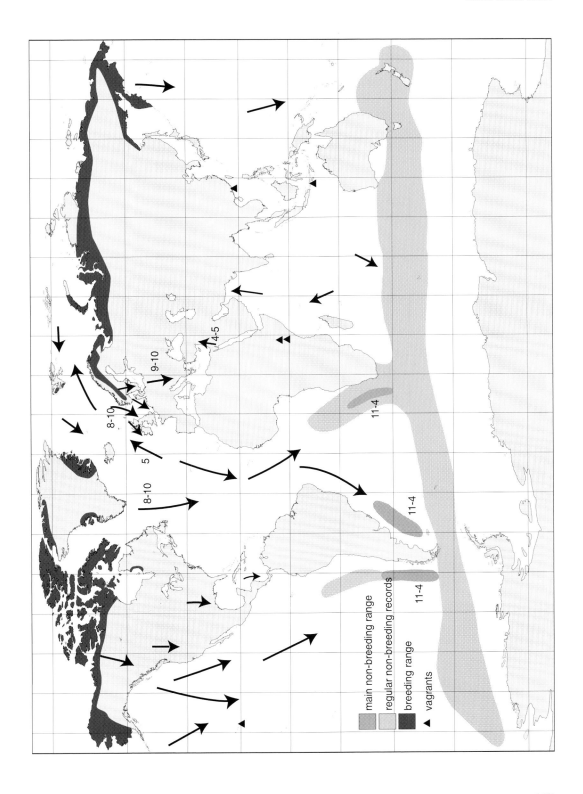

main non-breeding range

regular non-breeding records

breeding range

11-4

vagrants

Figure 136. Great Skua, adults. Note distinct dark cap (but also traces of pale spotting on crown) against yellow streaking on neck sides. Mantle and upperwing-covert pattern varies; on left-hand bird mantle is strongly pale-spotted, but when this is the case coverts also are strongly pale-patterned (unlike on southern *Catharacta* skuas). Shetland, June 1993. *Gordon Langsbury*.

Figure 137. Great Skua, adult in aggressive display. Note irregular pale spotting on head and breast, variation in head and mantle pattern, and sometimes brown tinge to underwing-coverts. Shetland, June 1993. *Gordon Langsbury*.

Figure 138. Brown Skua, adult of ssp. Subantarctic Skua *lonnbergi*. Note blackish-brown overall impression, with dark hood, irregular whitish blotching on mantle and scattered pale streaks on otherwise dark coverts. Flat crown and very heavy bill create fiercer appearance than on other skuas. Torrett Point, Antarctica, December 1995. *Phil Palmer.*

Figure 139. Brown Skua, displaying adults of ssp. Subantarctic Skua *lonnbergi*. Certain individuals show 'woolly' whitish patterning on hindneck (continuing to mantle). South Georgia, December. *Alan Tate.*

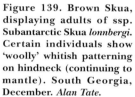

Figure 140. Brown Skua, adult of ssp. Tristan Skua *hamiltoni*. Similar to Subantarctic Skua, but smaller, with warmer tinge to hindneck and neck sides (and also mantle streaks). Tristan da Cunha, December 1993. *Anders Andersson.*

Figure 141. Brown Skua of ssp. Falkland Skua *antarctica*. Note coldish dark brown overall impression, pale frontal blaze, and cold yellow hindneck streaks. Upperwing-coverts typically more uniform, with restricted pale patterning compared with Great Skua. Carcass Island, Falklands, December 1995. *Phil Palmer.*

Figure 142. Brown Skua of ssp. Falkland Skua *antarctica*. Often uniformly dark-looking in flight. Note uniform dark upperwing and scattered goldish spots on mantle. Falklands, December. *Ko de Korte.*

171

Figure 143. Chilean Skua, adult. Note dark cap in good contrast to reddish head and underparts, strong yellow streaks on hindneck and neck sides, warm tinge to upperpart feathering, and slightly bicoloured bill. Beagle Channel, Argentina/Chile, August. *Ko de Korte.*

Figure 144. Chilean Skua, adult with Kelp Gull *Larus dominicanus*. Upperpart contrast similar to Great Skua, thus unlike most southern *Catharacta* species apart from certain Falkland Skuas. Note also dark hood against clean pale surroundings. Tierra del Fuego, February. *Alan Tate.*

Figure 145. Chilean Skua, adult. Note bicoloured bill and dark cap resembling Pomarine Skua, but strong reddish tint on underparts, and densely pale-spotted breast and overall shape as in other *Catharacta* skuas. Tierra del Fuego, November 1994. *Howard Nicholls.*

Figure 146. South Polar Skua, pale morph adult displaying. Note cold creamy head and underparts against all-dark-looking upperparts and wings. Deception Island, Antarctica, January 1978. *Ko de Korte.*

Figure 147. South Polar Skua, intermediate morph adult. Note dark face and traces of paler mantle, creating saddle against dark upperwing-coverts. Compare short gonydeal angle with that of Brown Skua. Peterman Island, Antarctica, December 1995. *Phil Palmer.*

Figure 148. South Polar Skua, dark morph adult. Note cold blackish-brown head and body apart from paler hindneck streaking. Hydrugga Rocks, Antarctica, December 1995. *Phil Palmer.*

Figure 149. Pomarine Skua, adult summer, pale morph. Note gull-like jizz with heavy, hooked bill and rounded head. Upperparts blackish-brown, the darkest among the *Stercorarius* skuas. Barrow, Alaska. June 1995. *Alex Halley.*

Figure 150. Pomarine Skua, adult summer pale morph. Note S-shaped outline to underbody, deep belly, blob-ended tail, and complete dark surroundings to belly, producing isolated white belly patch. North West Territories, Canada, June 1976. *Allan Kjær Villesen.*

Figure 151. Pomarine Skua, second-summer dark type. Ageing possible by pale tarsus spots and short tail projection. Spitsbergen, July. *Ko de Korte.*

Figure 152. Arctic Skua, adult summer dark morph. A particularly dark individual, almost lacking yellow streaks on sides of neck. Shetland, June 1993. *Gordon Langsbury.*

Figure 153. Arctic Skua, adult summer pale morph. Individual with only partial grey breast band. Shetland, June 1993. *Gordon Langsbury.*

Figure 154. Long-tailed Skua, adult summer of ssp. *longicaudus*. Note that upperparts and belly appear concolorous. Also very long tail projection. Northern Norway, July 1992. *R.F. Dickens.*

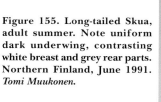

Figure 155. Long-tailed Skua, adult summer. Note uniform dark underwing, contrasting white breast and grey rear parts. Northern Finland, June 1991. *Tomi Muukonen.*

Figure 156. Long-tailed Skua, juvenile pale type. Note whitish head and underparts, cold grey upperpart barring, distinct dark barring on flanks, and dark distal half of bill. Zealand, Denmark, August 1996. *Peter Koch.*

BIBLIOGRAPHY

Ahlén, I., & Tjernberg, M. 1992. *Artfakta. Sveriges hotade och sällsynta ryggradsdjur 1992*. Databanken för hotade arter.

Ahlgren, C.-G. 1994. Fåglar i södra Älvsborg 1993. *Fåglar i Södra Älvsborg* 20: 70-98.

Ainley, D.G., Howell, S.H., & Wood, R.C. 1986. South Polar Skua breeding colonies in the Ross Sea region, Antarctica. *Notornis* 33: 155-163.

— & Jacobs, S.S. 1981. Seabird affinities for ocean and ice boundaries in the Antarctic. *Deep Sea Research* 28A: 1173-1185.

—, Spear, L.B., & Wood, R.C. 1985. Sexual color and size variation in the South Polar Skua. *Condor* 87: 427-428.

Alerstam, T. 1982. *Fågelflyttning*. Förlaget Signum i Lund AB.

—, Gudmundsson, G.A., & Larsson, B. 1995. Tundra-fåglarnas flyttning och flygvägar. *Vår Fågelvärld* 54/1: 18-21.

Ali, S., & Ripley, S.D. 1969. *Handbook of the Birds of India and Pakistan*. Vol. 3. Oxford University Press.

Andersen, C., *et al.* 1992. Fugle og dyr i Nordjylland 1991. Rapport nr. 28 fra Nordjysk Ornitologisk Kartotek. Skive, Denmark.

Andersson, Å., & Staav, R. 1980. *Den häckande kustfågelfaunan i Stockholms län 1974-1975*. pp. 145-147. Stockholm.

Andersson, M. 1971. Breeding behaviour of the Long-tailed Skua *Stercorarius longicaudus*. *Ornis Scandinavica* 2: 35-53.

— 1973. Behaviour of the Pomarine Skua *Stercorarius pomarinus* with comparative remarks on Stercorariinae. *Ornis Scandinavica* 4: 1-16.

— 1976a. Predation and kleptoparasitism in a Shetland seabird colony. *Ibis* 118: 208-217.

— 1976b. Population ecology of the Long-tailed Skua *Stercorarius longicaudus*. *J. Anim. Ecol.* 45: 537-559.

— 1976c. Social behaviour and communication in the Great Skua. *Behaviour* 58: 40-77.

— 1981. Reproductive tactics of the Long-tailed Skua *Stercorarius longicaudus*. *Oikos* 37: 287-294.

— & Götmark, F. 1980. Social organization and foraging ecology in the Arctic Skua: a test of the food defendability hypothesis. *Oikos* 35: 35-61.

Andrew, D.G. 1994. Spring passage of skuas in Outer Hebrides. *Scottish Birds* 17: 172.

Anon.1992. Bird News October 1992. *Birding World* 5: 368-369.

Arnason, E., & Grant, P.R. 1978. The significance of kleptoparasitism during the breeding season in a colony of Arctic Skuas *Stercorarius parasiticus* in Iceland. *Ibis* 120: 38-54.

Ash, J.S. 1983. Over fifty additions of birds to the Somalia list. *Scopus* 7: 54-79.

Ash, J.S., & Shafeeg, A. 1994. The birds of the Maldives. *Forktail* 10: 3-32.

Austin, D.L., & Kuroda, N. 1953. *The Birds of Japan, their status and distribution*. Cambridge, Mass.

Backström, P. 1990. Sixth spring record for Parasitic Jaeger. *Loon* 62: 163-164.

Bailey, R. 1966. The seabirds of the southeastern coast of Arabia. *Ibis* 108: 224-264.

Baillon, F., & Dubois, P. 1991. Seawatching from Cape Verde, Senegal. *Birding World* 4: 440-442.

Baker, K. 1993. *Identification Guide to European Non-Passerines*. BTO Guide 24. BTO, Norfolk.

Baker, R.H. 1947. Observations of the birds of the North Atlantic. *Auk* 64: 245-259.

Balch, L.G. 1981. Identifying skuas in the ABA area. *Birding* 13: 190-201.

Bannerman, D.A., & Vella-Gaffiero, J.A. 1976. *Birds of the Maltese Archipelago*. Museums Department, Valletta.

Barré, H. 1976. Le Skua Subantarctique *Stercorarius lonnbergi* (Mathews) à L'ile de la Possession (Iles Crozet). *C.N.F.R.A.* 40: 77-105.

Barthel. P.H. 1995. Rätselvogel 45. *Limicola* 9: 40-43.

Bartle, S. 1983. Wreck of Long-tailed Skuas. *Orn. Soc. of New Zealand News* 30: 6.

Barton, D. 1978. Birds seen at sea off southern NSW and eastern Victoria. *Aust. Seabird Group Newsl.* 10: 17.

— 1982. Notes on skuas and jaegers in the western Tasman Sea. *Emu* 82: 56-59.

Bayes, J.C., Dawson, M.J., Joensen, A.H., & Potts, G.R. 1964. The distribution and numbers of the Great Skua (*Stercorarius s. skua*) breeding in the Faroes in 1961. *Dansk Orn. Foren. Tidsskr.* 58: 36-41.

Beaman, M. 1994. *Palearctic birds: A checklist of the birds of Europe, North Africa and Asia north of the foothills of the Himalayas*. Harrier Publications, Stonyhurst, England.

Behn, E-G. 1993. A Parasitic Jaeger *Stercorarius parasiticus* at the Arend Lake, Saxony Anhalt. *Falke* 40: 270.

Bell, D.G. 1965. Studies of less familiar birds 133: Long-tailed Skua. *British Birds* 58: 139-145.

Belopolskii, L.O. 1961. *Ecology of Sea Colony Birds of the Barents Sea*. Trans. Israel Programme for Scientific Translations, Jerusalem.

Bengtsson, S.A., & Owen, D.F. 1973. Polymorphism in the Arctic Skua in Iceland. *Ibis* 115: 87-92.

Bent, A.C. 1921. *Life Histories of North American Gulls and Terns*. United States National Museum Bulletin 113. Smithsonian Institution, Washington.

Bentz, P.G. 1980. Fler exempel på hur labbars kleptoparasitism utnyttjas av andra fåglar. *Anser* 19: 38.

Berry, R.J., & Davis, P.E. 1970. Polymorphism and behaviour in the Arctic Skua *Stercorarius parasiticus*. *Proc. Roy. Soc. London* B 175: 255-267.

Bertel, B. 1994. *Fugle over Skagen*. European Faunistical Press, Jyllinge.

Betzholtz, P.-E., & Swenzén, A. 1992. *Sörmlands fåglar*. Föreningen Sörmlands Ornitologer, Katrinehamn.

Beusekom, R.F.J. 1985. Foerageergedrag van een Kleinste

Jager *Stercorarius longicaudus. Limosa* 58: 33-34.

Bezzel, E. 1994. Seltene Larolimikolen in Bayern: Anmerkungen zur Auswertung und Interpretation langer Zeitreihen. *Limicola* 8: 281-297.

Biermann, W.H., & Voous, K.H. 1950. Birds observed and collected during the whaling expeditions of the 'Willem Barendsz' in the Antarctic, 1946-1947 and 1947-1948. *Ardea* 37: suppl. 123 pp.

Birt, V.L., & Cairns, D.K. 1987. Kleptoparasitic interactions of Arctic Skuas *Stercorarius parasiticus* and Black Guillemots *Cepphus grylle* in Northeastern Hudson Bay, Alaska. *Ibis* 129: 190-196.

Blake, E.R. 1977. *Manual of Neotropical Birds*. Vol. 1. The University of Chicago Press, Chicago & London.

Blechschmidt, K., Peter, H-U., de Korte, J., Winke, M., Seibold, I. & Helbig, A. 1993. Investigations on the Molecular Systematics of Skuas (Stercorariidae) *Zoologisches Jahrbuch für Systematik* 1993, 120: 379-387.

Blinkow, J. 1985. The Buckinghamshire skua. *British Birds* 78: 669-671.

Block, D., & Sørensen, S. 1984. *Yvitlit øver Færoya fuglar*. Torshavn.

Boesman, P. 1985. Juvenile kleinste en kleine jagers (*Stercorarius longicaudus* en *S. parasiticus*) te Zeebrugge: een vergelijkende studie. *Ornis Flandria* 4: 107-119.

Boertmann, D. 1979. Ornithologiske observationer i Vestgrønland i somrene 1972-77. *Dansk Orn. Foren. Tidsskr.* 73: 171-176.

Bonner, W.N. 1964. Polygyny and supernormal clutch size in the Brown Skua, *Catharacta skua lönnbergi* (Mathews). *Br. Antarct. Surv. Bull.* 3: 41-47.

Borgo, E., Truffi, G., & Verner, A. 1992. First record of Long-tailed Skua *Stercorarius longicaudus* in Liguria (NW Italy). *Riv. Ital. Ornitol.* 62: 181-182.

Boulinier, T. 1988. Feeding behaviour and employment of time of a pair of Bonxies *Stercorarius skua* parasitizing Puffins *Fratercula arctica. Alauda* 56: 409-410.

Bourne, W.R.P. 1986. Late summer seabird distribution off the west coast of Europe. *Irish Birds* 3: 175-198.

— 1989. McCormick's Skua in north-west European Waters. *Sea Swallow* 38: 63-64.

—, & Curtis, W.F. 1985. South Atlantic seabirds. *Sea Swallow* 34: 18-28.

—, & — 1994. Bonxies, barnacles and bleached blondes. *British Birds* 87: 289-299.

Bowman, M.J., & Esaias, W.E. (eds.) 1978. *Oceanic Fronts in Coastal Processes*. Springer-Verlag, New York.

Brady, A. 1988. Possible presence of an Antarctic Skua in New Jersey waters. *Cassinia* 62: 7-11.

— 1994. Kleptoparasitism of Long-tailed Jaeger on Wilson's Storm-Petrel. *Cassinia* 65: 19-20.

Brazil, M. 1991. *The Birds of Japan*. A&C Black, London.

Breife, B. 1989. Speglar massuppträdanden av bredstjärtad labb *Stercorarius pomarinus* i södra Skandinavien under hösten en god lämmeltillgång på den ryska tundran? *Calidris* 8: 3-10.

—, Holmström, N., & Blomquist, L. 1993. Sjöfågelboken. Fältbestämning av sträckande sjöfåglar. *Vår Fågelvärld* supplement 18. Stenåsa.

Brockman, J.H., & Barnard, C.J. 1979. Kleptoparasitism in birds. *Animal Behaviour* 27: 487-514.

Brooke, R.K. 1977. The South Polar Skua is a probable visitor. *Cormorant* 3: 14.

— 1978. The *Catharacta* skuas (Aves, Laridae) occurring in South African waters. *Durban Museum Nov.* 11: 299-308.

— 1981. What is *Stercorarius madagascariensis* Bonapartei? *Auk* 94: 664-665.

Brooks, A. 1939. Migrations of the Skua family. *Ibis* 3: 324-328.

Broome, A. 1987. Identification of juvenile Pomarine Skua. *British Birds* 80: 426.

Brouwer, P., Brouwer, S., & Binning, B. 1987. Skuas mobbing Black-backed Gulls. *Notornis* 34: 306.

Brown, R.G.B. 1979. Seabirds off the Senegal upwelling and adjacent waters. *Ibis* 121: 283-296.

— 1981. Seabirds in northern Peruvian waters, November-December 1977. *Bulletin de Institu del Mar del Peru*, Volumen Extraordinario.

—, Cooke, E., Kinnear, P.K., & Mills, E.L. 1975. Summer seabirds distribution in Drake Passage, the Chilean Fjords and off southern South America. *Ibis* 117: 339-356.

Bruns, H. 1984. Zur feldornithologischen Unterscheidung von Raubmöwen. *Orn. Mitt.* 35: 54-60.

Bundy, G., & Warr, F.E. 1980. A check list of the birds of the Arabian Gulf States. *Sandgrouse* 1: 4-49.

Burger, J., Olla, B., & Winn, H.E. (eds.) 1980. *Behaviour of Marine Animals*. Vol. 4. Plenum Press, New York.

Burton, R.W. 1968. Breeding biology of the Brown Skua *Catharacta skua lonnbergi* (Mathews) at Signy Island, South Orkney Islands. *Br. Antarct. Surv. Bull.* 15: 9-28.

Butler, A., & McLaughlin, J. 1989. Identification of a dark juvenile Long-tailed Skua. *Birding World* 2: 362-364.

Caldow, R.W.G. 1988. Studies of the morphology, feeding behaviour and breeding biology of skuas (family Stercorariidae) with reference to kleptoparasitism. PhD dissertation, Univ. Glasgow, Glasgow.

—, & Furness, R.W. 1991. The relationship between kleptoparasitism and plumage polymorphism in the Arctic Skua *Stercorarius parasiticus. Funct. Ecol.* 5: 331-339.

Campbell, K.F., Bailey, S.F., & Erickson, R.A. 1988. The changing seasons: Middle Pacific county report. *American Birds* 42: 127-134.

Camphuysen, C.J. 1988. Invasie van de Middelste Jager in Nederland in November 1985. *Dutch Birding* 10: 54-65.

—, & van IJzendoorn, E.J. 1988. Influx of Pomarine Skuas in northwestern Europe in autumn 1985. *Dutch Birding* 10: 66-70.

Cassol, M., & Farra, A.D. 1989. Interesting records at the S. Croce Lake (Belluno, NE Italy). *Riv. Ital. Ornitol.* 59: 281-282.

Caughley, G. 1960. Observations on incubation and chick rearing in the Antarctic Skua. *Notornis* 8: 194-195.

Cech, R.B. 1986. Identification of juvenile Long-tailed Jaeger from photographs. *Bird Observer East. Mass.* 14: 15-23.

Cherkas, N.D. 1993. Observations of Arctic Skua *Stercorarius parasiticus* (L) at the Byelorussia. *Parki Nat. Rez. Przyr.* 12: 79-80.

Christensen, L., Hansen, L.G., & Søby, E. 1996. Fugle i Danmark 1994. Årsrapport over observationer. *Dansk Orn. Foren. Tidsskr.* 90: 49-88.

Christophersen, H. (ed.) 1989. *Fugle og dyr i Nordjylland 1988.* Rapport nr. 25 fra Nordjysk Ornitologisk Kartotek. Skive, Denmark.

— (ed.) 1990. *Fugle og dyr i Nordjylland 1989.* Rapport nr. 26 fra Nordjysk Ornitologisk Kartotek. Skive, Denmark.

Clancey, P.A. 1982. Miscellaneous taxonomic notes on African birds. *Durban Museum Nov.* 13: 132-134.

Clegg, M. 1972. Partial albinism in skuas. *British Birds* 65: 530-531.

Coates, B.J. 1985. *The Birds of Papua New Guinea.* Vol. I. Dove Publications.

Commisie van de Belgische Avifauna. 1967. Avifauna van België. *Le Gerfaut* 57: 273-363.

Cooke, F., & Mills, E.L. 1972. Summer distribution of pelagic birds off the coast of Argentina. *Ibis* 114: 245-251.

Cornwallis, L., & Porter, R.F. 1982. Spring observations of the birds in North Yemen. *Sandgrouse* 4: 1-36.

Court, G.S., & Davies, L.S. 1990. First report of the Southern Great Skua *Stercorarius skua lonnbergi* at Cape Bird, Ross Island, Antarctica. *Notornis* 37: 25-27.

Cox, J.B. 1973. Long-tailed Skua at Tobe. *The South Australian Ornithologist* 26: 85-86.

Cramp, S., & Simmons, K.E.L. (eds.) 1977. *The Birds of the Western Palearctic.* Vol. I. Oxford University Press.

— & — (eds.) 1980. *The Birds of the Western Palearctic.* Vol. II. Oxford University Press.

— & — (eds.) 1983. *The Birds of the Western Palearctic.* Vol. III. Oxford University Press.

Crossland, A.C. 1993. Do Arctic Skuas sometimes roost on land at night? *Notornis* 40: 305-306.

Curtis, W.F. 1996. McCormick's Skua *Stercorarius maccormicki* off west Scotland, 14 May 1994. *Sea Swallow* 45: 101-102.

Custer, T.W., & Pitelka, F.A. 1987. Nesting by Pomarine Jaegers near Barrow, Alaska 1971. *J. Field Ornithol.* 598: 225-230.

Darefeldt, G. 1995. Sjöfågelsträcket vid Vänern och Vättern hösten 1994. Fågelåret 1994: 63-66. *Vår Fågelvärld* supplement nr. 22.

—, & Johansson, B. 1994. Vänersborgsviken. Högklassig sträcklokal i inlandet. *Vår Fågelvärld* 53/4: 8-16.

Darling, P. 1991. Great Skua killing Brent Goose. *British Birds* 84: 507.

Davenport, D.L. 1975. The spring migration of the Pomarine Skua on British and Irish coasts. *British Birds* 68: 456-462.

— 1979. Spring passage of skuas at Balranald, North Uist. *Scottish Birds* 10: 216-220.

— 1981. The spring passage of Pomarine and Long-tailed Skuas at the south and western coast of Britain and Ireland. *Irish Birds* 2: 73-79.

— 1984. Large passage of skuas off Scotland and Ireland in May 1982 and 1983. *Irish Birds* 2: 515-520.

— 1991. The spring passage of Long-tailed Skuas off North Uist in 1991. *Scottish Birds* 16: 85-89.

— 1992. The spring passage of Long-tailed and Pomarine Skuas in Britain and Ireland. *Birding World* 5: 92-95.

David, R.E. 1988. First state record of Long-tailed Jaeger, with a note on the occurrence of Arctic Terns in Hawaii. *Elepaio* 48: 27-29.

Davis, J.F.W., & O'Donald, P. 1975. The Arctic Skua project on Fair Isle: a progress report. *Fair Isle Bird Obs. Report* 28: 73-76.

Dean, F.C., Valkenburg, P., & Magoun, A.J. 1976. Inland migration of jaegers in North-eastern Alaska. *Condor* 78: 271-273.

DeBenedictis, P.A. 1997. Gleanings from the Technical Literature: Skuas. *Birding* 29: 66-69.

de Fraine, R., & Leisen, K. 1988. Determinatie van een eerstejaars kleinste jager. *Oriolus* 54: 162-165.

de Korte, J. 1972. Birds, observed and collected by 'De Nederlandse Spitsbergen Expeditie' in West and East Spitsbergen, 1967 and 1968-69; second part. *Beaufortia* 19: 197-232.

— 1972. Birds, observed and collected by 'De Nederlandse Spitsbergen Expeditie' in West and East Spitsbergen, 1967 and 1968-69; third and last part. *Beaufortia* 20: 23-58.

— 1977. Ecology of the Long-tailed Skua *Stercorarius longicaudus* Vieillot, 1819, at Scoresby Sound, East Greenland. Report of the Nederlandse Groenland Expeditie Scoresbysund 1973, 1974 and 1975. Part 1: distribution and density. *Beaufortia* 25: 201-219.

— 1984. Ecology of the Long-tailed Skua *Stercorarius longicaudus* Vieillot, 1819, at Scoresby Sund, East Greenland. Part 2: arrival, site tenacity and departure. *Beaufortia* 34: 1-14.

— 1985. Ecology of the Long-tailed Skua at Scoresby Sound, East Greenland. Part three: clutch size, laying date and incubation in relation to energy reserves. *Beaufortia* 35: 93-127.

— 1986. Ecology of the Long-tailed Skua *Stercorarius longicaudus* Vieillot, 1819, at Scoresby Sund, East Greenland. Part 4: breeding success and growth of youngs. *Bijdr. Dierk.* 56: 1-23.

—, & Wattel, J. 1988. Food and breeding success of the Long-tailed Skua at Scoresby Sound, Northeast Greenland. *Ardea* 76: 27-41.

del Hoyo, J., Elliott, A., & Sargatal, J. (eds.) 1996. *Handbook of the Birds of the World.* Vol. 3. Lynx Edicions, Barcelona.

Delin, H., & Svensson, L. 1988. *Photographic Guide to the Birds of Britain and Europe.* Hamlyn, London.

Dementiev, G.P., & Gladkov, N.A. (eds.) 1951. *Birds of the USSR.* Vol. 3. Israel Prog. Sci. Translations, Jesusalem (1969).

de Roo, A., & van Damme, B. 1970. A first record of the Long-tailed Skua from the Ethiopian region. *Rev. Zool. Bot. Afr.* 82: 157-162.

de Schauensee, R.M.L., & Phelps, W.H. 1978. *A Guide to the Birds of Venezuela.* Princeton University Press, New Jersey.

de Silva, R.I. 1989. Identity of skuas *Catharacta* in Sri Lanka. *Cormorant* 17: 79-81.

— 1991. A new specimen of the Subantarctic Skua *Catharacta antarctica lonnbergi* from Sri Lanka. *Mar. Ornithol.* 19: 139.

Deutsche Seltenheitenkommission. 1994. Seltene

Vogelarten in Deutschland 1991 und 1992. *Limicola* 8: 153-209.

— 1995. Seltene Vogelarten in Deutschland 1993. *Limicola* 9: 77-110.

Devillers, P. 1977. The skuas of the Northern American Pacific Coast. *Auk* 94: 417-429.

— 1978. Distribution and relationship of South American Skuas. *Le Gerfaut* 68: 374-417.

Dinsmore, S.J. 1989. Pomarine Jaegers at Saylorville Reservoir. *Iowa Bird Life* 59: 20-21.

Dittberner, H., & Fiebig, J. 1986. The Skua *Catharacta skua* on the west coast of the Black Sea. *Faun. Abh. (Dresden)* 14: 102-103.

Divoky, G.J., Dakley, K.L., & Huber, H.R. 1979. Pomarine Jaeger preys on adult Black-legged Kittiwake. *Wilson Bulletin* 91: 329.

Dixon, C.C. 1933. Some observations on the albatrosses and other birds of the southern oceans. *Trans. Roy. Can. Inst.* 19: 117-139.

Domagalski, R.C. 1992. Parasitic Jaeger *Stercorarius parasiticus* 19 October 1991, Ozaukee County, at Concordia College. *Passenger Pigeon* 54: 177.

Dott, H.E.M. 1967. Numbers of Great Skuas and other seabirds of Hermaness, Unst. *Scottish Birds* 4: 340-350.

Douhan, B. (ed.) 1995a. Fågelrapportering, Uppland 1994. *Fåglar i Uppland* 22: 111-146.

— 1995b. Den 18 september 1994 - labbdagen. *Fåglar i Uppland* 22: 147-149.

Downes, M.C., Ealey, E.H.M., Gwyun, A.M., & Young, P.S. 1959. *The Birds of Heard Island: Australian National Antarctica Research Expeditions.* Anare reports, series B, vol. 1.

Drennan, S.R. 1988. 87th Christmas Bird Count. *American Birds* 41: 519-1350.

— 1990. 89th Christmas Bird Count. *American Birds* 43: 551-1236.

Driessens, G. 1995. Recente meldingen België Januari-Maart 1995. *Dutch Birding* 17: 85-87.

— 1995. Recente meldingen België September-Oktober 1994. *Dutch Birding* 16: 262-264.

Drury, W.H. 1960. Breeding activities of Long-tailed Jaeger, Herring Gull and Arctic Tern on Bylot Island, Northwest Territories, Canada. *Bird-Banding* 31: 63-79.

Duncan, C.D. 1994. First-summer record of Parasitic Jaeger in Quintara Roo. *Euphonia* 3: 19-20.

Dunn, P.J., & Hirschfeld, E. 1991. Long-tailed Skuas in Britain and Ireland in autumn 1988. *British Birds* 84: 121-136.

Durinck, J., & Lausten, M. 1990. Effekten af overvågningsindsats på beskrivelsen af havfugles træk, Blåvandshuk 1978-1988. *Pelagicus* 5: 8-16.

Dymond, J.N., Fraser, P.A., & Gantlett, S.J.M. 1989. *Rare Birds in Britain and Ireland.* T. & A.D Poyser, Calton.

Eckert, J. 1990. Skuas inland. *S. Aust. Ornithol.* 31: 55.

Egnett, G., & Elmberg, J. 1990. Sträcket av labb och bredstjärtad labb genom Norra Kvarken våren 1989. *Vår Fågelvärld* 49: 95-97.

Eigenhuis, K.J. 1987. Moult and identification of South Polar Skua. *Dutch Birding* 9: 124-125.

Eisenhauer, J.H., & Paniyak, J. 1977. Parasitic Jaeger preys

on adult Ptarmigan. *Auk* 94: 389-390.

Ekberg, B., & Nilsson, L. (eds.) 1994. *Skånes fåglar i dag och i gången tid. Del 1: Lommar till och med alkor.* Skånes Ornitologiska Förening/Bokförlaget Signum, Lund.

Eklund, C.R. 1961. Distribution and life history studies of the South Polar Skua. *Bird Banding* 32: 187-222.

— 1964. The Antarctic Skua. *Sci. Amer.* 210: 94-100.

Elkins, N. 1983. *Weather and Bird Behaviour.* T. & A.D. Poyser, Berkhamsted.

Elmberg, J. 1992. Cooperative nest defence by trios of Arctic Skuas *Stercorarius parasiticus. Ibis* 134: 298.

Emslie, S.D., Karnovsky, N., & Trivelpiece, W. 1995. Avian predation at penguin colonies on King George Island, Antarctica. *Wilson Bull.* 107: 317-327.

Engler, J. 1990. Long-tailed Jaeger at Fish Springs NWR. *Utah Birds* 6: 28-31.

Ensor, P.H. 1979. The effect of storms on the breeding success of South Polar Skuas at Cape Bird, Antarctica. *Notornis* 26: 349-352.

Escalante, R. 1970. *Aves marinas del Rio de La Plata. Y aguas vecinas del oceano Atlantico.* Barriero Y. Ramos S.A., Montevideo.

— 1972. First Pomarine Skua specimen from Brazil. *Auk* 89: 663-665.

— 1985. Los salteadores menores *Stercorarius parasiticus* y *S. longicaudus* en el Uruguay. *Coom. Zool. del Museo de Hist. Natur. de Montevideo* 11: 1-8.

Evans, L., & Millington, R. 1993. 1993: the review of the birding year. *Birding World* 6: 469-487.

Evans, P.G.H. 1984. The seabirds of Greenland: their status and conservation; and Status and conservation of seabirds in Northwest Europe. pp. 49-84 and 293-322 in Croxall, J.P., Evans, P.G.H., & Schreiber, R.W.: *Status and Conservation of the World's Seabirds.* ICBP, Cambridge.

Evans, R.M. 1980. Development of behaviour in seabirds: an ecological perspective. In Burger, J. (ed.): *Behaviour of Marine Animals.* Vol. 4. Plenum Press, New York.

Ewins, P.J., Ellis, P.M., Bird, D.B., & Prior, A. 1988. The distribution and status of Arctic and Great Skua in Shetland 1985-86. *Scottish Birds* 15: 9-20.

Falla, R.A. 1964. Distribution patterns of birds in the antarctic and high-latitude subantarctic. In Carrick, R., Holdgate, M., & Prévost, J.: *J. Biologie Antarctique: Compt.-rend. Premier Sump. Organ,* SCAR, Paris, 2-8 Sept. 1962: 367-376. Paris.

—, Sibson, R.B., & Turbott, E.G. 1967. *A Field Guide to the Birds of New Zealand.* Riverside Press, Cambridge.

Faxon, D. 1994. Jaegers. *Oregon Birds* 20: 49.

ffrench, R. 1973. *A Guide to the Birds of Trinidad and Tobago.* Asa Wright Nature Center, Trinidad.

Finlayson, C. 1992. *Birds of the Strait of Gibraltar.* T. & A.D. Poyser, London.

Fleming, C.A. 1939. Birds of Chatham Islands. *Emu* 38: 492-509.

Folkedal, S., & Ness, J.K. 1994. Året som gikk - art for art. Årsrapport 1993, del 2. *Utsira Fuglestasjons årbok* 1993: 10-31.

Forsten, P., & Tuominen, A. 1967. The colour phases of the Arctic Skua *Stercorarius parasiticus* in the archipelagos of the Bothnian Sea. *Ornis Fennica* 44: 1-6.

— & — 1969. Merikhu *Stercorarius parasiticus* Selkämerella ja pohjoisella Saaristomerellä. *Porin Lintitiet. Ydh. vuosikirja* 1968: 35-37.

— & — 1984. Vuosikynnen merikihuja - pesamäkanta paikkauskollisus ja saalistustavat. *In Satakunnan Linnusto* 61-69. Pori.

Fox, A.D., & Aspinall, S.J. 1987. Pomarine Skuas in Britain and Ireland in autumn 1985. *British Birds* 80: 404-421.

Fraser, M.W. 1984. Foods of Subantarctic Skuas on Inaccessible Island. *Ostrich* 55: 192-195.

Fraser, P.A., & Ryan, J.F. 1994. Scarce migrants in Britain and Ireland (part 2). *British Birds* 87: 605-615.

Friedmann, H. 1945. Birds of the United States Antarctic service expeditions 1939-41. *Proc. Amer. Phil. Soc.* 89: 305-313.

Fuhrmann, K. 1988. Eine sehr helle junge Falkenraubmöwe. *Limicola* 2: 196-197.

Fullager, P.J. 1976. McCormick's Skua *Catharacta maccormicki*, in the North Atlantic. *Australasian Seabird Group Newsletter* 7: 18-19.

Furness, B.L. 1983. The feeding behaviour of Arctic Skuas *Stercorarius parasiticus* wintering off South Africa. *Ibis* 125: 245-251.

Furness, R.W. 1977. Effects of Great Skuas on Arctic Skuas in Shetland. *British Birds* 70: 96-107.

— 1978. Kleptoparasitism by Great Skuas *Catharacta skua* Brünn. and Arctic Skua *Stercorarius parasiticus* L., at a Shetland seabird colony. *Anim. Behav.* 26: 1167-1177.

— 1987. *The Skuas.* T. & A.D. Poyser, Calton.

— & Monaghan, P. 1987. *Seabird Ecology.* Blackie, Glasgow & London.

— 1990. Evolutionary and ecological constraints on the breeding distributions and behaviour of skuas. *Proceedings of the International Centennial Meeting of the Deutsche Ornithologen-Gesellschaft. Current topics in avian Biology.* R. van den Elzen, K.-L. Schuchmann & K. Schmidt-Koenig (eds.).

— & Hislop, J.R.G. 1981. Diets and feeding ecology of Great Skuas *Catharacta skua* during the breeding season in Shetland. *J. Zool. London* 195: 1-23.

Gabrielson, I.N., & Lincoln, F.C. 1959. *The Birds of Alaska.* The Stockpole Company, Harrisburg, Pennsylvania.

Gain, J. 1914. *Oiseaux antarctiques. Deuxième expédition antarctique française (1908-1910).* Sci. Naturelles: Documents scientifiques, Paris.

Gantlett, S., & Harrap, S. 1992. Identification forum: South Polar Skua. *Birding World* 5: 256-270.

Garrett, K.L., & Dunn, J. 1981. *Birds of Southern California: status and distribution.* Los Angeles Audubon Society.

Gibbons, D.W., Reid, J.B., & Chapman, R.A. 1993. *The New Atlas of Breeding Birds in Britain and Ireland 1988-91.* T. & A.D. Poyser, Calton.

Ginn, H.B., & Melville, D.S. 1983. *Moult in Birds.* BTO, Tring.

Gjershaug, J.O., Thingstad, P.G., Eldø/y, S., & Byrkjeland, S. 1994. *Norsk Fugleatlas. Hekkefuglenes utbredelse og bestandsstatus i Norge.* Norsk Ornitologisk Forening.

Gloe, P. 1985. Zu dem Kennzeichen junger Falken-

Raubmöwen. *Orn. Mitt.* 37: 329-331.

Glutz von Blotzheim, U.N., & Bauer, K.M. 1982. *Handbuch der Vögel Mitteleuropas 8/I.* Wiesbaden.

Godfrey, W.E. 1966. *The Birds of Canada.* Ottawa.

Golley, M., & Millington, R. 1994. 1994: the review of the birding year. *Birding World* 7: 478-495.

Goodman, S.M., & Meininger, P.L. (eds.) 1989. *The Birds of Egypt.* Oxford University Press.

Grant, P.J. 1986. *Gulls - a guide to identification.* T. & A.D. Poyser, Calton.

— 1988. Solution to Quizbird 1. *Birding World* 1: 34.

Grant, P.R. 1971. Interactive behaviour of Puffins *Fratercula arctica* and Skuas *Stercorarius parasiticus*. *Behaviour* 40: 263-281.

Grembe, J. 1981. Auftreten und Durchzug von Raubmöwen in Schwartzmeergebiet und im Ostmediterranean Raum. *Ornithol. J. Berlin Mus. Hein* 5/6: 13-36.

Grossman, R. 1978. Beobachtungen an der Falkenraubmöwe in Schwedisch-Lappland. *Orn. Mitt.* 30: 34-39.

Gudmundsson, F. 1954. Icelandic Birds 4. The Great Skua. *Náttúrufraedingurinn* 24: 123-136.

— 1954. Icelandic Birds 8. The Arctic Skua. *Náttúrufraedingurinn* 24: 16-21.

Götmark, F., Andersson, M., & Hildén, O. 1981. Polymorphism in the Arctic Skua *Stercorarius parasiticus* in NE Norway. *Ornis Fenn.* 58: 49-55.

Hagen, Y. 1952. The Birds of Tristan da Cunha. *Res. Norweg. Sci. Exped. Tristan da Cunha 1937-38.* 20: 1-248.

Hake, M. 1983. Labbar. Havsfåglar i Kattegatt. *Rapp. KOF, Suppl.* 5: 24-29.

— 1984. Labbar. Havfåglar i Kattegatt. *Rapp. KOF, Suppl.* 6: 26-32.

— 1985. Labbar. Havsfåglar i Kattegatt. *Rapp. KOF, Suppl.* 7: 23-26.

Halkier, E. 1961. Usædvanlige observationer af måger på Vest-Spetsbergen. *Dansk Orn. Foren. Tidsskr.* 47: 193-197.

Halle, L.J. 1973. Eagle of the South Pole. *Audubon* 75: 89.

Hamilton, J.E. 1934. The sub-antarctic forms of the Great Skua *Catharacta skua skua*. *Discovery reports* 9: 161-174.

Hancey, R., & Boosey, E. 1995. *Norfolk Bird Report 1994.* Norfolk & Norwich Naturalists Society, Norwich.

Hansen, J.M. 1984. The population of Long-tailed Skuas at Kærelv, Scoresby Sund, East Greenland, 1979. *Dansk Orn. Foren. Tidsskr.* 78: 99-104.

Hansen, M.M. (ed.) 1994. *Fugle på Sjælland 1993.* DOF, Copenhagen.

— 1995. *Fugle på Sjælland 1994.* DOF, Copenhagen.

Hansson, P. 1995. Sträckande sjöfåglar längs Västerbottens kust hösten 1994. *Fåglar i Västerbotten* 20: 32-38.

Hardwick, M. 1993. A Long-tailed Skua with extensive white wing flashes. *Birding World* 6: 403-404.

Hario, M. 1985. *Stercorarius*-kihujen lajan - ja iänmääritys. *Lintumies* 20: 2-20.

— 1986. *Itämeren lokkilinnut. Määritys ja esiintyminen.* Lintutieto.

— 1986. Art- och åldersbestämning av *Stercorarius*-labbar. *Calidris* 15: 91-118.

Harrap, S. 1990. Quizbird nr. 30 solution. *Birding World* 3: 435-436.

Harris, M.P., &. Hansen, L. 1974. Seabird transects between Europe and Rio Plate, South America. *Dansk Orn. Foren. Tidsskr.* 68: 117-137.

Harrison, P. 1983. *Seabirds - an identification guide.* Croom Helm, Beckenham.

—1987. *Seabirds of the World. A photographic guide.* Christopher Helm, London.

Harrop, H.R. 1993. Massive skua passage off Shetland. *Seabird Group Newsletter* 64: 11.

—, Mellor, M., & Suddaby, D. 1993. Spring passage of Pomarine Skuas off Shetland in May 1992. *Scottish Birds* 17: 50-55.

Hemmings, A.D. 1984. Aspects of the breeding biology of McCormick's Skua *Catharacta maccormicki* at Signy Island, South Orkney Islands. *Br. Antarc. Surv. Bull.* 65: 65-79.

Heubeck, M. 1992. Great Skuas attacking a flock of moulting Eiders. *Scottish Birds* 16: 284-285.

Higgins, P.J., & Davies, S.J.J.F. 1996. *Handbook of Australian, New Zealand and Antarctic Birds, vol. III: Snipe to pigeons.* Oxford University Press.

Hildén, O. 1971. Occurrence, migration and colour phases of the Arctic Skua *Stercorarius parasiticus* in Finland. *Ann. Zool. Fennici* 8: 223-230.

Hinde, S. 1990. A record of Long-tailed Jaeger at Bear River Refuge. *Utah Birds* 6: 32.

Hirschfeld, E. 1985. Sträcket av labb genom Sverige augusti 1982-januari 1983. *Vår Fågelvärld* 44: 21-30.

Holden, P. 1985. Measurements of wing-span. *British Birds* 78: 403-404.

Hollom, P.A.D., Porter, R.F., Christensen, S., & Willis, I. 1988. *Birds of the Middle East and North Africa.* T. & A.D. Poyser, Calton.

Hoogendoorn, T., Mullarney, K., & van den Berg, A.B. 1993. (Comment). *Dutch Birding* 15: 174-175.

Howell, S.N.G., & Webb, S. 1995. *A Guide to the Birds of Mexico and Northern Central America.* Oxford University Press.

Hudson, R. 1968. The Great Skua in the Caribbean. *Bird Study* 15: 33-34.

Hulsman, K. 1976. The robbing behaviour of terns and gulls. *Emu* 76: 143-149.

Humphrey, P.S., & Parkes, K.C. 1959. An approach to the study of molts and plumages. *Auk* 76: 1-31.

Hunt, G.L. 1980. Mate selection and mating systems in seabirds. pp. 113-151 in Burger, J., Olla, B.L., & Winn, H.E. (eds.): *Behaviour of Marine Animals, Vol. 4: Marine birds.* Plenum, New York.

Hutchinson, C.D. 1989. *Birds in Ireland.* T. & A.D. Poyser, London.

Hytönen, O., & Wikström, D. 1933. Nuorten kihujen, *Stercorarius* Brisson, määräämisestä. *Ornis Fennica* 11: 1-6.

Il'icev, V.D., & Zubakin, V.A. 1990. *Handbuch der Vögel Sowjetunion - band 6/Teil 1.* A. Ziemsen Verlag, Wittenberg Lutherstadt.

Isakson, E., Kjellén, N., & Wiklund, C.G. 1995. Rovfåglar och lämlar på ryska ishavstundran. *Vår Fågelvärld* 54/1:

Jackson, E.E. 1966. The birds of Foula. *Scottish Birds* 4, spec. suppl. 1-56.

James, P. 1996. *Birds of Sussex.* Sussex Ornithological Society.

Jehl, J.R. 1973. The distribution of marine birds in Chilean waters in winter. *Auk* 90: 114-135.

—1974. The distribution and ecology of marine birds over the Continental shelf of Argentina in winter. *Trans. San Diego Soc. Nat. Hist.* 17: 217-234.

—, Todd, F.S., Rumboll, M.A.E., & Schwartz, D. 1978. Notes of the avifauna of Southern Georgia. *Le Gerfaut* 68: 535-550.

Jensen, J.-K. 1982. Muligt overvintringsområde for Sydpolarkjove *Stercorarius maccormicki*, ved Flemmings Kap. *Dansk Orn. Foren. Tidsskr.* 76: 148.

Jensen, J.V., & Kirkeby, J. 1980. *The Birds of the Gambia.* Aros Nature Guides.

Jespersen, P. 1930. Ornithological observations in the North Atlantic Ocean. *Danish Dana Exp. 1920-1922 Rept* 7: 1-36.

—1933. Observations on the oceanic birds of the Pacific and adjacent waters. *Vidensk. Medd. fra Dansk Naturhi. Foren.* 94: 187-221.

Joensen, A.H. 1966. *Fuglene på Færøerne.* Rhodos, Copenhagen.

Johanson, J. 1984. Fältkaraktärer hos ungfåglar av bredstjärtad labb och vanlig labb. *Gavia* 10: 96-107.

Johnson, D.P. 1986. Jaeger identification. *Loon* 58: 141-142.

Johnson, R. 1987. Parasitic Jaeger on Wisconsin Point. *Passenger Pigeon* 49: 157.

Jonsson, L. 1976. *Fåglar i Naturen: Hav och kust.* Wahlström & Widstrand, Stockholm.

—1984. Identification of juvenile Pomarine and Arctic Skuas. *British Birds* 77: 443-446.

—1992. *Birds of Europe with North Africa and the Middle East.* A&C Black, London.

Jönsson, P.-E., Nilsson, K.-G., Oldén, B., Peterz, M., & Strid, C. 1990. Nordvästskånska fåglar. *Fåglar i Nordvästskåne*, supplement 2. Helsingborg.

Jouventin P., & Guillotin, M. 1979. Socio-écologie du skua antarctique à Pointe Géologie. *Terre Vie Rev. Ecol.* 33: 109-127.

Källander, H. 1979. Labben på truten och truten på labben. *Anser* 18: 299.

Kampp, K. 1982. Notes on the Long-tailed Skua in West Greenland. *Dansk Orn. Foren. Tidsskr.* 76: 129-136.

Kapanen, M. 1977. Merikihui *Stercorarius parasiticus* muutosta Juensuu seudulta. *Ornis Fennica* 54: 123-136.

Kaufman, K. 1990. *A Field Guide to Advanced Birding.* Houghton Mifflin, Boston.

Kemp, J.B., Sellors, G., & Smith, T.G. 1984. Identification of first-winter Pomarine Skua. *British Birds* 77: 27.

Kinder, T.H., Hunt, G.L., Schneider, D., & Schumacher, J.D. 1983. Correlations between seabirds and oceanic fronts around the Pribilof Islands, Alaska. *Estuarine Coastal and Shelf Science* 16: 309-319.

King, W.B. 1967. *Seabirds of the Tropical Pacific Ocean.* Smithsonian Institution, Washington D.C.

Kitson, A.R. 1979. Separation of adult pale-phase Arctic and Long-tailed Skuas. *British Birds* 72: 120-121.

Kiørboe, T. 1991. Seabirds observed in the Andaman Shelf Sea off Phuket, Thailand. *Nat. Hist. Bull. Siam Soc.* 39: 85-90.

Kjellén, N. 1980. Labbar. In Axelsson, P. (ed.): Fåglar i Skåne 1979. *Anser* Suppl. 6. Lund.

Klafs, G., & Stübs, J. 1979. *Die Vogelwelt Mecklenburgs.* 2. Aufl. VEB Gustav Fischer Verlag, Jena.

Klomp, N.I., & Furness, R.W. 1992. A technique which may allow accurate determination of the age of adult birds. *Ibis* 134: 245-249.

Knolle, P. 1994. Kanttekeningen bij herkenning van juveniele Kleinste Jager. *Dutch Birding* 16: 202-205.

Kochanov, W.D. 1970. Materialen zum Zug der Spatelraubmöwe vor Murman. *Trudy Kandalakschokogo gos. Sapowed.* 8: 182-189.

Köhler, U., & Köhler, P. 1994. Zanzibar records of Arctic Skua *Stercorarius parasiticus* and Pomarine Skua *Stercorarius pomarinus. Scopus* 18: 116-117.

Korducki, M. 1992. Parasitic Jaeger *Stercorarius parasiticus* - 19 October 1991, Ozaukee County, at Concordia College. *Passenger Pigeon* 54: 177-178.

Korol, B., & Wapple, R. 1995. Pomarine Skua at Lac La Plonge, Saskatchewan. *Blue Jay* 52: 33-35.

Koskimies, P. 1992. Population sizes and recent trends of breeding birds in the Nordic countries. *Bird Census News* 5: 41-79.

Krabbe, N. 1980. *Checklist to the Birds of Eilat.* Priv. publ., Copenhagen.

Kranendonk, H. 1981. Een cladistische analyse van de soorten van der familie Stercorariidae. 1-27. Inst. v. Tax. Zool. Amsterdam.

Krasnov, Y.V. 1990. Alternative foraging strategies in seagulls. *Zool. Zh.* 69: 67-72.

— 1993. Great Skua *Stercorarius skua* nesting in the USSR. *Seabird Group Newsl.* 64: 11.

Kulstead, M. 1992. Parasitic Jaeger. *Spoonbill* 41: 7-8.

Kumlin, B. 1984. Två sällsynta fågelarter observerade vid Vänersborgsviken hösten 1983. *Gavia* 10: 108.

Kuroda, N. 1955. Observations of pelagic birds of the Northwestern Pacific. *Condor* 57: 290-300.

— 1960. Analysis of seabird distribution in the Northwestern Pacific Ocean. *Pacific Sci.* 14: 55-67.

— 1962. On the melanic phase of the McCormick Great Skua. *Misc. Rep. Yamashina Inst. Orn. Zool.* 3: 212-217.

Kuyken, E. 1970. De Kleinste Jager in Belgie, met een beschijving van de eerste augustusvangst, 1969. *Le Gerfaut* 60: 188-197.

Kwater, E. 1990. Parasitic Jaeger: Eric County. *Pa. Birds* 4: 97-98.

Lack, P. 1986. *The Atlas of Wintering Birds in Britain and Ireland.* T. &. A.D. Poyser, Calton.

Laine, L.J. 1996. *Suomalainen Lintopas.* Helsinki Media.

Lambert, K. 1969. Hinweise zu feltornithologische Bestimmung der Raubmöwen. *Der Falke* 16: 42-51.

— 1971. Seevogelbeobachtungen auf zwei Reisen im östlichen Atlantik mit besonderer Berücksichtigung des Seegebiets vor Südwestafrika. *Beitr. Vogelkunde* 17: 1-32.

— 1980. Ein Überwinterungsgebiet der Falkenraubmöwe, *Stercorarius longicaudus* Vieill. 1819, vor Südwest- und Südafrika entdeckt. *Beitr. Vogelkunde* 26: 199-212.

Lange, P. 1990. Forekomsten af Storkjove *Catharacta skua* i Kattegat 1978-1988. *Pelagicus* 5: 1-7.

Langrand, O. 1990. *Guide to the Birds of Madagascar.* Yale University Press, New Haven.

Languy, M., & Lambin, X. 1988. Record of Pomarine Skua *Stercorarius pomarinus* at Naivasha Lake, Kenya. *Alauda* 56: 73.

Lansdown, P. 1993a. Separation of South Polar Skua from Great Skua. *British Birds* 86: 176-177.

— 1993b. Mystery photographs 188: Great Skua. *British Birds* 86: 218-219.

Le Baron, G.S. 1989. The 88th Christmas Bird Count. *American Birds* 42: 505-1198.

Lee, D.S. 1989. Jaegers and skuas in the Western North Atlantic: some historical misconceptions. *American Birds* 43: 18-20.

— & Booth, J.R. 1979. Seasonal distribution of offshore and pelagic birds in North Carolina waters. *American Birds* 33: 715-721.

Lewis, A., & Pomeroy, D. 1989. *A Bird Atlas of Kenya.* A.A. Balkema, Rotterdam/Brookfield.

Lewis, M. 1991. The status of the Long-tailed Skua *Stercorarius longicaudus* in Australian waters. *Aust. Bird Watcher* 14: 119-122.

Lewis, M.J. 1987. An Arctic Skua taking passerines at sea. *Notornis* 34: 83-84.

Lippens, L., & Wille, H. 1972. *Atlas van de vogels in België en West Europa.* Tielt, Lanoo.

Lockie, J.D. 1952. The food of the Great Skua on Hermaness, Unst. *Scot. Nat.* 64: 158-162.

Löfgren, L-E. 1985. *Oceanernas fåglar.* Wahlström & Widstrand, Stockholm.

Lönnberg, E. 1906. Contributions to the fauna of South Georgia. *Kungl. Sv. Vet. Akademiens Handlingar* Vol. 40/5.

Løppenthin, B. 1943. Systematic and biologic notes on the Long-tailed Skua *Stercorarius longicaudus* Vieill. *Meddelelser om Grønland* 131 (12).

Lovegrove, R., Williams, G., & Williams, I. 1994. *Birds in Wales.* T. & A.D. Poyser, London.

Luchner, G.D. 1992. Parasitic Jaeger. *Spoonbill* 41: 7.

Lund-Hansen, L.C., & Lange, P. 1991. The numbers and distribution of the Great Skua *Stercorarius skua* breeding in Iceland 1984-1985. *Acta Nat. Isl.* 34: 16 pp.

Lust, P., & Rappé, G. 1980. Zeevogels, huidige status in België. *Stentor* 16: 30-37.

Madsen, S.T. 1990. Skuas *Stercorarius* sp. on the West Coast. *J. Bombay Nat. Hist. Soc.* 87: 292.

Maher, W.J. 1970. Ecology of the Long-tailed Skua at Lake Hazen, Ellesmere Island. *Arctic* 23: 112-129.

— 1970. The Pomarine Jaeger as a Brown Lemming predator in northern Russia. *Wilson Bull.* 82: 130-157.

— 1974. Ecology of Pomarine, Parasitic and Long-tailed Jaegers in Northern Alaska. *Pacific Coast Avifauna* 37: I-VIII.

Malling Olsen, K. 1987. Labbar - en bestämningsguide till

släktet *Stercorarius*. *Anser* supplement 20.

— 1987. Expertkommentar till fjällabbfyndet i Asker. *Fåglar i Närke* 10: 72-73.

— 1989. Field identification of the smaller skuas. *British Birds* 82: 143-176.

— 1989. Die Bestimmung der Raubmöwen Stercorariidae. *Limicola* 3: 93-137.

— 1992. Jagers. De jagers van het Noordelijk Halfrond. *Dutch Birding* Vogelgids 1. GMB Uitgeverij, Haarlem.

— 1992. *Danmarks fugle - en oversigt.* DOF København.

— 1993. Sträcket av måsar och tärnor förbi Falsterbo höstarna 1991 och 1992. *Anser* 32: 253-262.

— & Christensen, S. 1984. Field identification of juvenile skuas. *British Birds* 77: 448-450.

— & Larsson, H. 1995. *Terns of Europe and North America.* A&C Black, London.

Manning, T.H. 1964. Geographical and sexual variation in the Long-tailed Jaeger. *Biol. Pap. Univ. Alaska* 7: 1-16.

Manolis, T. 1981. First sight record of South Polar Skua *Catharacta maccormicki* for Trinidad, West Indies. *American Birds* 35: 982.

Marr, T., & Porter, R. 1992. Spring seabird passage off Senegal. *Birding World* 5: 391-394.

Martin, M., & Barry, T.W. 1978. Nesting behaviour and food habitats of Parasitic Jaegers at Anderson River Delta, Northwest Territories. *Can. Field-Nat.* 92: 45-50.

Martinez-Vilalta, A., Ferrer, X., & Carboneras, C. 1984. Situación de los pigalos (*Stercorarius* sp.) en el litoral Catalán (ne de la Peninsula Ibérica). *Misc. Zool.* 8: 217-223.

Mather, J.R. 1981. Mystery photographs 54: Long-tailed Skua. *British Birds* 74: 257-259.

Mathews, G.M. 1913. *Birds of Australia.* Vol. II. Witherby, London.

Mattocks, P.W. 1989. The changing seasons: North Pacific Coast Region. *American Birds* 43: 157-161.

— & Harrington-Tweit, B. 1987. The changing seasons: North Pacific Coast. *American Birds* 41: 132-136.

Maxton, S.J., & Bernstein, N.P. 1982. Kleptoparasitism by South Polar Skua on Blue-eyed Shags in Antarctica. *Wilson Bull.* 94: 269-281.

McGeehan, A. 1991. South Polar Skua - more questions than answers. *Irish Birds* 2: 15-28.

— 1995. Telling tails. *Birdwatch* 37: 23-29.

McCaskie, G. 1971. Spring migration, southern Pacific coast region. *American Birds* 25: 799-804.

McWilliams, J. 1990. Jaeger (Pomarine or Parasitic), Erie County. *Pa. Birds* 4: 98-99.

Meek, E.R., Booth, C.J., Reynolds, P., & Ribbands, B. 1985. Breeding skuas in Orkney. *Seabird* 8: 21-33.

Meininger, P., & Mullie, W.C. 1981. Some notes on bird migration in the area of the Gulf of Suez (Egypt), autumn 1980. *Sandgrouse* 3: 84-86.

Meltofte, H. 1976. Ornithologiske observationer i Scoresbysund-området, Østgrønland 1974. *Dansk Orn. Foren. Tidsskr.* 70: 107-122.

— 1979. Forekomsten af kjover ved Blåvandshuk 1963-1977. *Dansk Orn. Foren. Tidsskr.* 73: 293-304.

Melville, D.S. 1985. Long-tailed Skua in New Zealand.

Notornis 32: 37-51.

Mitchell, C.D. 1990. Parasitic Jaeger in Southwestern Montana. *Northwest. Nat.* 71: 63.

Mocci, D.A. 1986. A new record of the Great Skua *Stercorarius skua* in Sardinia. *Riv. Ital. Ornitol.* 56: 271-272.

Møller, A.P. (ed.) 1978. *Nordjyllands Fugle - deres yngleudbredelse og trækforhold.* Klampenborg.

Moors, P.J. 1980. Southern Great Skuas on Antipodes Island, New Zealand: observations on foods, breeding and growth of chicks. *Notornis* 27: 133-146.

Morosov, N.S. 1987. The Bewick's Swan *Cygnus bewickii*, the Brent Goose *Branta bernicla* and the Parasitic Skua *Stercorarius parasiticus* on the Piros Lake, Novgorod Region. *Ornitologiya* 22: 189-190.

Morvan, P. le, Mougin, J.L., & Prévost, J. 1967. Ecologie du skua antarctique (*Stercorarius maccormicki*) dans l'Archipel de Pointe Géologie (Terre Adélie). *L'Oiseaux et R.F.O* 37: 193-220.

Moynihan, M. 1959. A revision of the family Laridae (Aves). *Amer. Mus. Novitates* 1928: 1-42.

— 1962. Hostile and sexual behaviour patterns of South American and Pacific Laridae. *Behaviour* 8 (suppl.): 1-365.

Munkebye, O. 1973. First proof of breeding Great Skua (*Catharacta skua*) on Bjornoya. *Nor. Polarinst. Årbok* 1971: 122.

Murphy, R.C. 1936. *Oceanic Birds of South America.* Vol. II. The American Museum of Natural History, New York.

Murray, R. (ed.) 1994. 1993 *Scottish Bird Report.* The Scottish Ornithologists Club.

Myers, B. 1986. Parasitic Jaeger at Saylorville Reservoir. *Iowa Bird Life* 56: 31.

Naveen, R. 1989. First record of Long-tailed Skua for South Georgia. *American Birds* 43: 17.

Newton, I. 1979. *Population Ecology of Raptors.* T. & A.D. Poyser, Berkhamsted.

Norderhaug, M. 1989. *Svalbards fugler.* Dreyer, Oslo.

Norman, D.M. 1985. A white-headed juvenile Long-tailed Skua. *British Birds* 78: 453-454.

— & Tucker, V.R. 1979. Abnormally plumaged Great Skuas off Cornwall. *British Birds* 72: 476.

Norman, F.I., McFarlane, R.A., & Ward, S.J. 1994. Carcasses of Adelie Penguins as a food source for South Polar Skuas; some preliminary observations. *Wilson Bull.* 106: 26-34.

Nyrup, H. 1992. Forekomsten af kjover i Nordjylland 1975-1989. *Dansk Orn. Foren. Tidsskr.* 86: 257-261.

O'Donald, P. 1983. *The Arctic Skua. A study of the ecology and evolution of a seabird.* Cambridge University Press.

— 1987. Polymorphism and sexual selection in the Arctic Skua. In Cooke, F., & Buckley, P.A. (eds.): *Avian Genetics: A population and ecological approach.*

— & Davis, J.W.F. 1975. Demography and selection in a population of Arctic Skuas. *Heredity* 35: 75-83.

Oreel, G. 1981. On bill colour of Pomarine Skua. *Dutch Birding* 3: 57.

— 1981. Mystery bird: Pomarine Skua. *Dutch Birding* 2: 130.

Ortiz-Von Halle, B. 1990. Additions to the Avifauna of Colombia - New species on Gorgona Island. *Caldasia* 16: 209-214.

Osmolowskaja, W.I. 1948. Ecology of predatory birds of the Yamal peninsula. *Trudy Inst. Geogr. Akad. Nauk SSSR* 61: 5-77.

Ouweneel, G.L. 1987. Great Skua *Stercorarius skua* feeding on victims from power transmission lines. *Limosa* 60: 42.

Parmelee, D.F. 1985. Polar adaptions in the South Polar Skua (*Catharacta maccormicki*) on Anvers Island, Antarctica. *Acta XVIII Congressus Internationalis Ornithologici* 1: 520-529. Moscow.

— 1988. The hybrid skua: a southern ocean enigma. *Wilson Bull.* 100: 345-356.

— 1992. *Antarctic Birds.* Univ. Minnesota Press, Minneapolis.

—, & MacDonald, S.D. 1975. Recent observations on the birds of Isla Contramaestre and Isla Magdalena, Straits of Magellan. *Condor* 77: 218-220.

—, Fraser, W.R., & Neilson, D.R. 1977. Birds of the Palmer Station area. *Antarctic Journal of the United States* 12: 14-21.

Pasquier, R.F. 1973. Parasitic Jaegers seen from Great Gull Island, New York. *Kingbird* 23: 75-78.

Paterson, A.M. 1986. Kleptoparasitic feeding by migrating skuas in Malaga Bay, Spain. *Ringing & Migration* 7: 51-55.

Pedersen, J. 1967. 2 kjovearter fundet døde på Præstø Fed. *Dansk Orn. Foren. Tidsskr.* 61: 188.

Pehrsson, O. 1966. Inventering av häckande sjöfågel i Göteborgs och Bohus län. Stencil.

Pennie, I.D. 1953. The Arctic Skua in Caithness. *British Birds* 46: 105-108.

Perdeck, A.C. 1960. Observations of the reproductive behaviour of the Great Skua or Bonxie in Shetland. *Ardea* 48: 111-136.

— 1963. The early reproductive behaviour of the Arctic Skua. *Ardea* 51: 1-15.

Perry, R. 1948. *Shetland Sanctuary.* Faber & Faber, London.

—1949. Natural history of the skuas. *Discovery* 10: 389-392.

Peter, H.U., Blechschmidt, R., Furness, R.W., Cohen, B., Wilson, R., & de Korte, J. 1994. Molecular Systematics of Skuas. *Journal für Ornithologie* 135: 320.

Petersen, I., & U.G. Sørensen, U.G. 1981. *Migration studies from the eastern part of the lagoon 'Sabhket el Bardawil' on the north coast of the Sinai peninsula.* Privately printed, Copenhagen.

Pettersson, D. 1987. Fynd av ung fjällabb i Asker, Närke 10.9-13.9 1985. *Fåglar i Närke* 10: 27-30.

Peturson, G. 1994. *Bliki: skrå yfir islenska fugla.* Reykjavik.

Pietz, P.J. 1985. Long call displays of sympatric South Polar and Brown Skuas. *The Cooper Ornithological Society* (1985): 316-326.

— 1987. Feeding and nesting ecology of sympatric South Polar and Brown Skuas. *Auk* 104: 617-627.

— & Parmelee, D.F. 1994. Survival, site and mate fidelity in South Polar Skuas *Catharacta maccormicki* at Anvers Island, Antarctica. *Ibis* 136: 32-38.

Pitelka, F.A., Tomich, P.Q., & Treichel, G.W. 1955. Breeding behaviour of jaegers and owls near Barrow, Alaska. *Condor* 57: 3-18.

—, — & — 1955. Ecological relations of jaegers and owls as lemming predators near Barrow, Alaska. *Ecol. Monogr.* 25: 85-117.

Pizzey, G. 1980. *A Field Guide to the Birds of Australia.* Collins, Sydney.

Porter, R.F., Christensen, S., & Schiermacher-Hansen, P. 1996. *Field Guide to the Birds of the Middle East.* T. & A.D. Poyser, London.

—, Martins, R.P., Shaw, K.D., & Sørensen, U. 1996. The status of non-passerines in southern Yemen and the records of the OSME survey in spring 1993. *Sandgrouse* 17: 22-53.

Post, W. 1986. First inland record of Pomarine Jaeger from the Carolinas: a collection. *Chat* 50: 125.

Powers, K.D. 1983. *Pelagic distribution of marine birds of the northeastern United States.* NOAA Techn. Memo. NMFS-F/NEC 27. Woods Hole, Mass.

Preuss, N.O. 1983. Storkjove i Danmark. *Fugle* 3/1: 21.

Pringle, J.D. 1981. *The Shorebirds of Australia.* Angus & Robertson, Sydney.

Prize, L.W. 1973. The local ecological effect of Long-tailed Jaegers nesting in the subarctic. *Arctic* 26: 253-255.

Pulliam, B. 1986. Pomarine Jaegers observed at Cumberland Island, Georgia. *Oriole* 51: 19.

Rankin, M.N., & Duffey, E.A.G. 1948. A study on the bird life of the North Atlantic. *British Birds* 41: suppl. 42 pp.

Rasmussen, E.V. 1980. Forekomsten af kjover i Kattegat - efteråret 1979. *Rapp. KOF*, Suppl. 2: 21-25.

— 1981. The occurrence of the Great Skua *Stercorarius skua* in Southern Scandinavia, especially Denmark, during 1970-1978. *Dansk Orn. Foren. Tidsskr.* 75: 41-46.

Richardson, C. 1990. *The Birds of the United Arab Emirates.* Hobby Publications, Dubai and Warrington.

Richdale, L.E. 1965. Biology of the birds of Whero Island, New Zealand, with special reference to the Diving Petrel and the White-faced Storm Petrel. *Trans. Zool. Soc. London* 31: 1-155.

Risberg, L. 1990. Sveriges Fåglar. *Vår Fågelvärld*, supplement nr 14. Stockholm.

Ritchie, R.J., & Ambrose, R.E. 1992. The status of selected birds in east-central Alaska. *Can. Field-Nat.* 106: 316-320.

Robel, D. 1991. Is identification in the field hopeless? On the identification characters of juvenile *Stercorarius longicaudus*. *Falke* 38: 184-189.

— 1992. Evidence of *Stercorarius longicaudus* in Turkey. *Beitr. Vogelkunde* 38: 355-356.

Roberts, T.J. 1991. *The Birds of Pakistan, Vol. 1. Regional status and non-passeriformes.* Oxford University Press.

Roller, J., & Nikas, M. 1992. Third Colorado record of Long-tailed Skua *Stercorarius longicaudus*. *Colorado Field Ornithol.* 26: 147-151.

Root, T. 1988. *Atlas of Wintering North American Birds: An analysis of Christmas bird count data.* The University of Chicago Press.

Ryan, P.G. 1989. The distribution and abundance of Long-tailed Skua off South Africa. *Ostrich* 60: 89-90.

— 1989. Common Nighthawk *Chordeiles minor* and new records of seabirds from Tristan da Cunha and Gough Islands. *Bull. Br. Ornithol. Club* 109: 147-149.

— 1986. Records of skuas and Sabine's Gulls ashore in Southern Africa. *Cormorant* 13: 107-111.

—, Dean, W.R.J., Moloney, C.L., Watkins, B.P., & Milton, S.J. 1990. New information on seabirds at Inaccessible Island and other islands in the Tristan da Cunha group. *Mar. Ornithol.* 18: 43-54.

Salomonsen, F. 1927. Ornithologiske studier i Nordskandinavien. *Dansk Orn. Foren. Tidsskr.* 21: 87-108.

— 1967. The South Polar Skua *Stercorarius maccormicki* at Saunders in Greenland. *Dansk Orn. Foren. Tidsskr.* 70: 81-90.

— 1967a. *Fuglene på Grønland*. Rhodos, Copenhagen.

Saunders, H. 1876. On the Stercorariinae or Skua Gulls. *Proc. Zool. Soc. London* (1878): 317-332.

Schaaning, H.T.L. 1916. Bidrag til Novaja Zemlias fauna. *Dansk Orn. Foren. Tidsskr.* 10: 145-190.

Schlatter, R.P. 1984. *The status and conservation of seabirds in Chile*. In Croxall, J.P., Evans, P.G.H & Schreiber, R.W. (eds) *Status and Conservation of the World's Seabirds*. ICBP Technical Publication Nr. 2, Cambridge.

Schmidt, G. 1954. Zum Rauben der Schmarotzer-Raubmöwe. *Vogelwelt* 75: 147-151.

Schnell, G.D. 1970. A phenistic study of the suborder Lari (Aves) 1,2. *Sys. Zool.* 19: 35-37, 264-302.

Schuster, S., *et al.* 1983. *Die Vögel des Bodenseegebietes*. Ornithologische Arbeitsgemeinschaft Bodensee, Konstanz.

Schüz, E. 1933. Über die Kennzeichen der beider kleinen Raubmöwen in Jugendkleid und ihr Vorkommen in Ostpreussen. *Orn. Mber.* 41: 77-81.

Sears, J., Ellis, P.M., Suddaby, D., & Harrop, H.R. 1995. The status of breeding Arctic Skuas *Stercorarius parasiticus* and Great Skuas *S. skua* in Shetland in 1992. *Seabird* 17: 21-31.

Seitz, E., & von Wicht, U. 1980. Der Einflug von Raubmöwen ins mitteleuropäische Binnenland in Spätsommer/Herbst 1976. *Der Ornithologische Beobachter* 77.

Serventy, D.L., Serventy, V., & Warham, J. 1971. *The Handbook of Australian Seabirds*. A.H. & A.W. Reed, Sydney.

Sharrock, J.T.R., & Sharrock, E.M. 1976. *Rare Birds in Britain and Ireland*. T. & A.D. Poyser, Berkhamsted.

Shirihai, H. 1996. *The Birds of Israel*. Academic Press, London.

Sibley, C.G., & Monroe, B.L. 1990. *Distribution and Taxonomy of the Birds of the World*. Yale University Press, New Haven.

Sick, H. 1993. *Birds in Brazil*. Princeton University Press, New Jersey.

Sinclair, I., Hockey, P. & Tarboton, W. 1993. *Illustrated Guide to the Birds of Southern Africa*. New Holland, London.

Sinclair, J. C. 1980. Subantarctic Skua *Catharacta antarctica* predation techniques on land and at sea. *Cormorant* 8: 3-6.

Sirois, J., Alexander, S.A., & Westover, S.E. 1991. Breeding sites of gulls, terns and jaegers at Iles du Large, Resolution Bay, and along the West shore of Great Slave Lake, Northwest Territories. *Can. Wildl. Serv. Prog. Notes* 192.

Sladen, W.J.L. 1954. Pomarine Jaeger in the Antarctic. *Ibis* 96: 315-316.

Slater, P., Slater, P., & Slater, R. 1986. *The Slater Field Guide to Australian Birds*. Rigby, Dee Why West, NSW.

Slepkov, M.M. 1963. Juzno-polrnyi pomornik v vocach SSSR. *Ornitologiya* 6: 482.

Small, A. 1974. *The Birds of California*. Winchester Press, New York.

SOF. 1990. *Sveriges Fåglar*. Stockholm.

Soloviev, M. Yu., & Talanina, E.B. 1991. Spring record of the Pomarine Skua *Stercorarius pomarinus* in Moscow Region. *Ornitologiya* 25: 175.

Sonobe, K. (ed.) 1983. *A Field Guide to the Birds of Japan*. Wild Bird Society of Japan, Tokyo.

Sørensen, E.H. 1996. Kjover. In Andersen, C., *et al.*: *Fugle og Dyr i Nordjylland 1995*. Rapport nr. 32 fra Nordjysk Ornitologisk Kartotek. Skive, Denmark.

Southern, H.N. 1943. The two phases of *Stercorarius parasiticus*. *Ibis* 85: 443-485.

— 1944. Dimorphism in *Stercorarius pomarinus*. *Ibis* 86: 1-16.

Spear, L., & Ainsley, G. 1993. Kleptoparasitism by Kermadec Petrels, jaegers and skuas in the eastern tropical Pacific: evidence of mimicry by two species of *Pterodroma*. *Auk* 110: 222-233.

Spellerberg, I.F. 1967. The distribution of the McCormick's Skua *Catharacta maccormicki*. *Notornis* 14: 201-207.

— 1970. Body measurements and color phases of the McCormick's Skua *Catharacta maccormicki*. *Notornis* 17: 280-285.

— 1971. Breeding behaviour of the McCormick's Skua. *Ardea* 59: 189-230.

Spence, I. 1992. Exceptionally bold Pomarine Skua. *British Birds* 85: 311.

Stawarczyj, T. 1985. Rozpoznawanie wydrzykow w szatach mlodocianychi spoczynkowcho. *Notatki Ornitologiczne* 26: 179-191.

Stead, E.F. 1932. *The Life History of New Zealand Birds*. Search, London.

Stenlund, J. 1988. Var labben bredstjärtad? - problemet att bestämma ung bredstjärtad och vanlig labb i fält. *Fåglar i Uppland* 15: 135-137.

Stevenson, H. 1890. *The Birds of Norfolk*. Van Voorst, London.

Stiles, F.G., & Skutch, A.F. 1989. *A Guide to the Birds of Costa Rica*. Christopher Helm, London.

Stonehouse, B. 1956. The Brown Skua *lonnbergi* of South Georgia. *Sci. Rep. Falkland St. Dep. Survey* 14: 1-25.

Størkersson, Ø.R. 1985. Feltbestemming av unge joer. *Trøndersk Natur* 12: 73-75.

Stresemann, E., & Stresemann, V. 1966. Die Mauser der Vögel. *J. Ornithol.* 107, Sonderheft.

Summerhayes, C.P., Hofmeyer, P.K., & Roux, R.H. 1974. Seabirds off the southwestern coast of Africa. *Ostrich* 45: 83-109.

Svensson, L. 1984. Nytt från raritetskommittén. *Vår Fågelvärld* 43: 57-61.

Svingen, P. 1994. Pomarine Jaeger at Park Point. *Loon* 66: 209-210.

Taylor, D. 1996. *Birding in Kent*. Pica Press, Sussex.

Taylor, I.R. 1979. The kleptoparasitic behaviours of the

Arctic Skua *Stercorarius parasiticus*, with three species of terns. *Ibis* 121: 274-282.

Taylor, P. 1993. Mid-continental jaegers: A Manitoba perspective. *Blue Jay* 51: 157-164.

Thom, V.M. 1986. *Birds in Scotland*. T. & A.D. Poyser, Calton.

Thomsen, P., & Jacobsen, P. 1979. *The Birds of Tunisia*. Nature Travels, Copenhagen.

Thomson, A.L. 1966. An analysis of recoveries of Great Skuas ringed in Shetland. *British Birds* 59: 1-15.

Tickell, W.L.N., & Woods, R.W. 1972. Ornithological observations at sea in the South Atlantic Ocean, 1954-1964. *British Antarctic Survey Bulletin* 31: 61-84.

Timmermann, G. 1949. *Die Vogel Islands*. Reykjavik.

Tostain, O., & Dujardin, J.L. 1988. Nouveaux oiseaux de la mer en Guyane Française. *Alauda* 56: 67-78.

Tranda, E. 1961. Wystepowanie wydrzykow Stercorariidae w Polsce. *Acta Ornitologizwe* 6: 41-45.

Trillmick, F. 1978. Feeding territories and breeding success of South Polar Skuas. *Auk* 95: 23-33.

Trivelpiece, W., Butler, R.G., & Volkman, N.J. 1980. Feeding territories of Brown Skua *Catharacta lonnbergi*. *Auk* 97: 669-676.

— & Volkman, N.J. 1982. Feeding strategies of sympatric South Polar *Catharacta maccormicki* and Brown Skuas *C. lonnbergi*. *Ibis* 124: 50-54.

Tuck, G., & Heinzel, H. 1978. *A Field Guide to the Seabirds of Britain and the World*. Collins, London.

Tucker, G.M., & Heath, M.F. 1994. *Birds in Europe: their conservation status*. BirdLife International (Birdlife Conservation Series Nr. 3). Cambridge, U.K.

Tyrberg, T. 1993. Fågelrapport för 1992. - Fågelåret 1992: 35-79. *Vår Fågelvärld* supplement nr. 19.

— 1994. Fågelrapport för 1993. - Fågelåret 1993: 51-99. *Vår Fågelvärld* supplement nr. 20.

— 1995. Fågelrapport för 1994. - Fågelåret 1994: 66-123. *Vår Fågelvärld* supplement nr. 22.

Ulfvens, J., Hildén, O., & Hästbäcka, H. 1988. Marked population increase in the Arctic Skua *Stercorarius parasiticus* from 1957 to 1987. *Ornis Fennica* 65: 86-88.

—, — & — 1989. Labben i Kvarken - färgfaserna år 1957-1987. *Lintumies* 24: 78-80.

Ullman, M. 1984. Field identification of juvenile Pomarine Skuas. *British Birds* 77: 446-448.

— 1985. Fjällabb *Stercorarius longicaudus* i Ystad sommaren 1984 - samt något om åldersbestämning av subadulta fjällabbar. *Anser* 24: 149-158.

— 1985. Fältbestämning: adult fjällabb. *Vår Fågelvärld* 44: 380-381.

— 1990. Long-tailed Skua identification. *Birding World* 3: 28-29.

Unitt, P. 1984. *The Birds of San Diego County*. San Diego Society of National History.

Urban, E.K., Fry, C.H., & Keith, S. 1986. *The Birds of Africa*. Vol. 2. Academic Press, London.

Vader, W. 1980. The Great Skua in Norway and the Spitsbergen area. *Cinclus* 3: 49-55.

van Balen, S. 1991. Jaegers in Indonesian waters. *Kukila* 5: 117-124.

van den Berg, A.B. 1987. Mystery photographs 22: South Polar Skua. *Dutch Birding* 9: 13-14.

— 1991. Mystery photographs 40: Arctic Skua. *Dutch Birding* 13: 106-108.

Vandenbulcke, P. 1973. Tier jaar zeefogeltrek langs de Belgische kust. *Veldornitologisch Tijdschrift* 2: 35-57.

van der Elst, D. 1987. A propos de l'identification de labbe à longue queue *Stercorarius longicaudus* juvenile. *Aves* 24: 112-119.

van Dongen, R.M., Gebuis, H., & de Rouw, P.W.W. 1992. Recente meldingen September-Oktober 1992. *Dutch Birding* 14: 234-238.

van IJzendoorn, E.J., & de Heer, P. 1981. Over herkenning van onvolwassen Kleine end Kleinste Jager. *Dutch Birding* 3: 10-12.

Vaughan, T. 1995. Critical approach to skua identification. *British Birds* 88: 155-156.

Veit, R.R. 1978. Some observations of South Polar Skuas on Georges Bank. *American Birds* 32: 300-302.

— 1985. Long-tailed Jaegers wintering along the Falkland current. *American Birds* 39: 873-878.

Vittoz, P. 1992. A jaeger at 2350 metres in Valais. *Nos Oiseaux* 6: 372.

Voisin, J.F., Voisin, C., Bock, W.J., & Théry, M. 1993. Case 2816: *Catharacta antarctica lonnbergi* Mathews, 1912 (Currently *Catharacta skua lonnbergi*, Aves, Charadriiformes): proposed conservation of subspecific name. *Bull. Intern. Comm. Zool. Nom.* 50 (1): 48-51.

Vooren, C.M., & Chiaradia, A. 1989. *Stercorarius longicaudus* and *S. parasiticus* in southern Brazil. *Ardea* 77: 233-235.

Vyrut, J. 1989. The second documented sighting of *Stercorarius pomarinus* Temminck in West Bohemia (Czechoslovakia). *Zpr. Muz. Zapadoces. Kraje* 38-39: 65-66.

Walker, F.J. 1981. Notes on the birds of northern Oman. *Sandgrouse* 2: 33-35.

Waller, G. (ed.) 1996. *Sealife: A Complete Guide to the Marine Environment*. Pica Press, Sussex.

Walter, H. 1962. Vergleichende Untersuchungen an den Raubmöwen *Stercorarius parasiticus* und *longicaudus*. *J. Ornithol.* 103: 166-179.

Wang, Z., & Norman, F.I. 1993. Timing of breeding, breeding success and chick growth in the South Polar Skuas *Catharacta maccormicki* in the eastern Larsemann hills, Princess Elizabeth Land, Antarctica. *Notornis* 40: 189-203.

Warr, F.E. 1989. A check-list of the birds of Arabia. Unpublished typescript. Tring, UK.

Watson, G.E. 1975. *Birds of the Antarctic and Sub-Antarctic*. Amer. Geophys. Union, Washington D.C.

Webster, J.D. 1988. Some bird specimens from Sitka, Alaska. *Murrelet* 69: 46-48.

Welch, G., & Welch, H. 1984. Birds seen on an expedition to Djibouti. *Sandgrouse* 6: 1-23.

Wetmore, A. 1926. Observations on the birds of Argentina, Paraguay, Uruguay and Chile. *U.S. Nat. Mus. Bull.* no. 133. Smithsonian Insitute.

Whittle, J. 1992. Pomarine Jaeger. *Spoonbill* 41: 7-8.

Wiegant, W.M, Steinhaus, G., & CDNA. 1994. Rare birds in the Netherlands in 1992. *Dutch Birding* 16: 133-148.

Willett, G., & Howard, H. 1934. Characters differentiating certain species of *Stercorarius*. *Condor* 34: 158-160.

Williams, A.J. 1980. Aspects of breeding biology of the Subantarctic Skua at Marion Island. *Ostrich* 51: 160-167.

Williams, E.H., Jr., & Bunkley-Williams, L. 1992. Two unusual sea bird records from Puerto Rico. *Caribb. J. Sci.* 28: 105.

Williams, L.E. 1965. Jaegers in the Gulf of Mexico. *Auk* 82: 18-25.

Williamson, K. 1957. The Bonxies of Fair Isle. *Bird Notes* 27: 164-169.

Wilson, E.A. 1907. Aves. *National Antarctic Expedition. Natural History* 2 (2): 1-121.

Wood, K.A. 1989. Seasonal abundance, marine habitats and behaviour of skuas off New South Wales. *Corella* 13: 97-104.

Wood, R.C. 1970. A population study of South Polar Skuas (*Stercorarius maccormicki*) aged one to eight years. *Proc. XV Int. Orn. Congr. The Hague* 1970: 705-706.

— 1971. Population dynamics of breeding South Polar Skuas of unknown age. *Auk* 88: 805-814.

Wourinen, J.D. 1992. Do Arctic Skuas *Stercorarius parasiticus* exploit and follow terns during the fall migration? *Ornis Fennica* 69: 198-200.

Wynne-Edwards, V.C. 1935. On the habitats and distribution of the birds of the North Atlantic. *Proc. Boston Soc. Nat. Hist.* 40/4: 233-346.

Yosef, R. 1995. Foraging behaviour of Arctic, Pomarine and Long-tailed Skuas on migration in the Red Sea. *Bulletin OSME* 34: 12-13.

Young, E.C. 1963a. The breeding behaviour of the South Polar Skua *Catharacta maccormicki*. *Ibis* 105: 203-233.

— 1963b. Feeding habits of the South Polar Skua. *Ibis* 105: 301-318.

— 1978. Behavioural ecology of *lonnbergi* skuas in relation to environment on the Chatham Islands, New Zealand. *N.Z. J. Zool.* 5: 410-416.

— 1994. *Skuas and Penguins.* Cambridge University Press.

Zang, H., Grosskopf, G. & Heckenroth, H. 1991. *Die Vögel Niedersachsens und des Landes Bremen. Raubmöwen bis Alkes.* Naturschutz und Landschaftspflege in Niedersachsen, Hannover.

Zink, R.M. 1981. Observations of seabirds during a cruise from Ross' Island to Anvers Island, Antarctica. *Wilson Bull.* 93: 1-136.

INDEX